BEYOND SATIRE
Julia Caesar &
the Kevin Sutra

beyond
satire

Julia Caesar & the Kevin Sutra

ROWAN DEAN

connorcourt
PUBLISHING

Published in 2013 by Connor Court Publishing Pty Ltd

Copyright © Rowan Dean 2013

Connor Court Publishing
PO Box 224W
Ballarat VIC 3350
sales@connorcourt.com
www.connorcourt.com

ISBN: 9781922168726 (pbk.)

Printed in Australia

To Claire,

who taught me how to paint in words

Preface

On 7 September 2010, Rob Oakeshott made the "juicy and sexy decision" as to who should govern Australia. I remember the moment distinctly. It struck me as faintly absurd that such an easily lampooned character should be deciding the fate of the entire country, and more out of amusement than anything else I instructed the creative department of the multinational advertising agency I worked at to gather around a computer screen to watch the momentous event unfold. And unfold. And unfold.

"This is a joke," muttered one of my team, around about the eight minute mark as the Independent member for Lyne explained how "my four-year-old and six-year-old are split on this decision".

"Not a joke. It's pure satire," chimed in another, instinctively upping the ante, as advertising writers tend to do.

"It's been an absolute line ball, points decision, judgment call, six-of-one, half-a-dozen-of-the-other, this could not get any closer," Rob droned on, relishing his moment in the sun.

"It's going to be ugly, but it's going to be beautiful in its ugliness."

Finally I could take no more of Mr. Oakeshott, and irritably I switched him off.

"Hey! Leave it on!" yelled another creative. "We could do a spoof of that speech! It's hilarious."

I shook my head. "Some things are beyond satire. I suspect Mr. Oakeshott's new government will be one of them. Now get back to work before you all get the sack." As usual, I was completely wrong on both scores.

Six weeks later it was me who got the sack. In classic Mad Men style, I was given an hour to clear my desk, hand in my Blackberry, and pack my bags. My career as a highly paid Executive Creative Director had come to a crashing end. What would come next, I had no idea. ECD's, once dumped, rarely get another crack at it – damaged goods and all that.

So for several months I moped around. I read the papers. Watched TV. And became increasingly amused at the theatrics of the calamitous Julia Gillard, of the hapless Wayne Swan, of the baffling Kevin Rudd and the vast, delicious cast of comical cameos that made up the Labor/Green/Independent government. One morning, sitting bolt upright in bed, I decided that maybe, just maybe, they weren't beyond satire after all. It was at that moment that I decided it was time to return to my first love, writing.

With the world of advertising still fresh in my mind, I jotted down a piece of political satire and sent it off. Much to my delight, it was published.

Emboldened by the thrill of being read (as an advertising copywriter 90% of your output never sees the light of day), I started getting up early every morning to write some more. There was no shortage of amusing topics.

During 2011, I found myself being published more and more frequently. Soon I was writing every week for the Spectator Australia and in early 2012 was given the coveted satirical column in the weekend Australian Financial Review.

I am deeply indebted to all the editors who gave me a chance; above all, my mentor Tom Switzer at the Spectator Australia and Michael Stutchbury at the Australian Financial Review.

My eternal gratitude as well to Sarah Dudley, whose insights, ideas and inspiration permeate every page.

BEYOND SATIRE

Julia Caesar & the Kevin Sutra

For a brief period following the 2010 election, Kevin Rudd, who'd demanded the job of Foreign Minister in exchange for supporting the woman who had overthrown him, kept an unusually low profile.

Then came the 2011 Queensland floods, the Japanese tsunami and the Libyan civil war.

Suddenly, Kevin was everywhere.

National Times, 4 April 2011

IS KEVIN PUTTING HIS PORTFOLIO TOGETHER?

You can always tell when advertising types are getting restless. They start "putting their portfolio together". As the Creative Director of an ad agency, you learn to spot the signs pretty quickly. Suddenly, the unhappy Art Director – let's call him, say, Kevin – becomes feverishly active. Uninvited, he starts popping up all over the place. Weekend work? "No probs," he'll say. Late night meetings? "Count me in." Treading on toes and butting in on other people's business becomes the order of the day. You see, Kevin will do literally anything to get some more ads out. He's desperately putting his portfolio together.

Almost certainly, Kevin has been miserable in his job recently. Sure, he gets to travel a lot and go on all the glamorous overseas shoots. The expense account is good, too, with long lunches and fine wines galore. But creatively, well, Kevin feels stifled. And under appreciated. Nobody asks for his opinions anymore. Ever since he was stabbed in the back by that red-headed woman. Advertising is such a ruthless game. And despite the faux friendship they both feign, she is definitely getting on his nerves. That voice! Aaarrrrgggh. Worse, she keeps nicking his ideas and claiming them as her own. The chutzpah is unbelievable. So one lunchtime Kevin sneaks out to see a Headhunter. Furtively smuggling his "book" – the shiny black portfolio containing his very best work – out of the office, he hops in a cab for his secret rendezvous in a cafe on the other side of town.

Headhunters don't do a great deal, apart from make tons of money and the odd phone call. But you can rest assured they will immediately tell you one thing; that your portfolio isn't up to scratch. Kevin sits there, stunned. Spread out across the table is his most famous campaign from 2007. As everyone knows, it won every top award in town; Best Ad Campaign of the Year, Most Effective Campaign of the Year, Most Memorable Slogan. How much more up-to-scratch can you get, he protests, his voice rising unnaturally. The Headhunter casually lights up another cigarette, flicks the ash over her shoulder, and shrugs dismissively. "Yes, but that was way back in '07," she says. "This is 2011. That's a lifetime ago in today's high-pressured world. What stuff have you done recently? What on earth have you been doing with yourself all this time?"

Kevin frowns pensively, clears his throat and pushes his glasses up his nose. Of course, how could he forget? Eagerly, he starts describing the massive Anti-Carbon campaign he spent so long conceptualizing. It was brilliant! Ahead of it's time, unbelievably creative, dynamic… but the Headhunter cuts him off. "So what?" she says, dismissively, "that campaign never ran. Nobody cares how good it could have been," she snarls, cruelly emphasizing the 'could'. "If it didn't even get up, it counts for nothing." Kevin starts to sweat. It's true, he thinks to himself. Nor did the Mining campaign. Nor the… he stops himself. So many great campaigns he'd had in his head. Yet none of them had actually seen the light of day. Just loose ideas. Doodles and scribbles on the back of envelopes and beer coasters.

He starts to stammer. "The Grocery thing, that was really cool," he says, trying to sound enthusiastic. "And the, um… the Pink Batts was kind of an interesting approach to…"

"You can't put that in your portfolio!" sighs the Headhunter, wearily stubbing out her ciggie. "Those ads bombed. Big-time. They were a complete disaster. Nobody wants to see ads that failed."

Kevin gulps, lost for words. "The reality is," says the Headhunter, ordering dessert, "you can't put any of that junk in your portfolio. You got nothin'! What the top agencies are looking for these days are the big visual campaigns. Lots of dramatic footage. Raw emotion. Passion. That's what turns them on. And forget Australia. The really cool jobs are overseas."

Kevin nods, taking it all in. London, Geneva. Or even the really big one, New York. Forget piddly old Canberra. It's a crap joint anyway. Way too political, for starters. And they'd never appreciated him here, not really. Let's face it, he tells himself, you're far too good for this lot!

"So what do I have to do?" Kevin pleads, as the bill arrives and they agree to split it. The Headhunter looks thoughtful. "Get some new stuff out there," she says. "Visibility is everything. Make a noise. Get noticed. They've got to be topical ads, you know, current. Relevant! Make people sit up and take notice. Find some controversial campaigns you can get involved in. Natural disasters are good. Floods. Earthquakes. Wars are even better. Guns. Bombs. Nuclear terror is best! Scare the pants off everyone. Lots of opportunities for really graphic pictures. You're a heavyweight. So throw that weight around. Get them talking about you again. Write a few opinion pieces in the trade rags, too, just for good measure. Can't hurt."

Kevin hesitates. He's in a cushy job. What's the big hurry, after all? "Maybe I should just sit tight," he says, "and see how things play out? You never know – the red-head might get hit by a bus crossing Northbourne Ave." The Headhunter gives him a withering look. "Timing is everything in this game," she snaps. "You're in a great position now, you know, to put yourself out there. Capitalize on it. Who knows how long you'll be in this job? Aren't those bastards over at Abbott Bishop Turnbull sniffing around? Advertising's a fickle game. If those guys win the next big pitch, then you lot are out on the street. Yesterday's news."

Kevin nods, deep in thought. "As soon as you've got your portfolio together," says the Headhunter, "give me a shout. In the meantime, I'll start lining up a few interviews." She smiles. "There's a really tasty position coming up in New York pretty soon. Fantastic offices downtown. Massive expense account. Loads of travel. Korean bloke called Hanky or Banky or something is in there at the moment. He's completely useless. You'd be perfect for it."

Kevin grins, and thanks her profusely. Then he rushes back to the agency as fast as he can. There's not a moment to lose when you're putting your portfolio together.

On the night she overthrew Kevin Rudd, Julia Gillard promised four things: to sort out climate change, fix up a mining tax, bring back a surplus and solve the problem of boat people and border-security by "breaking the people-smuggler's model".

Less than a year later, her plan to open a processing centre in Timor floundered when she apparently forgot to ask their President if he minded, which he did.

Gillard and her Immigration Minister Chris Bowen then opted for a bilateral agreement whereby 800 boat people be taken to Malaysia and swapped for 4000 refugees.

The Spectator Australia, 21 May 2011

MY BRILLIANT NEW CAREER IN PEOPLE-SMUGGLING

I'm thinking of going into the people smuggling business. After all, times are tough, and we've all got to earn a crust. I used to think the ad game was an easy way to make a quick buck. However, this boat people caper just gets more and more tempting by the day.

The easiest way to sell something to somebody is when somebody else does it for you. Thanks to Julia and Chris Bowen's 1-for-5 Refugee

Bonanza – now available in all good South East Asian nations – business will soon be booming.

All I've got to do is set up a rickety stall in some far-flung Middle East market town, and knock out a few brochures. That's pretty much it for overheads – other than, of course, purchasing a vaguely sea-worthy vessel for the journey. Here's how my all-important sales pitch goes: "Want a new life? In an awesome country? Well, have I got a deal for you: Australia! Full of sun, surf and scantily clad girls (except your sister, who can wear her burqa to go swimming if you want her to). And the best bit? You can pretty much waltz straight on in."

To which the wary customer, nervously fingering his hard-earned greenbacks tucked into the lining of his goatskin satchel, will raise a suspicious eyebrow. "Australia? I've heard horror stories about that place. I don't want to sit in some detention centre in the desert for years on end. Not happening, dude."

"Those days are long gone," I'll say, with a reassuring smile. "We got rid of that horrible little man with the bushy eyebrows. Besides which, there's a new government incentive scheme. A new guarantee! I'll show you. Straight from the Prime Minister's mouth, no less!"

"The Prime Minister is a woman?" the startled refugee will exclaim, as Julia pops up on my iPad. I wink. "I told you this place was a soft touch."

And then I'll let Julia deliver the sucker punch and close the deal, with the clip of her announcing her "tough" new policy: "If someone seeks to come to Australia, then they are at risk of being sent to Malaysia and going to the back of a very long queue."

My potential client will look at me in disbelief. And then burst out laughing. "It's that easy?" he'll say, pulling out his roll of bank notes. And I will nod. "It's that easy."

As anyone who has ever done business in South East Asia knows, telling someone they are going "to the back of a very long queue" is about as menacing as telling them "a limo will pick you up at 7 and take you straight to your front row seats." The rules are very different once you leave the air-conditioned comfort of Kingsford Smith and touch down in the sticky, humid world of our nearest neighbours.

I remember my first job in KL. We'd just left the airport when we were pulled over by an irate policeman. "What does he want?" I asked, puzzled. My driver sighed irritably as he fumbled in the glove-box for a wad of crumpled notes. "Just the usual. Baksheesh."

Ostensibly a form of charity giving, 'baksheesh' is anything from small tips to large, outright bribes, without which South East Asian business and politics would grind to a halt. According to a recently published survey of expat businessmen, nearly 50% believe Malaysian corruption is a "significant" problem.

Here's how Julia's "Malaysian Solution" looks to the people who will be implementing it. No; not the government bureaucrats, although they must still be shaking their heads in bewilderment at our naivety, but those who run the refugee camps.

"The Australians pay me money to take 10 boat people. Cool. And in return I get to offer 50 people in my camp the opportunity to make a charitable donation to me so that they can go to Australia. Cool. And then as soon as the 10 people from Australia arrive I will give them the opportunity to make a charitable donation to me so that they can be part of the next 50 who will go straight to Australia. Cool."

That's assuming, of course, that the Australian boat people sent to Thailand or Malaysia actually go into detention. It's just as likely they'll hop off the plane and hightail it straight down to the nearest port, where, luckily, I'll have another boat waiting. I'll offer a 20% discount, naturally, because repeat customers are the lifeblood of any new business. I may even offer frequent sailing points.

No wonder the Thais and Malaysians jumped at the offer. It's a win-win-win situation. Soon, there won't be a government in the region that hasn't grabbed our blank cheque-book with eager hands. And wisely or unwisely, Australia's refugee intake will go through the roof as every tin-pot Asian country seizes this golden opportunity to offload onto us their most troublesome and problematic illegal immigrants, including – you watch! – some of the very same ones we send to them.

Julia Gillard is desperate to do the decent thing on this issue. In fact, you can tell by the whispery, earnest way she speaks and her slightly flushed pink cheeks that for once she genuinely believes in what she's selling. Unfortunately, after a career spent in the confines of Canberra, shuffling agenda items and bureaucratic decrees from one folder to another, Julia is, quite simply, far too nice and trusting.

Corruption and South East Asia go hand in hand. Neither Malaysia nor Thailand are signatories to the UN Convention on Human Rights. Both their track records on treatment of illegal immigrants are woeful, with Thailand pushing unwanted Muslims back out to sea.

Doing his best to prove he's even more gullible than Julia, Chris Bowen came out with this gem: "We've talked these issues through (and) Malaysia's given that very firm commitment about dignity and humanity for asylum seekers." Really? Human Rights Watch thinks differently: "Malaysia cannot present itself as a responsible member of the international community while continuing to refuse to ratify core UN treaties, including… the Convention Against Torture. The government (needs to) upgrade the appalling conditions in immigration detention centers."

So are we trying to discourage asylum seekers by threatening them with the vile conditions awaiting them in Malaysian and Thai refugee camps? No, although that might actually work. Instead, we are lying to ourselves that Asian refugee camps are perfectly acceptable places to traffic people to at the taxpayer's expense, whilst officially handing control of our borders to foreign countries rife with corruption. And then kidding ourselves that this ill-considered policy will act as a deterrent.

My new career is looking very rosy indeed.

Climate change was the second challenge Julia Gillard set herself to resolve. Despite telling Rudd to ditch the ETS, and promising before the 2010 that "there will be no carbon tax under the government I lead", to secure power she did a deal with the Greens, promising them a carbon tax.

The Australian, 16 June 2011

HERE COMES THE EVIL DENIER MONSTER

When you've run out of positive things to say in advertising, the easiest trick is to make up a monster. The uglier and more repulsive the better.

Think of toilet cleaning ads. Take those imaginary, microscopic, horrible, slimy things that make guttural noises and squirm disgustingly as they salivate over your ceramic bowl.

Animation and special effects studios have a lot of fun designing and creating these grotesque visual metaphors with which to terrify the consumer, to the delight of advertising executives and their clients alike. Ugly monsters allow you to avoid having to spell out your own positive selling points, if indeed you have any.

It would appear the advocates of the carbon tax have cottoned on to this trick. Through a relentless and combined effort they have created their very own grotesque creature to terrify us. The hideous "climate change denier" is as ugly and repulsive as any toilet germ gremlin.

The climate change denier has become the Left's favourite bogeyman, pursued with all the zeal of a witch-hunt in 17th century Salem. Stupid, vain, ugly and mendacious, the climate change denier monster is anyone who questions any or all aspects of the anthropogenic global warming theory and rejects the urgent requirement of a carbon tax or ETS. This repugnant creature lurks in your neighbourhood and threatens life on earth as we know it.

"The agents of ... planetary death will be the climate change deniers," asserted one Sydney Morning Herald columnist recently. What, even more so than say, viral mutations, nuclear war, poverty, over-population, peak oil or even the odd asteroid? Yep. And so dangerous are these critters that he helpfully suggested "Surely it's time for climate change deniers to have their opinions forcibly tattooed on their bodies" before being "lashed to a pole at a certain point in the shallows off Manly? If they are right and the world is cooling ... their mouths will be above water." After this piece attracted a great deal of unwelcome attention the journalist apologised and pointed out the obvious; he was only joking.

But the joke's wearing a bit thin. Only weeks earlier the same journalist had another stab at humorously depicting so-called climate change deniers, eagerly conflating them with the "trolls" who clutter the internet. I'm sure esteemed individuals such as former British Chancellor of the Exchequer Nigel Lawson would be flattered to know that his opinions are of no more consequence than an "idiot who should be corralled".

And is it honestly the case that the likes of the former head of the civil service in Britain – who has demanded that his government stop terrifying the public about climate change – have their "heads in the sand and their bums defiantly aquiver as they fart their toxic message to the world"?

And is the physicist from Princeton University who claims it is far from clear there is any real threat from global warming – let alone a catastrophic one – really just a creature from "a septic tank teeming with snapping trolls"?

Another Herald journalist decided that rather than creating her own monster to terrify us with, she would borrow an existing one. Not even the best animation studios have managed to come up with anything as slimy, evil and repugnant as our very own cane toad.

With a cartoonist on hand to make sure you were suitably repulsed, the Herald applied the metaphor to 2GB's Alan Jones. Bemoaning the fact that Australia's highest rating broadcaster was "poisoning the logic well", "lowbrow", and will "irreparably harm our civilisation, as well as our climate", she chose to dismiss out of hand the points he has made about a) Julia Gillard having lied to the electorate about imposing a carbon tax and b) the nation's ability to have any measurable effect (negative or positive) on the world's climate.

Instead, we were treated to: "[Shock jocks] are the cane toads of contemporary culture: ugly, ubiquitous, toxic to most other life forms". There's that planetary death threat again. If only she'd had some Toilet Troll handy. It kills 99.9 per cent of all known climate change deniers. This particular journalist then gave us an accurate, but ironic, lecture on "dishonest tricks in argument, including caricature, anecdote and non sequitur" seemingly unaware that these are the precise tactics she and her fellow climate change denier demonisers (there! I've just created my own monster!) repeatedly use to demean anyone who happens to disagree with their point of view.

Yet another journalist conjured up the following imagery around someone who questioned climate change orthodoxy: "Pull out a few fingernails, stretch him on the rack, a bit of how's-yer-father with a red hot poker."

"The third lot of climate denial ratbags are those tabloid media pundits cynically banging the populist drum to drag in the hordes of bogan nongs out there.

"These are people who believe they are beset by a cabal of lefties, Greenies, gays, femi-Nazis, Muslims, venal and incompetent public servants and latte-sipping intellectuals conspiring to deprive them of all they hold dear, like their inalienable right to own a jet-ski and to name their children Breeyanna and Jaxxon."

That's a lot of condescension to pack into one paragraph. These wouldn't be those same people out in the western suburbs who are now lumbered with exorbitant electricity bills because of feel-good renewable schemes that, according to the Productivity Commission report, were ineffectual at best?

And let's not forget "the usual talkback shock jocks going feral and Rupert's opinionators lunging like a shoal of piranha". Is it possible for this debate to be conducted on the strength of the arguments alone? Or, like the toilet cleaning ads, do we have to create monsters in order to build our case?

By all means, counter every argument the climate change deniers, sceptics, carbon tax opponents and the rest put forward, and attack their opinions with passion and verve, or even better, with proven facts and irrefutable rebuttals.

But hysterically and repeatedly portraying them as ugly, stupid trolls, toads and ferals threatening life on earth as we know it, is intellectually (and morally) dubious at best.

Worthy of a toilet cleaning ad, perhaps. But not worthy of the future economic and environmental health of our country.

As scientists and environmentalists in Australia searched for ways to reduce greenhouse gas emissions, it was proposed that culling the country's estimated 1.2 million wild camels could form part of the solution.

The Spectator Australia, 16 June 2011

SHELTER FROM THE DESERT WIND

Finally, some common sense is being injected into the climate change debate. For too long, discussion has become bogged down in the existential and arcane intricacies of the carbon tax conundrum (how many compensated pensioners can you fit on the head of a pin?, how do you change peoples behavior without, um, changing their behavior?, and so on) whilst ignoring the very real threat to our atmosphere lurking insidiously in our own backyard.

I refer of course to the belching, farting camel.

Camels are one of our biggest carbon emitters. As far as bad guys go, they are right up there with BHP, Rio Tinto and Xstrata. Shivering in their under-heated, solar-paneled, pink-batted homes frantically fitting energy saving light bulbs and recycling their milk cartons, your average Aussie battler is woefully ignorant of the fact that a large part of their suffering is due to the thoughtless, selfish, dastardly lifestyle of the outback camel.

Roving unchecked across our sunburnt landscape, these burping, farting, native-vegetation guzzling grass munchers are emitting – as was reported in *The Australian* – "the same amount of carbon dioxide produced by a plane on a 7000km flight." Each and every one of them. Every year. And there's over a million of the buggers scattered across our vast continent. That's an awful lot of carbon dioxide.

But before you leap out of your seat in self-righteous indignation and climate change induced rage, relax: help is now at hand.

A doctor from an Adelaide-based firm that specializes in carbon has cracked it. His brilliant proposal will see this life-threatening hazard tackled with environmental zeal and Kyoto-style efficiency. Currently under review by the government's Domestic Offset Integrity Committee, with the blessing of the Parliamentary Secretary for Climate Change, the scheme combines the incentive structure of a "carbon credit swap" with the 19th century economic model known as "scalp-hunting".

The good doctor recommends an airborne assault on the camel population of Australia. For every camel you kill you get a credit for a tonne of carbon.

A crack team will soon be swooping down out of the clear blue Kimberley skies in a fleet of specially equipped helicopters. I might like to suggest that they exclusively employ returned Afghan servicemen, who at least should be able to spot the difference between a camel (the one with the lumpy bits) and say, a large red kangaroo or a water buffalo. I trust, too, that the marksmen will be specially trained to deliver the coup de grace (or should that be coup de grass?) as humanely as possible. No Indonesians need apply, thank you.

Gaia, I'm sure, will sigh with relief.

Another proposal will see the inoculation of cattle to stop them burping. About time, too. And a belated breath of fresh air in the vexed greenhouse emissions quandary. Perhaps, after all, Labor can afford to jettison the blighted carbon tax altogether. Let's face it, it's been a dog of an idea from day one. There isn't a politician on either side of the debate who hasn't rued the day he or she first mentioned the cursed thing, having in the past been caught on tape saying the complete opposite of what they now profess to believe in.

Julia can finally afford to ditch it. Because the common sense way forward is now clear.

Why stop at camels? Surely we should be targeting all those creatures who wantonly emit the most carbon dioxide and are thereby deliberately threatening life on earth as we know it? We need to do away with them as rapidly as possible. For the sake of the planet.

We can start with people who buy burgers. According to figures released last week by consumer watchdog Choice, a certain popular burger packs 80g of fat, 2386mg of sodium and 5085 kilojoules, and is "the most unhealthy option in a sample of major outlets." I can't say precisely how much carbon dioxide your average consumer of such a burger emits post degustation, but I bet it would make even the most hardened camel sit up and blush. I'm glad I'm not the one who will have to do the "emissions-measuring" that's for sure. Perhaps Tony Windsor or Rob Oakeshott could help out. Because if Greg Combet and his Multi Party Climate Change Committee are serious about making a difference to global warming, they should award each and every one of us our own Domestic Offset Integrity Value. After that, it's up to us. Overdo it on the Brussels sprouts and roast parsnips at gran's Sunday roast and you may well wake up the next morning to the ominous sounds of black Chinook helicopters circling overhead.

Pubs, too, could offer abundant opportunities to reduce emissions. A Pew Environment Group spokesman claims that "when feral animals belch they release methane, a particularly noxious greenhouse gas." You only need to spend a Friday afternoon at The Oaks to know that. There are certainly plenty of ferals at most of the pubs I drink in, and I think removing them from our lives altogether in the name of saving the planet is a fab idea. Win-win.

The government could even introduce a Dob-in-an-Emitter scheme. That greasy bogan squashed next to you on the bus who just let one rip? Take a snapshot of him on your iPhone and sms it to 1300 CARBONFARTER. If he's a repeat offender then, like the outback camel, an eager carbon offset hunter will quickly make sure he's history.

Hopefully then the planet – and the rest of us – will all be able to breathe a little easier.

With a broken promise on carbon pricing leading to demonstrations outside Parliament House and border security in tatters, less than a year in power the Gillard government was looking increasingly inept. Compounding its problems were allegations concerning the misuse of union funds and union credit cards on prostitutes by a Labor MP.

Meanwhile, despotic regimes had begun to crumble one by one in the 'Arab Spring.'

ABC *The Drum*, 26 August 2011

CANBERRA SPRING

As jubilant rebel forces declare the end is at hand, there are clear signs the government is on its last legs; with an unpopular leader nowhere to be seen and a palpable sense of "fin de regime" filling the air.

Are we witnessing the start of a Canberra Spring?

The streets of this lavishly built capital city remain ominously empty; where vast three lane motorways encircle a man-made lake of ostentatious fountains and grandiose buildings built for the sole purpose of impressing foreign dignitaries. Empty roundabouts bear witness to the folly and flamboyance of a powerful elite who for decades gave little thought to the rest of the country but squandered untold millions on themselves.

Reports filter in that the Supreme Leader has been spotted in her walled compound; El Lodge, a short drive from the parliament. Rumours abound that as the strain takes its toll she has taken to sporting ever-more flamboyant robes and to have dyed her hair bright red (with blonde streaks) at the behest of her ever-dwindling coterie of fanatical loyalists. Desperate to cling on to power, she remains fearful of her rivals within the Party, preferring to stay close to her private hairdresser, who travels everywhere with her, and with whom she is rumoured to be having an affair.

This is contradicted by reports of in-fighting amongst her colleagues, all of whom are desperately plotting to replace her, as confusion reigns deep in the government's underground bunker; an amazing array of marble tunnels built decades ago and hidden underneath Capit-Al Hill.

The police have been forced to investigate a member of the ruling elite, with sordid reports of prostitutes, forged credit cards and misused funds adding to the air of decadence surrounding the crumbling morale of the government. Only days ago, as a convoy of grey nomads and truck drivers encircled the parliament, one of the party's most trusted lieutenants, Anthony Al-Ben-Ezi made a fiery speech, where he pounded his fist and declared there would be no surrender. "These traitors are foreign mercenaries who have been flown in by semi-trailer from far flung provinces in the west such as Dar-Whin and Khal-Goorly and do not belong here. They are a convoy of no consequence. These people are extremists and Hansonites. We will have no, um, truck with them."

Standing on top of a vehicle outside the government square, surrounded by placards which had all been carefully censored for the TV cameras, and waving a microphone, rebel leader Ton-ei Abb-aht had declared victory to a cheering mob of about 200, proclaiming he will not stop until he has stopped the boats and stopped the taxes. Resting his hand on the shoulder of Al-ahn Jones, the fiery Mufti of T'oo Dji-be, he predicted the end of days had arrived. When a lone female journalist questioned whether the Mufti had been paid to attend the rally, the crowd visibly turned angry. She had to run, fearing for her life.

Yet again, the fractured history of this blighted land plays out before our eyes. It's only twelve months since the Supreme Leader, having been persuaded by a disgruntled coterie of unionists to seize power in a bloody coup, snuck up on her predecessor in the middle of the night and stabbed him in the back. Thus was born the Bath party, so called because they have been in hot water ever since. Cobbling together a coalition of loners and tree-worshippers, the new Leader immediately set about consolidating her power-base and calling an election, which – despite the Opposition's protests to the contrary – she has always claimed she "won".

Denying that she had lied to her people, she decided to introduce a Car Bomb Tax. "I have always said that we have to put a price on car bombs," she said. "There simply is no other way to change people's behavior, and I have made sure that there is adequate compensation for the poor as we move to a low car bomb economy." Defending the unpopular decision, she carried on in the face of frenzied talkback revolts, stubbornly telling her ever-dwindling group of political supporters that once the tax had been implemented, people would fall in love with it. As the pressure grows for her to step down, she must surely look back on the folly of this decision.

But there were other moments of madness, too. Dismissing international outrage that her Malaysian solution was inhumane and involved child trafficking, the Supreme Leader found herself being challenged by her own High Court to put a stop to the practice. Becoming increasingly erratic in her behavior, she caused havoc to Bedouin tribes and farmers on the land when she banned the sale of live cattle one day and then abruptly reinstated it the next.

Meanwhile at the United Nations in New York, Australia's long term ambassador Khe-vin R'houd announced his immediate defection from the government saying that he had never supported the current leader and wished it to be known that her government was totally illegitimate in his eyes. "This is a leader that regularly engages in torturing people (like me) and who overthrew the legitimate and much loved former leader of the country (me) and I therefore would also like it to be known that I stand ready to take control of the country again and restore proper, sensible, strong and reliable government (me again)."

These are turbulent days. Can the rebel forces succeed? Or will the Party turn on itself again, and a new leader emerge from the chaos and confusion? Will religious fundamentalists or climate change zealots attempt to seize power? In the ever-shifting sands of Canberra, history is there for the taking.

Having disappeared from public view since he lost his job, his government and his seat on the night of the 2007 election, John Howard tentatively re-appeared. As, indeed, did David Hicks, the ex-Guantanamo Bay prisoner.

The Spectator Australia editorial, 3 September 2011

HOWARD VS HICKS

This week, an attractive ABC newsreader suddenly started wearing glasses. But it's her employers who are clearly having problems seeing straight.

It's hard to think of a more myopic sense of perspective than that displayed by the decision to devote an hour's "special" on Tuesday night to telling the "Australian story" of David Hicks, and only nine minutes and eleven seconds to interviewing former Prime Minister John Howard. Is this the public broadcaster's idea of commemorating the tenth anniversary of 9/11?

Howard's brief interview with the impressive and skilled Chris Uhlmann made for compelling viewing. It included as succinct a diagnosis of the problems plaguing the current government as you will find anywhere. On Gillard: "She lacks authority." On the hung parliament: "The experiment of a new paradigm – this cosmopolitan Coalition – hasn't worked." On Tony Abbott's so-called negativity: "None of the big reforms of my government, none of them, were supported by the Labor Party in Opposition." On industrial relations: "Well, it's blindingly obvious that one of the worst mistakes Julia Gillard has made is to re-regulate the labour market. It is affecting our productivity and it will therefore affect our competitiveness." On the Greens: "They have a deep anti-Israeli streak in them which frightens and concerns a lot of people." On the Independents: "I think both Oakeshott and Windsor, if they run (again), will lose their seats." On China: "America and Australia will always be closer than China and Australia because we have shared values." There was even a bit of friendly banter, as John laughingly admitted to Chris that: "You haven't lost your touch."

All in a hurried nine minutes. Followed by a tedious, self-pitying and dissembling hour-long interview lauding David Hicks, built around such banalities as: "As a child, David was into the more natural side of things."

It's about time Auntie got her eyesight checked.

The Spectator Australia Diary, 3 September 2011

MOBBED WITH MARK LATHAM

The three girls sitting opposite can't take their eyes off us. Eventually it becomes too much for one of them (the pretty one) and she saunters over and shyly introduces herself. To Mark, of course, not the rest of us. Mark smiles and shakes her hand, and that's all it takes for the other two to rush over, pen and napkin poised for an autograph, mobile phones at the ready for the inevitable photograph.

"We really miss you," gushes one of them. She even grabs his hand. "You should *sooo* never have quit. You should be the PM, not her." The other two giggle in agreement. Mark smiles bashfully and gives a dismissive wave of his over-sized hand. "Naah," he says in his unmistakable western suburbs drawl, "I had my crack at it."

An evening with Mark Latham is an enlightening affair. The pub he has chosen is the Kirribilli Hotel, only a stone's throw from the large house on the harbour he nearly got to call home. He would have fitted in well. The locals can't seem to get enough of him. A man who introduces himself as "the Mayor of Kirribilli" is just one of the many patrons of the pub who finds an excuse to drift over and tell Mark the same two things: how much they like him. And how much they dislike Julia. "Come back, mate. All is forgiven!" he growls, to the nodding approval of those around him. Even as we attempt to leave the pub, Mark is bailed up by more people on the pavement, echoing the same sentiment. Like the best pollies with the common touch, he insists on chatting to each and every one of them in turn while the rest of us wait patiently on the sidewalk, shivering.

Over dinner we get the famous "taxi-driver-with-the-broken-elbow" yarn, complete with a visual re-enactment of the bone-snapping tackle and plate loads of humour and self-deprecation. He must've told it a thousand times before, but he makes the story sound as fresh as the tuna sashimi we tuck into. The meal is in a Japanese restaurant, around a low table, with dishes intended to share. Mark takes the beef hotpot and picks up a knife and fork. "What are you lot having?" he asks, tucking in. It suddenly occurs to me that the "handshake episode" that possibly cost him the election was completely misunderstood. Latham wasn't trying to intimidate Howard. He was probably quite pleased to bump into him and was just being himself – a brusque, forthright, no-frills Aussie bloke.

Listening to the radio on the way home, it's clear there's a new spirit in

Canberra. This one's called "defeat", and it must be hanging in the spring air as visibly as the pollen from the Floriade. "This is a dagger through the heart of the Gillard government," opines Graham Richardson, as the news comes through that the High Court has pronounced the Malaysian solution unlawful. Some months ago I wrote a spoof article in this magazine about how people smugglers would be encouraged, rather than deterred, by this ham-fisted policy. But even drawing on whatever meagre satirical skills I may possess, I couldn't have imagined how farcical this whole shemozzle would become.

Come back Mark, all is forgiven.

The Spectator Australia editorial, 10 September 2011

JUMPING THE SHARK

A fictitious TV sit-com called *At Home With Julia* has begun on the ABC, starring veteran Gillard impersonator Amanda Bishop and cult comedian Phil Lloyd. No doubt it will generate a few chuckles. But it will struggle to be anywhere near as dramatic, as tragic or even as downright funny as the real thing. Thus far, highlights of the 'Real Julia' show have included the Brutus-like slaying of a first term PM, the hanging-on-by-your-fingertips 2010 election results, the suspense-ridden pact with the Independents and Greens, the bare-faced lie of the carbon tax, and the bumbling will-she or won't-she confusion of banning live animal exports; all spiced up with titillating undercurrents of prostitution, embezzlement and union skullduggery.

But as with all great soap operas, there comes a point when the plotline becomes so ludicrous, the scenarios so unbelievable, and the dialogue so preposterous, that viewers start switching off in droves. In the classic 70's series *Happy Days*, it was the moment the Fonz famously went water-skiing in his leather jacket and jumped over a shark that signaled the end was nigh. Viewers could no longer suspend their disbelief; the ratings plummeted and it wasn't long before the series was axed. Clearly, the High Court's rejection of the Malaysian solution and the government's response is equally absurd. Indeed, is this the moment Julia "jumped the shark"? The farce has now gone on too long, and even for the most ardent fans, the whole show has become unbearable to watch.

Phillip Adams this week urged the PM to make way for the very predecessor she knifed little more than a year ago. (Who killed KR?) Mr. Rudd has long been suspected of briefing against the current Prime Minister, and the first weeks of her government were marred by cabinet leaks widely thought to have come from her predecessor. Mr. Adams' column, which gave Kevin Rudd full credit for steering Australia through the first global financial crisis, also questioned Gillard's ability to do the same when the next round of economic shockwaves hit. Was this article evidence that Rudd is now in full campaign mode to get his job back?

Should Labor panic and decide to replace Ms. Gillard, the fact remains that the party is in an untenable position. So long as it tries to straddle both its old, conservative working-class base and its socially progressive inner-city 'elite', the ALP will be unable to move forward whilst being eroded by the Greens on one side and the Coalition on the other.

No doubt, the anxious scriptwriters of the 'Real Julia' melodrama will hope to drag the ending out as long as they possibly can. As we speak, they are presumably arguing whether to spruce up the roles of some of the duller characters; like 'Cleanskin' Smith, 'Dreary' Combet or 'Junior' Shorten. They may even, in their desperation, attempt to emulate what the greatest soapie of them all, *Dallas*, so successfully did: resurrect Kevin and pretend that the last 12 months was all just a bad dream.

Throughout the entire Gillard government, Malcolm Turnbull and Kevin Rudd repeatedly dominated the opinion polls as the preferred leaders of the two parties.

ABC *The Drum*, 16 September 2011

KEVIN O'TURNBULL:
THE TEA PARTY TICKET

Prince Charles famously fantasized about being reincarnated as one of Camilla Parker-Bowles' tampons. For my part, I wouldn't mind coming back as one of Kevin Rudd's teabags.

Last night the ABC dangled before our eyes the tantalizing vision of Tea with Malcolm and Kevin. Malcolm Turnbull smiled with amused self-satisfaction when asked "is it true as reported that you and Kevin Rudd occasionally get together to talk about politics?" With a mischievous twinkle in his eye and a self-deprecating shrug Malcolm informed us somewhat primly that "Well we – not – you know, we've got together a couple of times and had a chat, had a cup of tea."

Oh, to have been a fly on the wall! Or even better, a soggy teabag on the side of the saucer; for surely whatever Mal and Kev discussed of any import would have been done in hushed tones and barely audible whispers in between carefully measured sips of tea:

Kevin: "Strange, isn't it? How similar you and I are, mate. And how entwined our fates."

Malcolm: "Indeed."

Kevin: "Has it ever occurred to you, hypothetically of course, what you and I could achieve if we worked together, in terms of logistical political specificity?"

Malcolm: "Absolutely."

For several long, drawn out seconds all we hear are the gentle sound of spoons tinkling against porcelain.

Malcolm: "In fact – dare I say it – we damn well did work well together! We nearly had that whole climate change thing done and dusted. In the bag."

Kevin: "Indeed."

Slow slurping sounds.

Kevin: "As I said, hypothetically speaking, off the cuff as it were, the question is this: were I to wrestle back the leadership, would you think about coming over? I could offer you whatever you wanted. Treasury? Foreign affairs? Climate change?"

Malcolm: "All three, perhaps?"

They both laugh.

Kevin: "The bottom line is this, to be fair dinkum about it. Would you and I make a formidable team? Yes, of course we would. And let's face it, there's no one else on my side of the fence I could trust! Haha."

Malcolm: "Funny you should ask. Because I was pretty much thinking the same thing myself."

Kevin: "Australia's Dream Team."

Malcolm: "Tony's nightmare!"

Alexander Downer and Graham Richardson have both already called on Julia Gillard to stand down. Kevin Rudd, it appears, is the only possible replacement if Labor is to avoid a NSW style implosion. He is the only one with the faintest hope of winning back Labor supporters, and of implementing the carbon tax with any credibility. With Malcolm by his side, it would be a walk in the park.

Could it be that Australia might soon see a major realignment of the political landscape? If only we could read the tea leaves.

The Prime Minister added a comedienne to her communications team.

The Spectator Australia editorial, 1 October 2011

STAND-UP COMEDY

News that Julia Gillard has enlisted onto her team the scriptwriting services of a popular stand-up comedienne comes as no surprise. But the woman in question will struggle to maintain the high comedic standards.

Who can forget gems such as "There will be no carbon tax under the government I lead," said with a straight face? Or the hilarious "I am the best person to lead this country", a line delivered with all the quixotic defiance of Python's Black Knight.

Julia's deft touch involves taking what we know and twisting it with biting sarcasm: "What I've said to Kevin is I think that this is the best (time for him) to spend more time with his family, which I know is one of his key priorities."

As any comic knows, the set-up is always important in writing a killer gag. Having dismissed the Howard government's Pacific Solution as "costly… and wrong in principle" Julia them embarked upon a series of sidesplitting alternatives. "In recent days I have discussed with President Ramos-Horta of East Timor the possibility of establishing a regional processing centre" got a few laughs, but nothing like the awesome satirical irony of the Malaysian solution.

Students of stand-up will study the Gillard technique for years. On tackling climate change: "A representative group of Australians drawn from all walks of life will help move us forward," was funny enough, but Julia milked it to the hilt: "The committee concluded that in view of the creation of this committee that the proposal of a citizens' assembly should not be implemented."

Every great comedian has a predictable catch-phrase. "Just like that!" was Tommy Cooper's, used whenever calamity struck. Julia has her own punchline for whenever she stuffs up: "Mr. Abbott will need to take the responsibility for that." It's a good gag, but it's getting a little repetitive.

After only twelve months, the Gillard experiment seemed to be in a constant state of crisis, whether over boat people, returning to surplus, climate change or the mining tax. The Age *reported on September 1: "Incompetence and disaster: another grim day for Gillard."*

ABC *The Drum*, 14 October 2011

SO, JULIA, WHY DON'T YOU TELL ME EXACTLY WHAT HAPPENED?

Having fired many people in my career, I know how difficult it is trying to get to the bottom of things when there's a stuff-up. Especially when it's a monumental one.

"Come in, Julia. Do sit down. Now tell me. What happened exactly?"

Invariably, Julia will start blubbing and I'll have to wait several moments while she dries her eyes with a tissue. To cover the awkward embarrassed silence, I buzz my secretary and ask her to bring in a pot of coffee for us both.

"I don't know where to begin," Julia finally says between sniffles. "I thought I had it all under control. But… I don't know… it was a disaster right from the start!"

That's when she'll look up at me with imploring eyes. "It was Kevin who started it all you know!" she'll finally blurt out. "It's all his fault."

"Of course it was," I nod, leaning back in my swivel chair. Already I can tell it's going to be a long drawn out meeting. I buzz my secretary again. "Better cancel lunch at Tetsuya's," I say.

Bit by bit the facts dribble out. Julia shakes her head in irritation. "I always said it was a stupid idea. But Kevin insisted. He had this massive hang up about asylum seekers, right from the word go, so first thing he does is he goes and cancels the Nauru contract. Just like that!"

I nod sympathetically. "Not, in hindsight, such I wise decision," I say, trying not to sound too judgmental.

She bristles. "But of course I told him at the time 'what on earth are we going to put in its place?' and he goes 'don't worry we'll sort it out later'."

I smile, and pour the coffees. Julia shrugs wearily. "For about a year or so, it was all hunky dory. Nothing much changed. Everyone agreed that Kevin had done the right thing."

"Sugar?" I say.

She ignores me, and carries on. "And of course, all that other stupid climate change stuff was going on and mining taxes and wotnot and next thing you know Kevin's gone and those faceless men from Sussex Street insist on giving me his job! Me?!? The next day all of his job sheets get dumped in my lap!"

"About the, er, stuff up?" I say, trying subtly to nudge her back on the track. She glares at me, and defiantly shakes her red bob.

"What was I to do? Suddenly there's boats arriving left, right and centre! I tried East Timor, but they didn't even bother returning my calls. Then I tried Manus, but no luck there either. So I got Chris to give the Malaysians a call and – hoorah!! – they were all up for it! So long as we did a bit of quid pro quo. You know, did a bit of 'contra'." She touches her (rather elongated) nose and gives me a wink.

"Chris?" I ask, puzzled.

She stares at me defiantly. "The nerdy guy from Accounts. He's my assistant now."

I try not to show any emotion. "Really?"

There's a long, awkward silence. "And, er, did you, and er, this Chris cover all the bases?" I ask as nonchalantly as possible.

Again, the steely glare.

"Did you check it all out with the legal department?" I demand.

There's a stifling silence.

I sigh wearily, and pick up my mug. This is always the hard part. It's not easy telling someone you had high hopes for that they have completely, utterly, irredeemably and – worse still – unnecessarily failed in their task.

"This is, um, kind of a monumental stuff up," I say, preparing her for the worst. "You do realize that it's now open season for people smugglers, don't you? We're going to be swamped. Inundated. From a business point of view, it's not a good look. We are a laughing stock." There. I've said it.

Julia starts to blub. I hate it when they blub.

"It's all Tony's fault," she says, wiping her eyes with her sleeve.

I frown. "Tony? I thought you said it was Kevin's fault?"

"Kevin's! And Tony's! And Chris's!" she sobs, shaking her head in dismay.

I rub my forehead, then discreetly buzz my secretary. "Have you got the number for those faceless men in Sussex Street?" I whisper as quietly as I can.

Wayne Swan was crowned 'the World's Greatest Finance Minister' by Euromoney magazine.

Heading off to the G20, the Treasurer warned European governments that the world economy will face years of stagnation if they don't tackle their debt crisis head on. He also re-iterated his boast of a surplus in 2012/13.

The Spectator Australia editorial, 22 October 2011

WORLD'S GREATEST TREASURER

A week may be a long time in politics, but so is thirteen minutes when you're up against Ali Moore, one of the ABC's sharpest interviewers. With an amused twinkle in her eye, Ali slowly grilled Wayne Swan to reveal that underneath his shiny new cloak of "The World's Greatest Finance Minister" lies… not very much at all.

"I believe there is a serious situation in the global economy," Wayne informed startled viewers, before enlightening us that he personally sees his main role as "getting on with making sure that we strengthen the global economy." Whew!

"Can you give us some detail?" Ms. Moore repeatedly begged, struggling in the face of a tsunami of bureaucratic jargon along the lines of "All of these things are part of the architecture of a comprehensive response" and "a sizeable facility to assist a European financial stability facility." Until Wayne finally confessed: "it's entirely a matter for the European ministers to talk about what they intend to do." And, er… that's it.

As for genuine insights into the global debt crisis, Australia's IMF role, cabinet leaks, the effects of onshore processing on the surplus and the legalities of the carbon tax – all raised by the determined Ms. Moore – Swan failed to deliver anything other than pre-rehearsed spin and obfuscation.

To the point where the interview tipped into satire: "I couldn't give you an update on that, but there will be an update on that in the normal processes through the mid-year review at the end of the year. That's the appropriate time to provide the update."

By the end, our world-famous Treasurer was left floundering that: "I don't know if those reports were accurate or not," "I'm not ruling anything in or out," and "I'm not going to speculate about what may or may not happen."

Even the amiable Ali struggled to keep smiling.

With Gillard and Swan looking increasingly chaotic, attention kept returning to Kevin and Malcolm.

The Spectator Australia, 22 October 2011

AH, THOSE WERE THE DAYS

'Ruddbullism' sounds like one of those infectious diseases such as botulism or toxoplasmosis that hints at much unpleasantness to come. First diagnosed by former Treasurer and Senator John Stone in *The Spectator Australia* over eighteen months ago, the term he coined describes an unhealthy merging of policy strains on climate change, work choices, boat people, the republic and other issues where supposed opponents Kevin Rudd and Malcolm Turnbull found common ground.

Much like botulism, a bacterium that enters the body through wounds, 'Ruddbullism' can also be viewed as a virulent strain that gains access through self-inflicted wounds upon the body politic. Perversely, it was the desire by Rudd and Turnbull to work together and stitch up an emissions trading scheme that eventually saw the two of them both lose their leadership positions. Similarly, Rudd's embrace of feel-good policies such as the apology to the "stolen" generation – which Turnbull was also strongly in favour of, going so far as to publicly criticise former leader John Howard over, maintaining that his former boss's position on the apology "was an error clearly" – weren't enough to save either of them from being turfed out by their own party-rooms. Both leaders lost their jobs not in spite of, but indirectly because of their support for 'Ruddbullist' principles.

Turnbull's tragedy, of course, is that he's either in the wrong electorate or the wrong party. Take your pick. His constituents are the one group in Australia who yearn for 'Ruddbullism'. A Labor party ticket with both Rudd and Turnbull together would be an answer to the sweetest dreams of the Wentworth crowd.

It's easy to see how the 'Ruddbullist' philosophy came about. In 2008-9, Kevin, confidently shedding his Howard-lite clothes, and Malcolm, eagerly donning the cloak of Liberal leadership under the mistaken belief that his own constituents expressed the desires of the larger electorate, found themselves dressed like a pair of slightly embarrassed identical twins. The majority of Australians suddenly woke up to the fact that the two leaders were prancing about in a manner utterly alien to them.

Although Rudd has now bounced back in the opinion polls, his popularity is probably as much due to the unfair manner in which he was dumped as to the policies he espoused. Call it the Short Poppy Syndrome. As is well known, we Aussies love an underdog. Where *Red Dog* endlessly roamed the outback looking for his deceased master, Rudd Dog now ceaselessly roams the globe, refusing to believe that his leadership is dead. And the audiences can't help but love him.

According to the online Medical Encyclopedia, botulism can lead to hypersensitivity, double vision, nervous exhaustion, nausea and finally paralysis of the entire system. It can be fatal.

Much like 'Ruddbullism' really.

In November, left-wing activist group GetUp! created a 'climate change time capsule'.

The Spectator Australia editorial, 19 November 2011

LAUGHING UNDERWATER

Perhaps they should include the video for 'Sexy and I Know It', by some dreadful electronic dance group, in GetUp's 2050 "carbon tax" time capsule. This current chart-topping hit features a bunch of young men in their undies wiggling their tackle around, and will tell future generations all they need to know about the value of the contemporary popular music scene.

Also waggling their tackle around, metaphorically speaking, are Wayne Swan, John Hewson, Bob Brown and, er, Penny Wong, who have all agreed to "be a part of history" by contributing their very own "letter to future generations" to be sealed in GetUp's time capsule to prove they "cared enough to speak up in an era when fear and cowardice almost won the day." You don't have to hang around to 2050 to imagine the earnest and unctuous words they, and others, will have penned. The air of self-righteous smugness will no doubt be as fresh as a daisy when the capsule is finally popped opened in the Museum of Australian Democracy thirty nine years hence.

Time capsules cut both ways. Although there is a faint possibility the Museum will be under water by then, there is a far greater likelihood that the prophesiers of doom will by 2050 have been shown to have exaggerated the scientific hypothesis of human-induced climate change in order to justify a reckless tax, and that without drastic and economically-suicidal actions by China, the US, India and others, the Gillard government's carbon tax will be acknowledged as having been deceptive, unnecessarily expensive and utterly futile.

"Well at least we did something," or "we thought we were doing the right thing" will be the awkward justifications when, and if, anybody ever bothers to open GetUp's latest gimmick. Hopefully they include the aforementioned hit single. It might, in the end, be less embarrassing than everything else in the capsule.

Julia Gillard addressed the 2011 ALP national conference, where her speech centered around the theme 'Labor says yes.'

Despite his 2007 victory over John Howard, Kevin Rudd's period as prime minister was deliberately omitted from Gillard's opening address.

The Spectator Australia, 19 November 2011

FULL OF SOUND AND FURY

"I have nothing to say, and I am saying it," said Julia Gillard this week, as she invited her Labor colleagues to make next month's conference a "noisy" one. Actually, it was John Cage, the American avant-garde composer who used those precise words, but in may as well have been our Prime Minister.

John Cage's most noteworthy contribution to contemporary culture was a piece entitled 4'33". Composed in three parts, it always features numerous diverse instruments, but it is famous because not a note is actually played during the performance. Instead, the audience get to listen to whatever noises (rustling of papers, someone coughing, a mobile phone going off and so on) that haphazardly occur over that period of time. One would struggle to think of a more apt metaphor for the "robust debates… full of energy and ideas" that Julia imagines the Labor conference will usher forth.

To put it bluntly, this government and this Prime Minister appear not only devoid of original ideas to put to the country, but are only dimly aware of what the real issues confronting us are. When a political party's one big achievement is to introduce a policy that they had no mandate for, and which by their own admission can be nothing more than a hopelessly tokenistic gesture aimed at getting other nations to "join in" combatting a "belief", then the avant-garde claim that we live in a world of surrealist absurdism starts to come uncomfortably close to being proven true.

Confusing "loving an argument" and "making a noise" with what she doesn't mention – coming up with fresh and unconventional ideas – the PM poses a series of questions that come with their own in-built set-piece answers. "As Australia becomes one of the richest countries in the world, how can we ensure a fair share for all?" she asks. And "how can we ensure no one is left behind by accident of birth or circumstance? How can we combine prosperity with stewardship of the environment?"

Clearly missing from these carefully scripted, meticulously "spun" questions are the far more fundamental ones. Such as "how do we actually generate the wealth to pay for all the things we want?" And "how do we avoid the debt crises faced by the rest of the West when we keep going further and further into debt ourselves?"

Already, the Gillard/Swan/Rudd team have destroyed the surplus that protected us first time around, have bloated the bureaucracy, have imposed crippling restraints upon productivity, and have committed the country to massively expensive and wasteful projects such as the National Broadband Network. Will any brave soul in the conference actually put up their hand and say "how do we increase the size of our nation's purse?" No, of course not. It is a given in Labor circles that wealth generates itself. It's the magic China boom pudding – Norman Lindsey's Dim Sum – and everybody can gorge themselves on as much of it as they want.

"A party able to hold robust debates is a party that's full of energy and ideas," claims Gillard, but the evidence is not there to support such a worthy claim. There will be no debate on the success or failure of Fair Work Australia. There will be no debate on the affordability of the ever-expanding health services, or education. Small business won't get a guernsey. The size of government and the need to reduce it won't get a look in, either. And then there are the taboo areas of immigration, reforming aboriginal welfare, building new dams, deterring asylum seekers, energy resourcing and pricing and so on.

None of these issues – all of which require serious, considered debate and analysis – appear to be on Julia's mind at the moment. But there is one issue that keeps her awake at night. Presumably, this will be the subject of the longed-for noisy, robust and passionate debate.

"The second issue is party reform. I want a Labor Party that is growing – with an extra 8000 members as a first step," Julia tells us.

Or, as John Cage saw it: "The highest purpose is to have no purpose at all."

Speaker of the House of Representatives Harry Jenkins tearfully and abruptly resigned. After accepting Labor's nomination to replace him, Peter Slipper quit the Coalition in a move that effectively shored up the government's wafer-thin majority and scuppered Tony Abbott's plans to force an election. As Speaker, Slipper would soon distinguish himself by bringing back some of the more traditional attire and arcane customs.

The Spectator Australia editorial, 3 December 2011

LOONEY TUNES IN CANBERRA

As the parliamentary season draws to a close, the political landscape of Canberra is beginning to resemble more and more a Looney Tunes cartoon. Every time Wily E. Tony sets one of his fearsome traps, the nimble Julia zooms straight past, and the leader of the Opposition's elaborate contraption inevitably blows up in his own face.

For months, the Acme Bring Down The Government weapon of

mass destruction has laboriously been constructed bit by bit in the scrubby wastelands behind Capitol Hill, ready to annihilate the Gillard government in an awesome puff of smoke. Early pre-selections put to bed? Check. Carbon tax to be repealed? Check. All systems for an early election ready to go.

The trigger? In Tony's clever plan, all that was needed was one teensy weeny defection from the motley crew of Roadrunner's cobbled-together coalition and her whole creaky edifice would come crashing down.

Just one defection.

Would it be Andrew Wilkie and his pokie reforms? Or would it be one of the NSW independents; a couple of Looney Tunes characters in their own right, who would stumble across the floor and set off the tripwire? Maybe it would be one of the whacko Greens, or the bloke in WA whose name nobody can remember? Rubbing his hands together in gleeful anticipation, Tony assured his eager troops that his latest plan could not possibly fail.

Just one defection.

BOOM! When the big bang finally happened, nobody saw it coming. Least of all Tony. As the dust settles, the leader of the Opposition stands dumbfounded with blackened face and singed eyebrows, blinking in confused astonishment. Yet again, her red hair glinting in the sunlight, cunning Julia has outclassed him, whizzing straight past and disappearing in a blur around the shores of Lake Burley Griffin, ready to fight another day. Meep meep!

The Spectator Australia, 31 December 2011

HOW TO DISMANTLE DEMOCRACY

Fed up with a democratic process that questions your every move and challenges your every ideological assumption? Despair no more.

Democracy may be a finely honed, intricate and complex mechanism that has been put together over thousands of years, but there's still no reason why you can't pull it to pieces. Just follow this handy step-by-step guide.

The key structural component of any democracy is capitalism, or rather, the process whereby individuals can harness their own skills, talents, desires and ambitions in order to improve their lot in life. In order to dismantle democracy, you must first switch off the capitalist power supply. There are a number of safe and proven ways to do this:

The Fannie Mae: Cleverly perfected by the immensely talented innovator William J. Clinton, this simple procedure will almost certainly bring your country's capitalist economy to a grinding halt. First, put in place legislation that requires mortgage lenders to lend money to people who have absolutely no means of repaying it. Second, ensure that there is no penalty for defaulting on your mortgage, allowing people to simply pack up and walk away from properties they can no longer afford. Third, allow government accreditation of mortgage lenders purely on the basis of the number of such loans they are prepared to hand out. Leave to simmer for about a decade or so, then sit back and watch the entire apparatus collapse in a heap.

The Brussels Sprout: Success has many fathers, and this elaborately cunning process is no exception. With special commendation going to H. Kohl, F. Mitterrand, J. Delors, T. Blair and numerous other inventive and dedicated individuals, this scheme involves a lengthy 'hoodwinking' period, during which the people of a variety of utterly incompatible and dysfunctional economies are ensured that tipping all their odorous economic ingredients into one big melting pot will create a magic pudding of peace, harmony and unending wealth. Crucially, any sceptics who question the wisdom of such a recipe must be labeled "radicals", "hardliners" and even "fools" by the press of the day.

The 'Brewster' (aka the 'Swan Dive'): In extremely rare circumstances, you may find you have inherited a large amount of money due to the frugality and caution of your predecessor. If so, it is obligatory that — as in the Richard Pryor comedy *Brewster's Millions* — you blow the entire lot in as little time as possible. Soon you will be safely back in debt.

Well done. Now that you've successfully thrown a spanner into the capitalist works, it is crucial that you repeatedly reinforce the negative connotations associated with it. Some suggestions:

Pen an essay, as did K. Rudd, claiming that "it now falls to social democracy to prevent liberal capitalism from cannibalising itself." Express sympathy, as did E. Miliband, for the goals of the 'Occupy' movement, emphasising the need to "rid the country of irresponsible, predatory capitalism."

Congratulations. You have now successfully unhitched capitalism from democracy in the public's mind, so you can start embellishing your own role. The following steps can be taken in any order:

Find a cause: Ideally, one that requires massive government taxation and involves a "doomsday" threat for people to get passionate about. Traditionally, wars and crusades have proven popular, but why not be more imaginative? Nowadays apocalyptic scenarios can be conjured up out of anything from Y2K viruses to a 12th century imam sitting at the bottom of a well — or even polar bears scurrying off ice floes.

Bloat your public service: If people rely on you for a living, they are hardly going to want to get rid of you.

Strengthen your unions: Get the public used to the idea that faceless men and backroom deals, as opposed to the ballot box, will decide who runs the country.

Rewrite history: Wherever possible, airbrush your opponents out of the picture.

Open your borders: Nothing undermines democracy faster than replacing controlled immigration with chaos and confusion.

Reduce individual wealth: Find a handy and oblique euphemism (we recommend "quantitative easing" or "expansionary monetary policy") for printing as much dosh for yourself as you want. Then spend it. Fast. Alternatively, just keep borrowing lots of money. (China's usually good for a touch up, but remember to call it a "stimulus package").

Redistribute the loot: With capitalism on the ropes, now is the perfect opportunity to ramp up those taxes on profitable companies and splash out the money bribing, er, sorry, "compensating" the great unwashed.

Don't forget — you need to start ignoring the electorate's wishes and begin imposing your own ideology upon them. If you're floundering, why not form a coalition and borrow someone else's whacko beliefs?

Remember, nothing thwarts the will of the voting population more than when the ruling party throws in their lot with a group of self-serving, hypocritical, un-mandated Independents, Greens, religious fanatics or whatever. This allows government to waste precious time and money on fringe issues, elitist lobby groups, nanny-state opinionators and so on, thereby removing the need to stick to any actual election promises. (Warning: if your coalition looks like coming unstuck, quickly purchase a Speaker. Any old one will do.)

You're almost there! For the final flourish, get a few disgruntled fellow travellers to come up with "alternative ideas" to "improve" democracy. These could include government by lottery, or even better, government by appointment of "interested parties" and "academic experts." Make sure you give them lots of fancy names.

And while you're at it, polish up your own sales pitch. Ensure that whatever you promise is actually devoid of any credible meaning. Stuck for ideas? Be brave. Try something really inane, like "moving forward," "say yes to the future" or even "we are us."

Well done! Have fun and enjoy your dismantled democracy for years to come.

On New Years Day 2012, following the release of cabinet papers, former Prime Minister Bob Hawke suggested it was his expertise on the economy and his consensus approach that saved Australia from becoming "the poor white trash of Asia." His successor and Treasurer Paul Keating quickly responded, blaming Hawke for presiding over wage explosions in the 1970's as the trade union leader who "nearly destroyed the economy twice."

Financial Review, 5 January 2012

ROCK'S OLD STAGERS REFUSE TO BURY THE AXE

"The sound you make is muzak to my ears," sneered John Lennon, as he savaged his former song-writing partner in the vitriolic 'How Do You Sleep?' His normally sweet-sounding voice which gave us 'All You Need Is Love' and 'Give Peace A Chance' was now laced with poison, as Lennon went on to claim that the only Beatles composition McCartney had been responsible for "was 'Yesterday'… and since you've gone you're just 'Another Day'."

Harsh words indeed. Almost as harsh as Keith Richards' criticism of his own former band-mate. Apparently, Mick Jagger, the great sex symbol of the 60's and 70's, could only boast a "tiny todger" according to his former best friend and drug-binging partner-in-crime. And the hits? Well, the implication is clear. 'Keef' would come up with the riff, the tune and the main idea of the song and leave Mick to polish it up a bit.

And now another famous duo whose glory days are long past have publicly fallen out. Aging rockers Bobby J. and Paulie K. have spent the last week squabbling over who came up with precisely which bit of their greatest hits.

"It was basically me what wrote the entire 'Float the Dollar' album,"

Paulie told me, lounging back in his gothic mansion, his eccentric rock star collection of antique French clocks all madly ticking away at different rhythms and chiming at different intervals. "It may as well have been a solo album. I wrote all the songs. Even designed the cover."

Bobby J. will have none of it, of course. "I don't wanna get into some Paulie slanging match over all that again," he said, downing a schooner of beer in his harbourside retreat, the beautiful Blanche curled up on the leopard-skin sofa beside him fondly stroking his silver mullet. "But Paulie really only played a minor part in the whole thing. It was a collaboration. I got all sorts of different people together, assembled 'em all in this big room together, and told 'em all to let rip. It was beautiful. Paulie never really liked the idea anyway. Me and the others had to talk him into it."

"You gotta be pulling my plonker!" explodes the ever-acerbic Paulie when I confront him with his former partner's comments. "Collaboration? The only thing that twat ever collaborated on was nearly bringing down the whole show! Not once, but twice! Way back before I came on the scene and it was just him running the act – or the ACTU as it was called then – he gave every two-bit hanger on and groupie as much dosh as they wanted and they nearly destroyed the label! I had to step in, crack a few skulls together and restore some common sense."

Bobby J. shakes his head and his craggy face breaks into a smile, a twinkle in his eye affording me a momentary glimpse of the charismatic idol who drove the fans wild all those years ago. "Paulie was very much under the sway of his guru, the Mahareshi Stone, back in those days. He was dead set against the whole thing. Said it would bring on a 'revolution'. I knew it was all bollocks. Me and the other guys had to basically talk them both into it."

But recently released documents tell a slightly different story. Dated 2 November 1983, the scribbles on the back of an envelope in Paulie's distinctive spider crawl handwriting make it clear that he was already flirting with the main concept six months earlier. In an unfinished couplet labeled 'Quantum Leap' Paulie wistfully points out that "Beyond these essentially technical changes/ Lies the possibility of a floating exchange rate."

Tensions between the two are not new, with Paulie claiming he "carried" Bobby through years of "emotional and intellectual malaise" in the mid 80's. Following a secret gig in Kirribilli, it was even rumoured Bobby had offered to let Paulie take over lead vocals.

So who is right and who is wrong? The answer, of course, is both are right and both are wrong. What made the Beatles and the Stones great is what made Bob and Paul great. That intangible, indefinable thing that happens when two great talents spark off each other. The sardonic humour of Lennon combined with the warmth and melody of McCartney. The gritty earthiness of Richards combined with the prancing sexuality of Jagger. The shopping-mall popularity of Hawke combined with the ruthlessness of Keating.

One of the rarest and greatest political couplings. Together they made magic. But in the end, it tore them both apart.

With the release of further cabinet documents, debate around the relative merits of policy decisions during the Hawke – Keating years continued to cause controversy.

Financial Review, 7 January 2012

TRUE BELIEVERS IN A WORLD LONG DEPARTED

Cabinet documents released on Friday have reignited the bitter feud between Julia Gillard and her former colleagues as to who can lay claim to the many policy decisions taken during the turbulent Rudd/Gillard/ Rudd/ Shorten/Combet government 30 years ago.

"Kevin's a dear friend of mine and I'm not going to get into some slanging match about trivial events that occurred so long ago, but the carbon tax was all his idea," said a defiant Gillard, outside her lakeside apartment as Canberrans shivered through their coldest summer on record.

"I made it very clear at the time that there would be no such tax under any government I led. Yes, I was forced to change my mind, but that was Bob Brown's fault."

But her former treasurer, Wayne Swan, enjoying a summer skiing trip in the Gold Coast hinterland, saw it differently. "What you have to remember is that all the Treasury advice at the time was that climate change gave us the perfect excuse to, er, make the numbers stack up again. How else was I going to balance the books after Rudd went and blew a perfectly good surplus?"

Former PM Kevin Rudd, who has just reappointed himself to another five-year term as UN Secretary-General, speaking at his lakeside home outside Geneva, was quick to dismiss the assertions as mischievous scuttlebutt from a bunch of "pretty crook cobbers."

"The record shows quite clearly I had nothing at all to do with any of it. When I spoke of a great moral challenge I was not speaking of any detailed programmatic specificity, but rather, merely articulating a widely held and popular view. Let's not forget – am I the guy who said sorry to the indigenous population of Australia? Yes. And am I the humble kid from Eumundi Plains who in my first term as Secretary-General of the World apologised to the Inuit, the Aztecs, the Armenians and the Orang Asli? You bet."

Former PM Bill Shorten takes an altogether different view.

"Basically, when the shit hit the fan and the country ground to a halt in the Winter of Discontent, let's not forget I was the go-to guy whom the party turned to. And I massively increased productivity almost overnight by repealing the carbon tax, repealing the mining tax and introducing Fair WorkChoices."

Former PM Greg Combet laughed dismissively at any suggestion that Shorten's short tenure as PM in the last two weeks of August 2013 had any impact whatsoever on the country's economic health: "The papers clearly show that it was under my leadership that we introduced the Super Profits Tax, the Medium Profits Tax, the Tiny Profits Tax and the No Profits Whatsoever Tax. These were all key Labor economic reforms that transformed the way we do, er, I mean did, business in this country."

However, Gillard was adamant the records proved she was the key prime minister of the period. "My revolutionary Open Borders Policy was a huge success, ushering in a new era of vibrant and colourful Islamic culture into all aspects of Australian life." But when questioned about rumours of mass drownings at sea during that era, Gillard was unequivocal. "Yes, but they were all Tony Abbott's fault."

Speaking from his tour bus on the Short Memories Anniversary Tour, Midnight Oil lead singer Peter Garrett called the release of the cabinet minutes "one of the greatest travesties of misinformation ever perpetrated upon the Australian people." Garrett, quivering with outrage and indignation, claimed: "When they said they were going to start digging up uranium and selling it willy-nilly to the Indians I stomped my foot really hard underneath the cabinet table. And when they said they were giving the nod to more US forces in Darwin I banged my fist really loudly on the table. Or it might have been the palm of my hand. But there's no mention of my steadfast opposition to both those thingies anywhere."

Meanwhile, speaking via wireless hologram from his farm in Tasmania, former communications minister Stephen Conroy defended the more than $200 billion blowout on the abandoned and obsolete NBN scheme as a tiny blip of no consequence in the bigger picture of the Gillard government's key economic platforms.

A Liberal backbencher said she was concerned about new migrants on 457 visas not integrating into the community because they hadn't been taught about cultural issues such as wearing deodorant and waiting in line politely.

"Without trying to be offensive, we are talking about hygiene and what is an acceptable norm in this country when you are working closely with other co-workers," she said.

Financial Review, 12 January 2012

ON THE NOSE IN DOWNTOWN CANBERRA

New arrivals to parliament need to be better taught how to fit in, particularly as regards such issues as personal hygiene and joining the queue, according to a Liberal backbencher.

"Some members of the government have a distinct whiff about them, which, to say the least, is not all that pleasant. Take the member for Dobell, for instance. He hasn't been around long enough to learn any common courtesy. He should have left his dirty laundry in the smoky backrooms and bordellos of the HSU rather than dragging it in here to stink the place out."

The MP's controversial remarks have caused a storm of outrage within the corridors beneath Capital Hill. Recently promoted Speaker-of-the-House Peter Slipper was one who immediately took umbrage at her insinuation that he had queue-hopped. "I waited very patiently for months on end until such time as Harry Jenkins was finally knifed in the back and bundled onto the back benches. Then of course I was able to hop straight in, roll up my sleeves and get to work," he said, speaking from a vineyard restaurant on the outskirts of Canberra. "As for fitting in with my co-workers, I feel perfectly at home sitting down for a long lunch with my new Labor Party colleagues."

Minister for Climate Change and All Sorts of Other Stuff Grog

Combat was equally contemptuous of her remarks. "It's well known that I have been politely waiting in a queue for several years now, without once complaining or ever raising my voice, behind both Kevin and Julia. But I have no doubt that my turn is coming up very soon now."

However, the MP has found some support for her criticisms of personal hygiene from unlikely quarters. Former PM Kevin Rudd was quick to point out that although the Heiner affair had threatened to hang around him like a bad smell for a couple of years he was able to get rid of it by taking a few simple precautionary steps, such as denying any wrongdoing whatsoever and shredding everything in sight. Picking some wax out of his ear and eating it, Rudd went on to say that he saw "nothing wrong at all" with his personal habits.

An elder statesman was quick to offer some timely advice. "Yes, indeed, there is a rather toxic odour wafting around the joint that we have to all face up to. It's not any one individual. Rather, it emanates from the rotting carcass that is today's Labor Party. We need to rebuild it from the ground up. That's the only way to get rid of the stench." Standing behind him with their noses pegged, a group of retired NSW Labor politicians reminded reporters that the nasty pong had nothing to do with any of them.

Tony Abbott, himself no stranger to the post-workout antiperspirant, was quick to defend his backbencher's comments. "Um, ah, different people have different lifestyles, and, ah, um, come from very different cultures. In fact, ah, one of my co-workers, Malcolm, struggles to fit in at all but, um, for some reason we still tolerate having him around." Sitting all alone by himself in the canteen, Malcolm fretfully admitted that deep down he longed to return to his natural birthplace, the left side of the political divide, from whence he'd fled many years earlier. "I've had a sniff around but they won't let me back in," he lamented.

Speaking from their adjacent New England electorates, former loners and outsiders Rob Oakeshott and Tony Windsor were unapologetic. "We both found it very easy to fit in, once Julia made it clear we could have as many millions of dollars as we wanted. Nothing smelly about that whatsoever."

Sweating profusely, Chris Bowen was quick to seize on the comments as a personal affront. "The only reason I sweat so much is nothing whatsoever to do with deodorant or a lack thereof," he said, his red face glistening under the harsh light of the TV cameras. "It's because I feel acutely embarrassed about what a disastrous job we've done." Standing stiffly behind him, Senator Conroy, a British immigrant, admitted that he still had problems adapting to some of the more outlandish Australian cultural norms. "Back in the old country we never bothered with such ridiculous rituals as a cost benefit analysis or a sound business model."

But Green's leader Bob Brown was unfazed by the controversy. "Everything around here smells pretty sweet to me. I get my own way on pretty much whatever I want and I only got 11% of the vote."

Julia Gillard was unavailable for comment, although rumours have it that some time in March she'll be taking a bath.

The Spectator Australia, 14 January 2012

TIME TO SAIL INTO THE SUNSET?

10,9,8,7,6,5,4,3,2,1. It's time for Peter Garrett to go. Now.

People enter politics either for the power or the passion, and hopefully a bit of both. Afforded every possible opportunity and advantage — a safe seat, celebrity status, the fast track to the front bench, numerous ministerial positions — Peter has shown beyond doubt he is not prepared to use his power to implement the things he once was passionate about. The excuse that is trotted out — from sympathetic commentators who claim Peter needs to be a "team player" in order to affect change "from the inside" — holds even less water than the now-defunct Traveston Crossing Dam.

It can't have escaped Peter Garrett's notice that not only has his party sacrificed nearly every principle he ever held dear, but also that he has been betrayed by nearly every political patron he trusted. Forget diesel and dust. His is a story of irony and pathos.

The erstwhile senate candidate for the Nuclear Disarmament Party has now agreed to expanding our uranium production and selling it to a nuclear-armed state. The messianic singer who railed against US forces being a "setback for your country" doesn't bat an eyelid at new Marine bases in Darwin. The political activist who sneered at those who toe the party line rather than fight for what they believe in ("politicians party line, don't cross that floor") now adheres to that very creed.

Kevin Rudd and Julia Gillard have walked all over Garrett, repeatedly demoted him or shunted him aside (from the one portfolio he really cares about — climate change) and, grotesquely, have allowed him to be the public scapegoat for the Pink Batts fiasco.

But at what point does repeatedly taking one for the team become a gang bang by the entire scrum? Acquiescing to the dredging of Port Phillip Bay? Ouch. Approving the Bell Bay Pulp Mill? Ouch! Expanding the Beverley uranium mine? Uuuggghh!! Agreeing to sell uranium to India? Aaaarrrggh!!! Allowing US forces to base themselves in Darwin? Noooo! Stop!

And that's ignoring such trivialities as withdrawing federal funding from the Australian National Academy of Music, an act which must surely have given him at least one sleepless night?

"I have protested, sung, marched, written, organised and campaigned on those things I simply believed were important, not just to me but to the life of the nation," Garrett reminded us in his maiden speech to parliament, just over seven years ago. And it was true. While the high point of his activism was probably the clever ambush advertising for the Reconciliation movement at the Sydney Olympics, both as leader of the Oils and as president of the Australian Conservation Foundation,

Garrett had become the angry spokesperson for any number of controversial issues, from environmentalism to indigenous welfare with a bit of 'occupy the street outside Exxon' thrown in. Our very own Bono.

Yet apparently the only time recently that Garrett has taken a strong stance on any issue of newsworthiness is his reported threat to cause a by-election if, yet again, he were to be demoted by his leader.

Rock stars disappoint. Rewind your memory to the Oils' hey- day. Whether it be a singalong at Selina's in '78 or an explosive gig at the Hordern in '87. And recall that shiver of excitement, that frisson of rebellion, from the dropout lawyer with the gangly physique, the awesome voice and the frenetic dance moves, who in every note and dance step savaged the complacency of mainstream white Australia, berating us for our subservience to uncle Sam, grabbing us by the throat and forcing us to face ourselves in the mirror over our neglect of our aboriginal brethren, and flaying us alive for our trashing of the environment. Feeble politicians, conniving capitalists, evil company executives. They were all there, in a rogues' gallery set to some of the most brilliant rock tunes ever written.

But what happens now? Does Garrett simply keep schtum, whither away and disappear in the wipeout of the next federal election?

Time is running out for Garrett to stand tall. Peter, pick an issue. Any one will do. And resign. Whether it be over your government's failure to genuinely improve indigenous wellbeing, or about the sale of uranium to India, or the basing of US forces in Oz, or offshore processing of asylum-seekers, or mandatory detention, or your government's inaction on whaling, or the threat of CSG mining, or any of the myriad issues you once were so passionate about.

Threaten to bring the whole show crashing down unless you get your way. Just this once. Better to die on your feet than to live on your knees.

Andrew Wilkie, the independent member for Denison, withdrew his support for the minority government, claiming the problem gambling proposals announced by Gillard were in breach of the agreement he signed with her after the 2010 election.

Wilkie said he felt "very disappointed" with the Gillard government. Independent Senator Nick Xenophon said the Prime Minister had lost all credibility.

Financial Review, 20 January 2012

HOUSE ALWAYS WINS IN POKIES REFORM GAME

Andrew blinked as he stepped into the gloom. He'd always avoided this sort of place. Huddled over the rows and rows of machines, their desperate, haunted features illuminated by a pallid glow, sat the hopeless, forlorn punters.

His heart went out to them and he felt a lump in his throat as he thought of the fortunes being frittered away every few seconds. All to no avail. It was time to put a stop to this madness.

"Welcome to Canberra, Mr. Wilkie," said the friendly looking red-headed woman at the door. "Would you care to play?"

Andrew swallowed hard. He'd always promised his constituents that he'd stay independent of this mob. That the sins of the flesh and political patronage were not for him. He knew that he would be able to resist it. He was different.

"Go on," said the woman, whose nametag labeled her simply as Julia. "Everybody likes a flutter. It's fun." A cheeky smile played on her thin lips. "Pick any game you like the look of," she whispered.

"It's very dark in here!" he replied, his voice betraying his nervousness. "Aren't there any windows?"

Julia laughed. "Of course not, Andrew. Parliament House was

specially designed that way – so pollies never know whether it's night or day and just keep on playing the game. Clever, isn't it? Come and meet the others."

Sitting at a bright, colourful machine, with a huge bucket of money next to him, a young man was frantically shoveling in what to Andrew looked like millions, if not billions, of coins.

"This is Stephen," cooed Julia. "He's playing National Broadband."

The man barely gave Andrew a glance.

"I'm winning!" he said, breathlessly. "I've already signed up 426 users!"

"And this is Wayne, who was recognised recently as The World's Greatest Gambler," Julia said proudly. "He borrows more than a hundred million dollars every day!"

Andrew glanced around at all the sad and lonely faces. "Why not have a go?" Julia asked sweetly.

He took a deep breath. He must be strong. "Not today, thank you, Julia," he said. "I just wanted to see how everything works down here. I'll just take a squizz, you know, have a bit of a poke around."

In the darkness Andrew couldn't read her expression, but the tone in her voice seemed slightly more sinister. "A poke, did you say? That's funny. We have a game called Pokie Reforms. Perhaps you'd like to try your luck?"

Before he could stop himself Julia had ushered him into his very own chair. Gently taking his hand, she placed it on the cool, shiny lever. The machine whirred and lights started to flash, almost as if the harmless box possessed a life of its own.

"Imagine if you were to win," Julia purred seductively into his ear. "The prestige, the power."

Andrew felt his heart racing.

"You could be a legend in your own lifetime. History books will sing your praises. Maybe name a statute after you – Wilkie's Law! The Man Who Won on Pokie Reform."

Andrew struggled to resist but the temptation was too strong. As the dazzling pictures and symbols flashed hypnotically before his eyes, he felt an exhilarating surge of adrenalin coursing through his veins. This was it! Finally, he was doing something important with his life. He was a player!

As he pulled on the lever a man at the next machine leaned over and started to say something, but Andrew wasn't listening.

He pulled again. The sound! The colour! It was more exciting than anything he'd ever experienced. He pulled again.

As the hours rushed past he was lost in a frenzied, glittering whirlwind of newspaper interviews, television studios and flashing lights.

And then there was silence. As abruptly as it started the game had stopped. Andrew stared at the blank, silent machine; stunned.

He called out for Julia, but she was far away, over the other side of the room, laughing and joking with another man; showing him which buttons to push on a glitzy game called Speaker of the House. Andrew started to panic. He wanted to keep playing.

Frantically he searched in his pockets but he didn't have any chips left to bargain with. They were all gone.

The man at the machine next to him leaned over again. "I'm Nick," he said, with a wry smile on his face. "I tried to warn you. Pokie Reforms is one hell of a game. I've been addicted to it for years. But I reckon it's rigged 'coz no matter what you do the House always wins."

In late 2010 Julia Gillard appointed a panel of experts to determine how best to recognise indigenous peoples in the Australian Constitution.

In January 2012 the 'Expert Panel on Constitutional Recognition of Indigenous Australians' issued its report to the Government, setting out its proposals for constitutional change.

Financial Review, 27 January 2012

CONSTITUTIONAL CONFUSION?
IT'S ALL BLACK AND WHITE

"Order, order, can we all please settle down," said the co-chair, squirming in his seat. "The Expert Panel has an important job to do here today. The hand of history lies delicately upon our shoulders, I think you'll all agree . . ."

Expert Panelist 2 rolled her eyes back. "When you say 'hand', could you not be a little more specific? It could be misconstrued as a white hand, and that would be paternalistic."

Around the room, heads nodded feverishly.

"Possibly even racist," muttered Expert Panelist 17 under her breath.

The co-chair felt beads of sweat breaking out on his forehead. The room was claustrophobic enough, 19 people all crammed around one long table, without the feeling of dread that had been creeping over him these past few minutes.

"Of course, of course. Allow me to rephrase that, er . . . let the minutes show that the black armband of history sits . . ."

Expert Panelist 13 slammed her hand down. "It's not the black armband. It's the black hand. We have to get these details right."

"I'm sure that's what my learned panelist meant," said the other co-chair, swiftly coming to the first co-chair's rescue. It had been a long, exhausting process. Tempers were frayed. He picked up his dog-eared copy of the constitution that lay forlornly on the table, covered in gigantic red crosses and angry red lines that made it look more like the victim of a road crash than the most important legal document in the land.

There was a hesitant cough. The thin expert panelist with the neatly trimmed beard sitting at the far end of the room adjusted his glasses as he summoned up the courage to speak. "I just think, perhaps, without overdoing it, but in, a, er, non-confrontational spirit of, er, mutual recognition, we might, er . . ."

"What?" said Expert Panelist 2, fixing him with her formidable gaze.

"I, er, just thought that perhaps we should, er, possibly consider, um, just simply changing one or two words . . . that was all."

Around the room the expert panelists all started angrily gesticulating and speaking at once.

"One or two words?" shouted one, grabbing the tattered document. "Look! Section 51. I'll read it to you: 'The Parliament shall, subject to this constitution, have power to make laws for the peace order, and good government of the commonwealth with respect to the people of any race, for whom it is deemed necessary to make special laws'."

"That is soooo racist," said Panelist 12, the youngest expert present. The rest of the room agreed, shaking their heads in disgust.

"Special laws for special races. Sick," said Panelist 9.

"In the bin!" yelled Panelist 14, screwing up the offending pages into a tight ball and lobbing them across the room.

"Whooaa!" yelled Expert Panelist 2, snatching back the document. "Not so fast. Not everything's gotta go. Not the new bits. They have to stay. The bit about 'advancement', for example."

"Which bit was that?" said one of the token MPs, stifling a yawn. Canberra politics was bad enough, but this mob were something else altogether.

Expert Panelist 2 glowered at him. "We have to have it legally enshrined that we can advance certain cultural groups."

"But isn't that, er ... racist?"

"Don't talk such rot! Some of them don't even speak English! Of course they need special treatment!"

"You mean like teaching them English?" said the shy developmental and educational expert, who'd been longing for an opportunity to get involved in the discussion.

Panelist 5, an expert in indigenous welfare and social deprivation issues looked aghast.

"How racist can you get?" she muttered, shaking her head in disbelief.

Expert Panelist 2 slumped back wearily in her chair.

"What I have in mind is a substantive section in the constitution that accords indigenous people recognition. And not some recognition-lite which involves interpretation by some future High Court or government. Got it?"

The independent MP reached for his glass of water. He'd always found Julia tough to negotiate with, but this woman was something else. "Of course, of course," he said, swallowing nervously.

"So. We remove sections 51 and 25 from the constitution because of their outdated racism. Agreed?"

Around the table, heads nodded enthusiastically.

"And we replace them with the proposed section 116A. Agreed?"

"Sorry, er, what was that again?"

"The making of laws to protect the cultures, languages or heritage of special groups."

"You mean, er, special laws for special races?"

"Don't be ridiculous," snapped Expert Panelist 2. "I mean special advancement policies for indigenous groups."

"Oh, I see."

"Well?" said the co-chair, swiftly wiping a bead of sweat from his brow. "Are we all agreed?"

One by one, the expert panelists turned and nodded.

The other co-chair gratefully shook his co-chair's hand. "Done," he said, sighing with relief. "Can't wait for the referendum."

The Wiggles announced the return of the original Yellow Wiggle, causing controversy over the shabby treatment of his stand-in replacement.

Speculation swirled around a possible Kevin Rudd challenge to Gillard.

The Spectator Australia editorial, 28 January 2012

LABOR'S WIGGLE ROOM

The world of children's politics was rocked to its foundation last week with news that Kev will return to the limelight, replacing "hired hand" Julia who has stood in for him for the past 18 months. Proudly donning his yellow skivvy, Kev announced that following his abrupt departure in 2010 he realised he had "unfinished business" and that over the Christmas break he had been asked to rejoin the original lineup. "It's our only hope of reconnecting with the fans," admitted 'Captain Magic Buttons' Arbib, 'Cocky Want a Cracker' Howes and 'I Want to Wear the Jacket' Shorten.

"The opportunity was too good to pass up," said Kev, grinning excitedly. "We always made beautiful music together and the kids love us. With such famous songs as 'Hot Potato — Ode to the Carbon Tax', 'Great Big Man In The Red (Wayne's Song)' and our Broadband hit 'Knead Some Dough', we brought politics to a whole new level of silliness." Tightly clutching her own tattered yellow skivvy, deposed band member Julia struggled to fight back the tears as she complained to a packed press conference that she had been ostracised and treated badly all along. "During my time I contributed enormously to the achievements of the group," she said, citing in particular 'We're The Cowboys', 'Wheels On The Bus (Have Come Off),' and her personal favourite 'Can You Point Your Finger (At The Opposition Leader)?'

"On top of that, I can single-handedly take credit for our best-selling DVD *Captain Featherbowen Fell Asleep on the Smugglers' Ship* and its mega-hit 'Our Boat Is Sinking on the Sea', which has been hugely popular as far afield as Indonesia, Malaysia and Afghanistan."

A spokesperson confirmed that Kev will rejoin the group for a sell-out national tour before the end of the year.

In a series of interviews, senior Labor minister Simon Crean, himself a former leader, said Mr. Rudd and his supporters must accept Rudd would never be prime minister again.

He said the ousted leader lost his position because he was not a "team player".

"One thing the Labor Party has got to learn is that it doesn't solve its polling problems by simply changing the leader."

Financial Review, 4 February 2012

THREE STOOGES

Australia now in effect has three prime ministers: the populist, the pragmatist and the politician.

All three were hard at work during the week, beavering away in front of the TV cameras as they sought to lead the nation in their three unique ways. One wants to be loved, one wants to be listened to, and one craves respect and legitimacy.

In some ways, we should be grateful. Who says you need only one leader? Plenty of European countries have run on troikas, including the USSR, briefly, after Stalin croaked, and it didn't do the Russians any harm (comparatively), so why should it bother us?

Our populist leader – the one recognised as Australia's PM by everyone overseas – returned to his favourite haunt this week, a school yard on the Gold Coast hinterland where, surrounded by adoring Aryan-looking, sun-bleached schoolkids in peaked hats and bright T-shirts, he was able to show off his brilliant PR and diplomatic skills.

Sounding nicer and more reasonable than any human being should ever have to, Kevin slid the knife ever so gently out of his own back and, with the greatest of aplomb, popped it squarely back where it belongs – between the shoulder blades of Simon Crean.

"Can I just say this … ?" began Mr. Ever-So-Humble-and-Exceedingly-Reasonable, and we knew we were in for a doozy. He didn't disappoint.

As the kiddies gazed up at him, with expressions normally reserved for Justin Bieber, Kevin neatly countered Crean's recent ambush of him and turned his graceless criticism that the former Prime Minister was "a prima donna" and "not a team player" abruptly on its head: "I am proud to be a member of this ministerial team, which is very strong, very dedicated, very hard-working and in which Simon himself plays a very positive role," said the Foreign Minister, humility, sincerity and prime ministerial magnanimity oozing out of every pore.

The kiddies, the journalists and the Queensland hinterland swooned as one.

Meanwhile, in the nation's capital, suitably attired in a smart suit and the same tie he wore to the Lobby punch-up on Australia Day, our pragmatic leader – the one who has dictated the government's agenda this past year and says what most people outside the beltway think – set out to prove to a sceptical audience of hardened journos that he's more than just a fluoro vest and a pair of tight-fitting togs.

Having spent most of the year telling the government what not to do and how not to do it, it was time for a bit of overdue "positivity".

Telling it like it is came easy to Tony, but utterly confounded the press gallery, so conditioned is it to a daily diet of deception and spin. Pragmatically – and honestly – Abbott pointed out that there wasn't a great deal any prime minister could readily commit to until the budget was back in strong surplus.

In other words, in a world that is being brought to its knees by mountains of government-generated debt, wouldn't it be a smart idea to sit tight and hold off on the overblown spending commitments, grandiose projects and novelty taxes that risk tipping our own perilously poised economy over the edge?

Explaining his aspirations, principles and priorities – practical measures he intends to see achieved on dental health, Aboriginal welfare, disability care and so on – clearly left the nation's top journalists confounded and more than a little frustrated. They'd far rather have a "core promise" to jot down in the cynical hope that they can string him up with it further down the track.

And finally, way down south, our nuts and bolts political leader – the one who gets to have all the fun doing backroom deals and backflips – went to work, mouthing carefully scripted words to sell us something nobody asked for and almost certainly nobody will ever see: her new economy. Taken straight out of the mouths of focus group groupies, the "new economy" is a sound-bite phrase carefully selected by the same mob who gave us "we are us" and "moving forward". It sounds thrilling and enticing but on closer inspection is devoid of meaning.

Attempting to steal credit from John Howard and Peter Costello for the rivers of gold that Labor found sloshing around in the vaults under Parliament House and promptly spent, at best the "new economy" is jargon for a robust mining boom being pilfered by a punitive couple of wealth redistribution measures.

All three speeches received the appropriate media coverage and varying degrees of acclaim. We are blessed to have three such gifted prime ministers. At some point, however, we might actually have to choose between them.

The Auditor-General announced significant problems with the Federal Government's $20 million carbon tax advertising blitz, including breaches of financial management regulations and "facts that were not properly sourced."
The campaign also failed to effectively sway public opinion.

Financial Review, 10 February 2012

MAD MEN

News that the auditor-general has found that the Labor government's carbon tax ad campaign had breached financial regulations and was largely ineffective has sent a resounding shockwave throughout the advertising and PR industries.

"The idea that we should be expected to stick to telling the truth in our ads goes against everything we stand for," said Bobby Spinne, chairman and chief creative officer of The Funky Ideas Factory.

"After all, as it makes clear on our website we are one of the most highly awarded ad agencies in the southern hemisphere, and have won more trophies and industry accolades than all our competitors put together, on top of which we are, to our mind, Australia's leading agency for digital effectiveness and creative innovation as well as one of the most strategic ad shops in the world thanks to our unique (and patented) Strato-think planning methodology.

"It's not as if we require exaggeration and hyperbole to get our message across."

Denying that there was anything misleading in his headline, "Why polar bears will get down on their knees and thank all Australians for the carbon tax," Spinne took issue with the auditor-general's findings that there was no "clear line of sight" between 52 of the claims made in the advertisements and the actual facts as they pertained to the introduction of the new legislation.

"At this agency, unlike all our rip-off competitors, we pride ourselves on the thoroughness of our approach in getting to the heart of the brief.

"Both at a strategic and a creative level we leave no stone unturned in our effort to dig out the nuggets of a compelling insight.

"For example, before we even discussed the carbon tax brief I made sure the entire agency sat down on a Friday night with a few bottles of red and watched the extraordinarily truthful, very moving and highly informative documentary by renowned international climate expert Al Gore, which I was able to download free off the internet."

The Minister for Climate Change and No Change Out of $20 million, Grog Combat, denied that the awarding of the campaign to Spinne's agency had been done in a panicky rush and without adhering to adequate processes and preparation.

"I'm sure I jotted down a complete budget breakdown and costs summary somewhere on the back of one of those coaster thingies that you put your drinks on in the business lounge," he said.

When questioned as to why the household mail-out distribution contract appeared to have been awarded to a different person in the department's system than the agency that carried out the work, Combat was quick to point out that "all these advertising types with their black jeans and silly tee-shirts look the same to me." Countering doubts expressed about his expertise in marketing strategies, Combat was quick to dismiss the suggestion that he had been taken for a ride.

"I make it my job to stay on top of these things. I am a big fan of *The Gruen Transfer* and I've even got the box set of *Mad Men*. There's no way some slick ad guy is going to pull the wool over my eyes."

On the ABC's Four Corners, Gillard awkwardly dodged questions about how early she was involved in the 2010 plot to remove Kevin Rudd.

Meanwhile, Newspoll showed public confidence in Labor's record of economic management was fast eroding.

Financial Review, 17 February 2012

ME AND JULIA DOWN BY THE SCHOOLYARD

The freckle-faced little girl with red hair and ponytails fidgeted nervously, squirming in the hard wooden chair. One sock lower than the other, a grazed knee and a telltale smudge of chocolate on the side of her mouth.

"I'm very disappointed in you," the headmistress said, sternly. "You seem to be getting into lots of strife recently."

The little girl stared defiantly back, a steely glint in her pale green eyes. "It wasn't my fault, Miss."

The headmistress glanced down at her notes. What was it about girls these days? So cocky and self-assured. Not like back in her day.

"Well, Julia, Kevin says you stole his chocolate crackles."

Under the chair, Julia clenched her fists tightly. So that's what this was all about. Yet again! Mr. Smarty Pants himself! Kevin-bloody-goody-two-shoes. Just wait till she ambushed him on the way home. She'd punch him so hard he'd blub all the way back to his stupid cane farm.

Julia swallowed.

She could still taste the yummy, chocolaty, crackly taste in her mouth. She forced herself not to smile. She'd trained herself to never show emotion, no matter how much trouble she got into.

"I don't even know what chocolate crackles are, Miss. I've never even heard of them."

The headmistress shook her head wearily. "Well, Kevin's not a very happy little Vegemite today. Did you know he brought them in specially for the whole class?"

"That's coz he's a crawler, Miss."

"Just answer the question, Julia."

"Miss, I've just given the best answer I can to your question."

The headmistress sighed.

"My question was simply whether or not you knew . . ."

"I heard your question and I've answered it," said the young girl, folding her arms defiantly across her chest.

"You have not answered the question," snapped the headmistress. "Don't make me go and fetch Mr. Slipper!"

"Well, I've given you the answer I'm going to give you."

The headmistress muttered under her breath.

Kids! She glanced back down at her notes. "And what about that dust-up on Australia Day outside the tuckshop? Kim says you made her go and tell the indigenous kids that Tony said they should all get lost, which wasn't true. And then you told Kim to tell them where Tony was sitting during lunch break so they'd go and bash him up."

Julia glowered, her thin lips sealed tightly together. If there was one thing she'd learned in this place it was to never own up to anything.

"Kim's a dobber. And I've never met her anyway."

"I'm sure I've seen you two together in the playground," replied the headmistress tentatively. "Often."

"Lots of girls hang around me all the time, Miss. Doesn't mean I know who they are, does it?" the seven-year-old said, triumphantly. She prided herself on her ability to think on her feet. That's how she'd stayed top girl in the playground for so long.

"And what about your science project?" sighed the headmistress.

"Before the holidays you promised everybody you wouldn't do a carbon tax this term but then on the first day back that's exactly what you did!"

Julia felt a tingle of perspiration on her top lip. She quickly licked it away with a flick of her tongue. As she did so, she again tasted the chocolate still lingering all down the side of her mouth. She quickly rubbed it away with her fist, hoping the headmistress hadn't noticed.

"I've dealt with that question numerous times before, Miss. I had to save the planet."

"I see. But there does seem to be a bit of a pattern here. Bobby Brown says you promised you'd look after the trees in his backyard but then you went and chopped them down. And that nice Wilkie boy says you broke your promise to him that you'd help him stop the other kids playing marbles so often. On top of that, Nurse said you promised the private school kiddies they could keep their pocket money rebates but now you've said they have to give it all to you." The headmistress stared at her sullen pupil, hoping to see some signs of contrition.

"Yes but I've already told you! Everything is Tony's fault. He keeps picking on me!"

The headmistress took a deep breath, wondering what on earth would become of this young thing. It was time to try another tack. "Well, let's just see if we can do better from now on, shall we? Think you can be a good girl and always tell the truth from now on?"

The young girl smiled sweetly.

"Of course I will, Miss."

"Promise?" said the headmistress.

"Promise."

In late February, leadership tension finally erupted.

First came a video of Kevin Rudd that was leaked online, possibly by someone within Gillard's office, that showed him swearing and frustrated whilst attempting to record a Chinese language message when he was PM.

The Spectator Australia editorial, 25 February 2012

SPEAKING A FOREIGN LANGUAGE

Hang on. There's something fishy in the won ton soup. We'd always been led to believe that one of Mr. Rudd's great skills was his talent for Mandarin, supposedly honed with first class honours at the ANU and finessed during his stint as a diplomat in Beijing. Yet it now turns out — if YouTube is anything to go by — that our once and (potentially) future PM can barely string a few words together in the language of the Middle Kingdom without exploding into a hissy fit of curses and f-bombs.

"Mate, this is just impossible," he snarled at his cameraman, as he struggled to get his tongue around a greeting video. But how hard could it have been? The words were displayed on an autocue for him to read in the privacy of his own studio. The editor was standing by to cut the good bits together and leave out the mistakes. The message was presumably along the lines of "Sorry I couldn't be there with you tonight, but I hope you all have a great time." Hardly an orthoepic dissertation on aspirated consonants in the Pinghua dialect.

Yet somehow the whiz-kid from Eumundi ended up all over the place, like a plate of left over dim sum at Sunday yum cha. "Just give me simple sentences! This f***ing language! How can anyone do this?" he dummy-spat, fretting like a Gonski-ite schoolkid who's just found out he's come bottom of the class. Was it all just a myth? Is Kevin's lauded mastery of mandarin no better than his mastery of economics ("save capitalism from itself"), diplomacy ("those Chinese f***ers are trying to rat-f*** us") or team management ("a psychopath with a giant ego")? Surely he hasn't been hoodwinking us all along?

Cabinet minister Simon Crean accused Kevin Rudd of destabilization and disloyalty, urging an "assertion of leadership" by Ms. Gillard.

At a late night televised press conference in Washington D.C., Mr. Rudd dramatically resigned as Foreign Minister citing Gillard's failure to repudiate Mr. Crean and the other 'faceless men' who had attacked his integrity. Rudd claimed he wanted no part in Labor's leadership 'soap opera'.

Financial Review, 24 February 2012

SECRET FRUSTRATIONS OF GLOBETROTTER KEV

A leaked video of Kevin Rudd's resignation speech has found its way on to the internet, believed to have been posted by none other than the former foreign minister himself.

Kevin Rudd: "Ah mate, this is just impossible (winces). I get to the very end of dinner and I'm explaining to Ban Ki-moon that he has my absolute full and total support and that I in no way intend to challenge him for his job as Secretary-General of the United Nations, which he is getting on with while I am getting on with mine because, honestly, I'm perfectly content being both prime minister-in-waiting and Foreign Minister of Australia and then, strike me dead, I've got to zip over to the f- - - ing Willard Hotel in the middle of the night and . . . (lifts hands in exasperation) . . . make a resignation speech before they go and sack me! (shakes head and looks away from camera, then takes a deep breath).

"All because of these f- - king hopeless time zone differences! I mean, what f- - -wit ever dreamt that one up? How f- - -ing inconsiderate! (takes a long slow sip of water, then mutters off camera). Mate, can you tell these dickheads in the embassy to just give me a simple backdrop, something plain and unobtrusive, not this gold flock wallpaper, I've said this before, tell that bloody seppo that . . . aarrrgghh, this f- - -ing language! I want a nice Aussie flag so I look like a normal, happy little Vegemite 'cos, you know, that's exactly what I am and ... and ... those faceless men on reception go and stick me in the bloody George Washington honeymoon suite with all these fancy gold patterns and swirls and floral motifs and it just complicates it SO MUCH!

"I'm human like anyone else, aren't I? (winces again, as if fighting back the tears). All the other rooms are shut up for the night and I can't even get into my own room 'cos I can't work that STUPID electronic swipe key!

"It might be easy for you to sit there and say it's easy to do but let me tell you, mate, it isn't (shakes his head from side to side, moaning). Nnnggghhh! (sits up straight and stares at the camera for several seconds, not blinking).

"Honestly, it's time for some plain speaking here; the simple truth is I cannot be expected to carry out my stealth campaign against the Prime Minister if she's going to sack me.

"I just think it's pretty sad for everybody when a soon-to-be-former leader of our party behaves in this way. I sat up for three days and three nights with 20 PR advisers from around the world to work out how to persuade those rat f- - -ers in the Labor Party who fancy keeping their f- - -ing jobs to just hurry up and draft me back and ... it's just, you know, this is becoming hopeless! (whacks table).

"Because I am absolutely passionate about ... I've been frustrated domestically, I've been frustrated politically by the lack of progress in my triumphant return to the Lodge but I will not be deterred and I will progress this matter and I will achieve the best possible means of bringing down this government (sighs and picks up a glass of water, then mutters off camera again).

"Tell them to cancel my six o'clock brekky with Barack Obama, you know I just don't have the f- - -ing patience to do that.

"Is this a f- - -ing Chinese interior decorator here or what? (stares at wallpaper).

"Just f- - -ing hopeless (grimaces). And the bottom line is this . . . the bottom line is this . . . let me tell you this, mate, there is no way I can be expected to stare in the mirror in the future and say, 'K. Rudd, you passed up the core opportunity to get your old job back as president' (slams fist down on desk, sending glass of water flying). Aaaarrggh! I f- - -ed up the last word."

Meanwhile, Julia Gillard has denied that members of her staff have been working for at least the last two weeks on a secret acceptance speech.

"I am not surprised that, whether it's people in my office or people more broadly in the Labor Party who are casting in their mind where circumstances might get to, but does that mean I know about it? Of course not," the Prime Minister said.

In the speech she accepts that she has lost the plot and accepts that someone else will have to take over.

At the leadership spill on February 27, Julia Gillard prevailed over Kevin Rudd by 71 votes to his 31. Following the vote, Mark Arbib resigned from the senate. A push to have the former NSW premier Bob Carr replace him appeared to founder, with Carr insisting he wanted the job of Foreign Minister. For several days, it seemed the whole idea had been killed off.

Meanwhile, nine months after the original Four Corners program that led to the suspension of live cattle exports to Indonesia, fresh footage emerged showing the continuing maltreatment of animals, presumed to be Australian.

In Syria, civil war raged.

Financial Review, 2 March 2012

CANBERRA CARNAGE: A HIDEOUS ACT OF CRUELTY

Shocking images smuggled out of Australia of sadistic, cruel and inhumane practices have yet again sparked a furore in neighbouring Indonesia.

Filmed in secret by undercover journalists from an Indonesian current affairs program, the grainy footage reaffirms that in Australia human beings are being humiliated, tortured and verbally abused before being savagely put down.

"We'd heard rumours of such barbarity, but we couldn't believe that this is how they treat their politicians in Australia," the program's producer said.

Airing tonight, the documentary features never-before-seen images taken on a mobile phone smuggled out of the notorious Labor Party boardroom known as "The Slaughterhouse".

"It was sickening," said the reporter, wiping away tears. "They dragged the poor beast in; I think his name was Kevin but I couldn't be sure, there was so much squealing and yelling going on."

Visibly shaken by her ordeal, the reporter looks mortified, recalling the grisly scenes. "The creature was clearly on his last legs, limping and bleeding, with big dark rings under his eyes. He looked like he'd just got off the red-eye from Washington.

"Apparently he'd been on his feet for hours, even days, staggering aimlessly through shopping malls and TV studios pathetically looking for some kind of support. It was heartbreaking."

Struggling to maintain her composure, the reporter went on to describe the final, brutal moments before the kill.

"He got up to make a speech, pleading for mercy, and reminding the baying mob – there were about a hundred of them – that he was the only one who could beat Tony Abbott. But they were in a frenzy. One woman was screeching 'let's move forward', then out came the knives and they all just started attacking him with these dreadful barbed comments."

Clips from the documentary, leaked onto YouTube, clearly show the Australian Treasurer, Wayne Swan, engaged in a vicious assault on his former school chum, in scenes of gratuitous violence that have horrified the Indonesian public.

"To put the boot in like that, over and over again; in most civilised countries they use a policy issue to bring down a leader humanely, but these savages go straight for the jugular," one viewer said.

Another viewer, dry retching in disgust said: "It was medieval. The whole gang laid into him. Not content with merely wounding him, they broke his spirit too, calling him all sorts of degrading names like 'psychopath' and 'prima donna'."

Indonesian animal activist (and animal) Abu Bakar Bashir said as he was whisked back to prison: "What distressed me the most was seeing that sweet, innocent K'hate Al-lis suddenly turn nasty, even after it was all over.

"She just got stuck right into his warm corpse on *7.30*. So what if Kevin went to some pub and called Gillard an atheist, childless, ex-

Marxist? It's not as if Australians live in some whacky, sharia-obsessed theocracy."

The video claims such practices are common throughout the Canberra meat belt. "First they stunned him back in 2010, without any warning. Then they just left him battered and bruised. The mistake was that nobody bothered to check whether he was really dead. I should have just slit his throat on the spot," said one of the faceless butchers, known only as "Bill".

With tears streaming down his cheeks, another participant in the savagery attempted to justify his actions. "I just want to kill Tories," said Albo Al-Banese. "But they keep saying 'No', so I have to slaughter my own people instead."

Soon after the killing, one of the perpetrators, Ar-Bh'ib, can be seen being persuaded to fall on his own machete. Visiting the abattoir yesterday, journalists were sickened to see the practices continuing unabated. "There was a fresh Bob Carrcass lying on the Senate floor, groaning and thoroughly humiliated. He never stood a chance."

Meanwhile, in unrelated news, an asylum seeker who arrived on Christmas Island by private jet has lashed out at Australian border police. "I am fleeing persecution in my own country – if I go back they will almost certainly string me up from the nearest lamp post simply because I went and butchered half my population," said Mr. Al-Assad, speaking on condition of anonymity.

Julia Gillard surprised everyone by announcing that Bob Carr would indeed be filling the vacant Senate spot, and that he would become the new Minister for Foreign Affairs replacing Kevin Rudd.

Financial Review, 5 March 2012

HE HAD HER AT HELLO

It's a marriage made in Labor heaven. The Master of Spin hooks up with the Mistress of the Backroom Deal. Two lonely hearts, who, in embracing, compensate for each other's glaring deficiencies. As Renée Zellweger said to Tom Cruise in the chick flick *Jerry Maguire*: "You complete me."

For Julia Gillard, her debilitating inability to connect with the public will now be handed over to the man of the mellifluous voice and headline-grabbing sound bites, while her complete lack of political nous will be more than compensated for by the wily former NSW premier's almost canine-like knack of sniffing every nuance floating on the political breeze.

For Bob Carr, who has fantasised about this job but was never prepared to put in the hard yards to earn it, he now has the queen of the late-night negotiations doing the dirty work for him, leaving him free to pester the newsroom in the wee hours of the morning before he "shoots off" overseas.

Of course, the fact that he is able to waltz into one of the cushiest, most high-profile gigs in Australia without actually having broken into a sweat says all you need to know about the political quagmire that is our current federal cabinet.

Already, Carr has put to good use his booming voice and new-found relevance to spruik Gillard's favourite obsession. "The horror of an

Abbott-led government," was his first classic sound grab, eagerly lapped
up by the newsroom.

No wonder he had her at "hello".

*Wayne Swan launched his class war with an attack on what he called the 'rising
influence of vested interests in Australia', also known as the mining magnates.*

The Spectator Australia editorial, 10 March 2012

WORLD'S GREATEST TREASURER (CONTD)

Our economy is lurching to the left, like a drunk staggering down the
sidewalk, keys in hand, looking out for the cops. Demonising sections
of the mining community as "poisonous" one minute yet calling the
Greens "irresponsible" the next, fanning the flames of class envy while
pretending to support democracy, pandering to conspiracy theories and
promoting a massive redistribution of wealth through a dishonest tax,
the federal Treasurer is tipping a toxic brew down the electorate's throat.

The "world's greatest finance minister" (who says Europeans have
no sense of humour?) has embarked on the lowest political strategy of
them all: demonising the rich. How fortunate for Mr. Swan — described
by the *Australian Financial Review* as the 'most left-wing treasurer since Jim
Cairns' — that at least two of his greedy 'vested interests', Gina Rinehart
and Clive Palmer, look like cartoon tycoons; all the easier to sneer at. Mr.
Swan's jittery, hyperventilating attack on mining magnates included such
deceptive and provocative statements as "I can tell you there's a lot of
unease in the Australian community about the activities of some of these
people." Really? Where? Or is it simply that the Labor party can't bear
any form of criticism from those who have the funds to broadcast them?

Fair Work Australia's investigation into HSU Victoria No 1 branch was completed, with three former officials said to face Federal Court action. There was much criticism about the length of time and amount of money it had taken Fair Work Australia to investigate the alleged misuse of union funds.

Federal Labor MP Craig Thomson was taken to hospital with unusual stomach pains, although Julia Gillard said she did not think Mr. Thomson's illness was serious.

Financial Review, 16 March 2012

MYSTERIOUS CASE OF THE VANISHING STOMACH PAINS

"Stomach pains, you say? Oh dear. They can be very painful. Take your shirt off and let me examine you," said the triage nurse to the man perched on the end of the bed.

"How long has this been going on?"

The man grimaced. "Years, but it just won't go away."

"Years?" said the nurse. "How many?"

The man stared at her, beads of sweat breaking out on his forehead. "They've been investigating my complaint for over three years."

"That sounds an unreasonably long time," replied the nurse, puzzled. She tut-tutted.

If there was one thing she couldn't stand, it was a lack of professionalism on the part of the health services. That's why she'd joined the union in the first place. To ensure that standards were maintained.

The man shrugged. "My boss, she's as tough as nails. 'At least I get the job done,' that's her motto. She says I'm not allowed to have a single day off work 'coz the whole place would go down the gurgler without me.

"The firm simply wouldn't have the numbers to stay in business."

"We'll see about that," the nurse said. "Lie down, and I'll have a feel."

There was a loud gasp from the patient as she gently prodded around his abdomen. "Oh dear, those feel like guilt pangs. Been a naughty boy, have you?"

The man looked away shiftily, and the nurse smiled sympathetically.

"We normally see these problems when people have been over-indulging. Long lunches. Boozy night clubs. That sort of thing. Been living the high life, eh?"

The man shook his head. "Not since they confiscated all my credit cards. Of course, before then . . ."

His voice trailed off, and he smiled ruefully, as the memory of those bacchanalian days and nights came flooding back.

"The good times," he said to her, with a twinkle in his eye. "Money for nothing and the chicks for free."

"Dire Straits," said the nurse.

"Yes," said the man, his smile fading. "I think so."

The nurse surreptitiously studied the patient's notes, pages and pages of them. It simply didn't make sense. She may not have had a medical degree but after a decade in triage she knew enough to realise that someone had simply avoided doing a proper investigation altogether.

Such negligence was verging on the criminal, she thought to herself. Even though, as far back as 2009, the notes clearly recorded "a clear prima facie case to proceed to an investigation".

The nurse frowned. What on earth was going on? Who was stalling?

It was almost as if there was a massive conspiracy – some kind of institutional go-slow. Her curiosity aroused, the nurse quickly flipped further back through the notes.

She couldn't believe her eyes. The hospital bills! Three years and nearly a million dollars later and they still hadn't come close to diagnosing the problem. It was scandalous! She knew full well that stomach cramps could lead to all sorts of nasty problems if they weren't treated quickly, such as vomiting or diarrhea.

Yet the only vague reference she could find to any kind of symptoms was the cryptic email that stated: "Thanks, that's awesome. Should minimise any runs he gets in the morning."

It was a real mystery. Made even stranger by the fact that several times over the past few years both the NSW and Victorian police had turned up at the hospital but the staff had refused to co-operate with them.

Surely that wasn't normal? What on earth had this patient done? Who on earth was he?

There was a knock on the door, startling both the nurse and her patient. Two policemen stepped into the room.

"Excuse us, nurse. We've been sent here by the ombudsman, he's asked us to investigate the 'gross delay' in the investigation of your patient."

"Thank goodness," said the triage nurse. "And about time, too! That's a relief, isn't it, Mr. . . . Mr. . ."

She turned around but her patient had gone.

Malcolm Turnbull yet again appeared on the ABC's Q&A.

The Spectator Australia editorial, 17 March 2012

COMEDY HOUR

Critics and fans alike of the ABC will be relieved that Aunty has finally delivered a genuinely funny comedy hour. Modeled on the British smash hit QI (where Stephen Fry tries to keep a straight face as his guests answer a series of ludicrous questions) the new show on ABC goes by the similar-sounding name of *Q&A*. Not to be confused with the ABC's former *Q&A* (a probing political commentary show), this latest Monday night offering is a laugh-a-minute side splitter where the show's host tries in vain not to smirk as contestants struggle to come up with the most absurd answers they can think of to seemingly innocent or just plain ridiculous questions.

Highlights of this week's show included regular panelist Malcolm Turnbull defending gay marriage while simultaneously opposing it (too funny!) and Malcolm mugging to the cameras over the hilarious suggestion he set up his own political party or take over Tony Abbott's. Equally amusing was the sly wit of Tanya Plibersek, who managed to twist a seemingly innocent question on asylum-seekers into a tired gag about the Libs' '$70 billion black hole'. Lots of fun.

Critics complain the audience seem to be in on the joke, knowing which gags to hiss at and which ones to rapturously applaud, but this misses the point. The sole aim of the new show, obviously, is to entertain rather than to inform.

The US Central Intelligence Agency was forced to deny claims by mining billionaire Clive Palmer that the CIA had secretly funded the Greens and other environmental groups in an attempt to destroy Australia's coal industry.

Financial Review, 23 March 2012

FICTION, FARCE, OR FACT?
THE PLOT SICKENS

"Do please come in and sit down, Mr. le Carré," said the pretty young editor, pulling out a chair for the distinguished-looking, white-haired man. "It was good of you to pop in."

He didn't reply.

She'd been warned about his legendary fiery temper, and offered him tea and a plate of freshly baked croissants from the Soho patisserie in the hope of softening him up for what was not going to be a pleasant conversation.

He took a chocolate pastry, eyeing both it and her suspiciously. She took a deep breath,

"It's about the plot of your new novel. I think we should, er, have a chat … "

The steely eyes gave nothing away. For all she knew, the last time anyone had dared to criticise one of the spymaster's masterpieces they'd ended up swinging from a bridge over the Thames with a poison dart lodged in their throat.

"The plot? Really?" the writer said, his voice betraying no emotion.

"Well," said the young woman, swallowing her tea nervously. "It's just that it's kind of … loopy." There. She'd said it.

"Loopy?" The famous novelist fixed her with his icy gaze.

"Yes," said the editor quickly. She may as well let it all out, get it over with. "And not only loopy, it's illogical. From start to finish. The whole story is farcical. Readers won't buy it. Literally. Let's start with the basic premise. Why would the CIA back the Greens when half of them hate Israel and the rest are KGB sleepers? And as if anyone would boycott a coffee shop to stop Israeli settlements. That's just plain whacko.

"Then you've got all these mining magnates running around buying up newspapers and football teams like they're playing Monopoly. Oh please! It's all so clichéd! And quite frankly, they're all a rather two-dimensional lot – stinking rich and suing their own children for billions of dollars. Hello? I'm sorry, but real people just don't do that. It's like a Jackie Collins novel.

"And don't get me started on those laughable characters you've got running the government. You're too late! Jeffrey Archer's already done the whole sleazy-prostitution-credit-card-cover-up thing.

"And the Prime Minister's a woman who 'gets things done'? Woopety-doo-dah! Ever heard of Indira? Or Golda? Or Maggie? OK, so at least this one's going out with a hairdresser. That pricked my interest for a nanosecond, but it's totally implausible.

"Then there's this other nerdy guy who used to be Prime Minister who she stabbed in the back a year ago. He just so happens to be married to a millionairess, and now he tries to get his old job back, but the PM beats him then appoints some other nerdy guy out of the blue to replace him. It's a mess. The entire backstory is contrived, preposterous and lacks all credibility. Then there's that guy straight out of Charles Dickens wandering around with a silk tie and a black robe. What the . . .? And that class-warfare Treasury dude who calls everyone Moe and Curly? C'mon, be a bit more imaginative. He puts in a mining tax and a carbon tax on the same day? That's just ludicrous.

The editor took a deep breath.

"We paid you one hell of an advance for a contemporary CIA thriller and this is what we get? It doesn't make sense – why would the CIA need to wreck the Australian economy when these clowns are doing it all by themselves?"

The old writer stared at her. Slowly, he took a bite of his croissant, the chocolate oozing malevolently from the crisp pastry. "I don't know what to say."

The editor shrugged. She glanced up at him and smiled weakly. "There was one thing I liked," she said.

The writer smiled. "And what was that?" he asked.

"The way you delivered the whole thing to me like it was the latest copy of an Australian newspaper. Cute"

Apple ran into compatibility and other problems with its new, third-generation iPad. And Future Fund chairman David Murray described the Gillard government's carbon tax as the worst piece of economic reform he had ever seen. In Queensland, Campbell Newman was elected in a landslide.

Financial Review, 30 March 2012

AN ALPple A DAY

Newsflash. Canberra, July 2. Political giant ALPple has been forced to offer refunds to more than 26 million Australians who last night purchased the latest iCarbonTax following complaints from customers that they were misled.

"Naturally, I'm devastated to learn that they lied about what it can do," said one irate customer, Glebe resident, environmental activist and rap artist Tre Hugga, who queued for hours at the weekend for the latest must-have accessory for those who are keen to save the planet.

"I've bought every single ALPple product since the ground-breaking iKevin07, which I loved to death," he said. "I didn't even mind when they changed it to the iJulia after only a year or two, although they were completely incompatible.

"I downloaded all the new software so I could move forward. Then they tried to bring back a new, smaller and less clunky iKevin but that never got off the ground. Now this!"

The furore began over prominent claims on the pack that the iCarbonTax would work on the international Global Warming network, help reduce carbon in the atmosphere, and stop the oceans from rising to threaten suburbs such as Newtown and St Kilda.

"It turns out it doesn't even do the basics," said another disgruntled customer. "It might work in countries like America or China, but the local version of the iCarbonTax does no such thing."

A red-faced spokesperson for ALPple, who went by the name of Wayne but spoke on condition of anonymity, confirmed that when it came to tackling climate change, the Australian version of the device was "next to useless."

"The Global Warming tag comes from the international advertising campaign, and has no relevance in such a tiny market as Australia, where even if you removed every single ounce of carbon from the atmosphere it would still account for only 1 per cent of global output.

"We understand consumers may be disappointed to find out they've bought something that doesn't work, but that's hardly our problem.

"Besides, with all the money we're making out of this new product we intend to invest billions in such exciting innovations as our new iWindTurbine."

A spokesperson for consumer group NoChoice said, "Most consumers going about their daily business would assume that because they are now paying through the nose for all sorts of things, the iCarbonTax would actually do something worthwhile.

"However, we can find no evidence to suggest it is having any impact on the climate whatsoever."

Critics have often pointed out that ALPple has a long history of products (and leaders) that quickly run out of power. When queried on how long it would be before any of the so-called iRenewables range would be capable of providing base-load electricity, Wayne explained that he had another urgent press conference to attend to announce another major innovation.

"It's not like we're standing still. I am pleased to announce today the iSurplus – so called because it is I who made it possible.

"The iSurplus means that we can go on spending as much money as we want to on anything that springs to mind. It's not for nothing that *Euromoney* put me on the front cover of their magazine. Along with my other innovations, such as the iMiningTax, it's no wonder they named the Genius bar after me."

Wayne also explained ALPple was giving "compensation vouchers" to everybody who had purchased the latest device but felt unhappy about the exorbitant price. "These vouchers are incredibly important in terms of reforming our economy, and mean working families can rush out and spend as much money as they like on flat-screen TVs and computer games, or holidays to Bali," he said.

Asked why ALPple had been forced to close most of its stores in Queensland, Wayne was quick to remind reporters it was purely a matter for local retailers and nothing to do with him.

But ALPple aficionado and keen blogger Steve No-More Jobs was quick to point out that such distinctions were irrelevant.

"The new iCarbonTax is designed to make the consumer feel good simply because they have one," he said. "Yes, it's ridiculously expensive and incredibly difficult to operate but having one of these things tucked into your pocket feels a lot better than not having one. Plus, it gives the user a warm, fuzzy feeling all over every time they use it."

Cardinal George Pell and self-confessed atheist Richard Dawkins go head to head on Q&A *with Tony Jones.*

Financial Review, 13 April 2012

Q&A: IT'S A HELL OF A DEBATE

Here are the redacted highlights of the *Q&A* debate this week featuring Cardinal George Pell, author and biologist Richard Dawkins, and host Tony Jones.

Pell: "For some extraordinary reason, God chose the Jews. They weren't intellectually or morally the equal of the Egyptians or the Persians. The poor little Jewish people were shepherds."

Jones: "But being a shepherd isn't a reflection on your intellectual capacity?"

Pell: "It is of your intellectual development."

Jones: "Are you including Jesus, who was Jewish? Not intellectually up to it?"

Pell: "For some reason God chose a very difficult (hesitates) … actually they're now an intellectual elite, because over the centuries they've been pushed out of every other form of work. Jesus is the greatest man that ever lived so I've got a great admiration for the Jews, but we don't need to exaggerate their contribution."

Question from the audience: "Explain how the universe came from nothing."

Dawkins: "When you have matter and anti-matter and put them together, they cancel each other out. If you start with nothing, the process can go into reverse. You can dispute exactly what is meant by nothing but it's very simple. (Audience laughs). Why is that funny?"

Pell: "It's a bit funny trying to define nothing."

Jones: "Do you accept humans evolved from apes?"

Pell: "Yeah, from Neanderthals."

Dawkins (outraged): "Neanderthals were our cousins! We're not descended from them . . ."

Pell: "Where will I find a Neanderthal today if they're my cousins?"

Dawkins: "They're extinct."

Pell: "That's my point."

Jones: "At what point was a soul imparted to humans from God?"

Pell: "A soul is not like putting a spot of gin in a tonic. We know the first humans developed in Africa because of cave drawings. No such thing from Neanderthals."

Dawkins: "Successive popes suggested the soul did get added, like gin to tonic."

Pell: "The soul is the principle of life. There are animal souls."

Dawkins: "Do jellyfish . . .?"

Pell: "All living things do. We have a voice box – one of the great miracles – so we can communicate our thoughts rather than grunting."

Jones: "Is it possible for an atheist to go to heaven?"

Pell: "Certainly. We will all be there as continuing persons in a new Earth."

Jones: "Billions of individual souls existing in some galactic space?"

Pell: "How it'll work, I've no idea."

Dawkins: "What happens when we die depends on whether we're buried or cremated. I don't believe you mean wafer turns into the body of Christ?"

Pell (indignantly): I don't say things I don't mean. The Son of God says, 'This is my body. This is my blood,' and I'd much prefer to take his word than yours."

Dawkins (snidely): "So you don't mean wafer turns into the body in any sense which normal English language usage understands."

Pell: "I remember when I was in England we were preparing some young English boys … (audience laughs). Thank you. Preparing them for communion. We Catholics believe in hell. I certainly believe in a place of purification. It will be like getting up in the morning and throwing the curtains back."

Jones: "Why create a world with so much suffering?"

Pell: "My first Easter as a priest was in Italy. Very sad village. All the men were away getting big money, home only for three weeks a year. I said: 'Well look, Christ suffered too. Christ had a bad run'."

Jones (shifting awkwardly): "Can I take it to a higher level? The holocaust? Genocide? Famine? Why does an omnipotent God let these things happen?"

Pell: "Probably no people in history have been punished the way the Germans were. It's a terrible mystery."

Jones (alarmed): "There's a strong argument saying the Jews of Europe suffered worse than the Germans."

Pell: "There was suffering in both."

Question from the audience: "Cardinal, how can you be against gay marriage when equality and respect are the foundations of love?"

Pell: "Christians love everybody."

Jones: "Do you believe homosexuality's part of God's natural order?"

Pell: "Creation is messy. Oriental carpet makers always leave a little flaw in their carpet."

Jones: "Are you suggesting homosexuals are flawed?"

Dawkins (tetchily): "I'm interested in whether God is actually there."

Pell: "So am I."

Some conversations defy satire.

As polls showed the increasing unpopularity of the carbon tax, budget speculation grew around the promised surplus.

The makers of Downton Abbey released a spectacular TV mini-series on the sinking of the Titanic.

Financial Review, 20 April 2012

GOOD SHIP LABOR HOLED
BY TITANIC TAX

A fascinating new mini-series that was launched this week depicts one of the great tragedies of our time: the sinking of the "unsinkable" Australian Labor Party. Each new episode explores the calamity from the point of view of a different character.

Scripted by Sir Julia Fellowes (author of long-running popular period drama *Downtown Canberra*) the series aims to set the record straight about the events that led to one of history's worst disasters.

Sir Julia, who controversially took over scriptwriting duties midway through the first draft because she was unhappy about the chaotic organisation and directionless approach to the project, has now taken full responsibility for how it pans out.

"There will be no happy endings in any production I lead," she famously (and accurately) predicted.

As the vessel heads inexorably towards the fateful night of the 2013 election, viewers get to experience repeatedly the extraordinary events leading up to those final calamitous moments as the Labor Party is struck by a gigantic, immovable carbon tax, and sinks without a trace into the darkness below.

In the final, horrific minutes, members of the party and fellow travellers attempt to scramble to safety but are sucked downwards by the sheer force of the anti-Labor vote. Even those clinging to floating preferences or hoping to clutch onto the passing debris of an Independent or inner-city Green are sucked under.

In one of the many flashbacks, a canny character known only as Barmy Bob manages to slip overboard and swim to safety in Tasmania. Sadly, his paramour, Christine, suffers a very different fate.

Ignoring all warnings, the hapless pilot of the doomed ship, Captain Swan, steers the vessel directly into the path of voter anger and treacherous cash floes. On a moonless night, he seems stubbornly insouciant to the dangers posed by the sea of taxes, imposts, and wasteful spending, any of which could punch a hole in the ship at any moment. Viewers learn that the shipbuilders were forced to borrow $100 million a day just to keep the enterprise afloat while, incredulously, squandering billions more on an archaic wireless message network.

Although the script is fast-paced, involving everything from a huge surge of illegal immigrants found hiding below decks to a luxurious ballroom where prostitutes frolic with credit card fraudsters, the dialogue is particularly cheesy, with lines such as "we're all moving forward" and "he has my full confidence" sounding insubstantial and trite.

For a costume drama, it leaves much to be desired. Grey suits are the norm, although one bizarre character inexplicably wanders the decks dressed in a long black robe and silk tie clutching a ceremonial mace. Visual relief comes from the exotic array of suit jackets and skirts worn by the enigmatic character known only as "Juliar", a tragic cameo role played by the scriptwriter herself.

The mini-series' great strength – and weakness – is that its plot is pre-determined. Indeed we know within the first few minutes of the 'Budget Back In Surplus' episode that most of the diesel rebates and other crucial business lifeboats have been jettisoned, leaving small and big companies foundering in a sea of red and green tape.

Meanwhile, vast sums of money have been wasted on extravagant projects such as wind turbines on the upper decks to try to keep the sinking vessel afloat, all to no avail. The series' overriding theme is an intricate study of the class prejudices glaringly prevalent at the time. The wealthy mining moguls who sip champagne on the western deck spend most of their time buying newspapers and even radio stations. Loud and boorish, they concoct all sorts of fanciful plots about CIA involvement in sabotaging coal supplies. Meanwhile, the working classes struggle to earn a crust below decks, their suffering only relieved by generous "compensation" packages that in the end still don't save them from drowning under the sheer weight of their energy bills.

The insidious class conflict, a device contrived by the script doctors for purely narrative purposes, is overworked and soon wears thin.

Nonetheless, crew members Wong, Shorten, Carr and Combet continually resort to class-ridden clichés, while blaming everything that goes wrong on the one vaguely credible character who toils away in the boiler room wearing nothing but a hard hat and a pair of speedos.

Critics have compared the series with filmmaker James 'Dougie' Cameron's 2007 blockbuster epic – unsuccessfully re-released earlier this year – in which Captain Rudd heroically steers the vessel to safety and is greeted at the docks by cheering throngs of Gold Coast school kiddies.

Timing his departure to perfection, Greens leader Bob Brown unexpectedly announced his retirement, on the eve of the implementation of the carbon tax.

The Spectator *Australia*, 21 April 2012

BOB DOES A BOB

There was something unsettling about watching Bob Brown ask Bob Carr his first questions in the Senate several weeks ago, but it only became apparent why it was such a creepy experience with Brown's abrupt resignation last week. The reason, of course, is that these two characters are so similar. It was like Tweedledee criticising Tweedledum. Like B1 having a go at B2. Or Herge's Thompson and Thomson trying to outfox each other. Oddly unconvincing. So it came as no surprise that Bob-with-a-B decided to exit the political fray in precisely the same manner as Bob-with-a-C so deftly did all those years ago. Brown's departure uncannily mirrors Carr's. Bob did a Bob.

The key to successfully "doing a Bob" is accurately gauging 'the tipping point' (no, not that one) that occurs in all political stories. This is the moment just before the chickens come home to roost; where your achievements have yet to be recognised as hollow, self-serving shams. If you jump at the right time, the failures that you have instigated will be sheeted home to one – or indeed all – of your hapless successors. Doing a Bob requires a sense of timing as acute as that of any actor or sportsman. Nail it, and your threadbare achievements will be eulogised and your numerous errors glossed over, leaving a glowing legacy that you can put to good use while the electorate pick up the hefty bill.

Not surprisingly, both Bobs share many of the same physical and political traits, which they have used as powerful tools in their respective careers. Their height, the deep voices and the ramrod stance have given them both an air of statesman-like gravitas that their policies belied. The well-honed soundbites and attempts at humour have seen them both labeled as "good communicators." Yet both are awkwardly unfunny. Think of Carr's tortuous "cheap hypnotist" routine, delivered in poor taste at a press conference after the Afghanistan massacre, or Brown's "here comes the washing up" shtick. Strangely, their deadpan expressions, ponderous pontifications and quirky obsessions have been confused by fans as "charisma" or "intellect".

Neither man has ever shown any real understanding of the humdrum concerns of average working men and women, or the tedious nuts and bolts of a functioning infrastructure that the vast majority of the population rely upon for a satisfactory existence. Rather, the two Bobs like to imagine themselves as out-of-this-world figures, saving the oceans and, of course, the planet. Alien civilisations, on this earth and elsewhere, are of great concern to them both. Bob's role as a peacemaker in the centuries-old schism with Islam is only matched in self-delusional silliness by Bob's role as intergalactic seer. The United Nations is the latest hobby of one, a One World Parliament and expanding the Greens into Africa are the fantasies of the other.

When doing a Bob, make sure you leave a crippling tax or two in place after you've gone. For Carr it was the land tax. For Brown, the carbon tax. Interestingly, when you successfully do a Bob, you yourself can sidestep the irksome imposts you have inflicted upon everyone else. Carr quickly bought his second home in New Zealand, out of reach of his own Treasury, while if Brown pursues his global dreams, they'll be unburdened by his own carbon price.

Both Bobs hate dams. Bob Brown's saving of the Franklin may be the shiny spot on his CV, but it led to the demonising of dams in this country, with hugely adverse effects on farming, industry and clean energy generation. Bob Carr was responsible for killing off the Welcome Reef dam, thereby condemning Sydney to water shortages and the farcical two billion dollars wasted on the Kurnell desalination plant. Both Bobs have saved a lot of trees, but at a significant cost.

In order to do a Bob, you must make your decision to step down appear spontaneous and unplanned. For Carr, it was "over a bottle of chardonnay" that he chose to "spend more time with my wife" and get "more recreation." "I've got no plans, no job offers," he claimed, only to quickly snaffle up a lucrative offer from Macquarie Bank.

For Brown, it was "during a trip to Africa" that he decided he needed to "get out more with Paul" for "bushwalking and photography."

The good thing about doing a Bob is that what politically occurs after you're gone is irrelevant. If your less-talented colleagues start fighting amongst themselves, it only makes you look better. If they do badly in the next election – which by definition they will – it only makes your wins more impressive. Which is, of course, the key point to doing a Bob.

What this apparently selfless and generous tactic enables you to do is to go out never having been voted out, thereby setting yourself up for the inevitable heroic comeback further down the track, preferably straight into a cushy job of your own choosing at the taxpayers' expense that offers a chance to indulge your fantasies on a far grander stage.

Want the world at your feet? Do a Bob.

As the carbon tax approached, and the rain kept falling, debate raged about the accuracy of earlier climate change predictions claiming the east coast of Australia would run out of water.

And a noted global warming expert admitted he had been overly alarmist in his predictions.

Financial Review, 27 April 2012

HOT AIR AND FAIR-WEATHER FRIENDS

Denying allegations by his former mentor James Poppycock that he had been "alarmist" in his best seller *The World Ends Next Year, Horribly!* global warming expert and Australian of the Century Professor Thomas

Weathervain defended his prediction that Parramatta would be washed away by the year 2013. "When I referred to western Sydney being entirely wiped out, I was of course referring to the Labor vote at next year's election," said the professor from his luxury acreage at Pacific Palms Waterfront Estate.

"Predicting future weather patterns and trends is an inexact science at the best of times," he explained, "which is why I have taken the precaution of buying up as much waterfront property as I possibly can. Obviously, my clear intention is to open a marine park in my front garden at some point in the future as a sanctuary for whales and other sea creatures that face extinction."

Contradicting assertions that he had exaggerated the dangers of global warming in his $180,000 a year role as The People's Climate Change Commissar, the professor maintained he had been misunderstood. "When I said that Brisbane's dams would all be bone dry by the end of the decade, I was speaking metaphorically. 'Bone dry' is a term we scientists use to describe a situation in which an awful lot of precipitation suddenly comes pouring out of the sky even though we weren't expecting it."

Professor Weathervain, who earned his doctorate in the study of the mating habits of the lesser-known wincing wombat, is Professor in Climate Risk and Sensational Doomsday Predictions Research Excellence at Westfield Technical College of the Arts.

Asked to give an example of a single prediction he had made that had come true, he pointed to his 2006 assertion that Sydney would soon face "devastating problems with water".

"As you can see, I was 100 per cent correct on that one. It's been bucketing down for at least the last two weeks and that's caused all sorts of problems with overflowing gutters and drains. My front lawn is like the Somme. You can't get more devastating than that."

When questioned about his claims that even if it did rain the soil would be so dry that water would simply cascade off, the professor explained that the expression "soil" referred to the irreversible environmental phenomenon known to scientists as "roads and pavements", in which a build-up of a sticky man-made substance called "tar" prevented moisture from penetrating the earth.

The professor, a major shareholder in renewable energy outfit HotRocks-R-Us, admitted having advised the government to invest billions of dollars in geothermal energy schemes. "I see no conflict of interest. This is the future. The technology is a doddle," he said. "All you do is tip some water over the hot rocks and, voila, you've got an infinite supply of energy. It couldn't be simpler."

When it was pointed out that the geothermal wells that taxpayers had thus far invested in had either blown up or been shut down due to excessive rainfall, the professor pointed the finger at man-made climate change.

"Mother Earth is a single entity and a sensitive female so if you go prodding Her in all the wrong places at the wrong time of the month and go sticking pipes into Her . . . well Gaia only knows what might happen," he said.

Posing for photographers in front of a giant Planatronic flat-screen TV, the professor said that although he accepted funding to his university chair from the Korean electronics giant, he in no way endorsed their products.

"In no way do I allow their sponsorship of my position to influence my attitude towards them or to compromise my firm ecological criticisms of them. Why would I? I mean look at this telly. It's a beauty! Really sharp picture quality. Slim eco-design. Bright green buttons. I love it. Good sustainable price, too. If you want to save a packet and save the planet, then this is the home entertainment package I'd recommend."

Asked if he was looking forward to the introduction of the carbon tax, the professor reminded his fans not to get too excited. "If we cut emissions today, global temperatures are not likely to drop for about a thousand years," he said. "And that's no exaggeration."

The Spectator Australia editorial, 21 April 2012

SNAKES AND LADDERS

If Julia Gillard is keen to salvage something worthwhile out of her period in office, she should quickly patent 'Gillard's Government' as a board game. Not since *Snakes and Ladders*, or *Dungeons and Dragons*, has a seemingly straightforward task – get from A to B by running the country competently and efficiently with a minimum of fuss and disruption – proved to be such a hair-raising ride. Full of twists and turns, sneaky backroom deals and dodgy alliances, scandal and subterfuge, sleaze and slipperiness. The game, at face value, will appear simple. Players are given plastic chips (called 'Taxpayers Squillions') they can throw around willy-nilly the moment they get into trouble. The idea is you have to keep a straight face as you explain to 'the public' what it is you are spending their money on and what it is you are trying to achieve, but of course, the rules forbid you from ever telling the truth. The bigger the fib, the more plastic chips you get to play with.

It's great fun. Every roll of the dice unleashes a torrent of mismanagement, chronic deception, tortuous semantics and mind-bending doublespeak. Every initiative backfires, every strategy unravels. What makes the game so diabolical is that every time you think you've done something clever it turns out to be a massive mistake and you go hurtling back down the Slippery Slope. Worse, the 'Get Out Of Jail Free' cards (called a Carbon Tax or an NBN) both turn out to be duds and it's back to square one. Want a tip? The only possible way to win is 'Advance Directly to 2013, Do Not Pass Any Further Legislation'. Your friends will love it. The last thing today's hipsters want is a dreary old turn of Relaxed and Comfortable. Where would be the fun in that?

With Craig Thomson, the Labor member for Dobell, denying charges that he misused Health Services Union funds to pay for prostitutes, and Peter Slipper denying claims he misused his cab charges, Gillard banished them both, saying "a line has been crossed." Speculation of more leadership turmoil focused on Bill Shorten, among others, or a possible return to Rudd.

Financial Review, 5 May 2012

JULIA CAESAR

A chill wind blew down from the Brindabellium mountains and over Capitoline Hill as footsteps echoed across the Forum in the pale light of the long-awaited dawn. Wrapping her cloak tightly around her, Julia Caesar shivered. How had it all gone so horribly wrong?

She gazed up at the statue of her illustrious predecessor, Bennelongus Imperium. "Relaxum et Comfortabilis" was his motto. How ordinary those words now looked, etched in stone and covered in bird shit. Yet, she now realised, they possibly represented the greatest triumph any leader could achieve.

Passing the vomitorium, she could hear squeals of delight and faint laughter intermingled with the sounds of dry-retching and puking. No doubt, she thought to herself, Slipperius was down there in his black toga regurgitating his cab charges.

Where on earth, she wondered, did he go on all those long journeys? And what debauchery went on in the back of the chariots that had so depleted the imperial coffers?

Swiftly walking past the Unionatis Hospitalis, she shuddered at the thought of her favoured son, the handsome rake Dobellius, taking tithes off the lowly slaves who toiled to clean soiled bed-sheets while he cavorted in the Via Bordello.

She turned abruptly, certain she could hear someone following her.

Treachery and subterfuge swirled around her, clothed in darkness. Her enemies were everywhere, plotting, waiting for the right moment to strike.

But she knew she could defeat them all, she was certain of that. "They may have knives," she thought to herself, "but they are as nothing compared to my formidable political skills – my acute sense of timing, my renowned judgment, my phenomenal ability to communicate with the masses and my mesmerising vocal skills." Her enemies didn't stand a chance.

But still, that nagging feeling kept creeping back: where on earth was Kevino Septimus hiding?

One by one, she mentally ticked off her foes. There was Minimus Shortus, the diminutive former slave master who had recently taken to mocking her in the Forum. "Whatever the Empress says, I support," he had proclaimed to roars of laughter from the crowds, "even though I have no idea what it is she said."

More cunning was Praetor Smith, with his cash-starved armies outside the city walls in the Fields of Duntroon. For 18 months he had patiently waited for the moment to pounce, like an adder in the grass.

And what of Senator Carrcero, the great orator with the booming voice, who as tribune of Nova South Walesium had razed it to the ground with his punic land taxes while entertaining the proletariat with extravagant Games in his specially built coliseum?

How smart had it been to let him back into the Senate? Had his ambitions been sated? Still on his travels to distant lands, imposing Roman Law on the Fijians, she was relieved she had sent him far away.

She turned to look at the foundation stones of the Basilica Julia, where her statue was being built, a magnificent testimony to her legacy, emblazoned with her own epithet: nos sunt nobis: "we are us". It would be the largest statue in Rome. After all, wasn't her most towering achievement, the introduction of the Carbonara Tax, a 23 dinar levy on all pasta production, a triumphant political victory that future generations would honour her for?

Most dangerous of all, she knew, were those closest to her. Such as Quaestor Waynium Swannus, the man she trusted more than any other with the regulation of marketplaces. His day of glory was fast approaching, when he would trick the plebeians by showering them with surplus bread and treasure. She felt an icy chill run down her spine. Somehow, she couldn't help thinking, whenever a leader was overthrown it was he who was always left standing.

Or Gregorius Combatus? A soldier of fortune who'd made his name on the wharves all those years ago, fighting injustice among the patrician galley-owners. He was now chief priest at the temple of the goddess Gaia, a powerful position from whence he could scrutinise the entrails. What had they really told him about her future? Even old Creanus, could she really trust him?

She stopped to listen, certain someone was close by. She froze as she heard the serpentine hiss of steel being drawn from leather. "Julia!" a voice whispered behind her. She spun around and couldn't believe her eyes. "You?" she said. "What on earth are you . . . ?"

But already it was too late.

The Spectator Australia editorial, 5 May 2012

UNDERBELLY RETURNS

Eager to capitalise on the success of TV series *Underbelly*, a Canberra production house is rumoured to be working on the most compelling Aussie crime drama to date. To be filmed on location in NSW, Victoria and Queensland, the true-to-life series is set to shock viewers as it explores sex, crime and corruption in the highest echelons of society.

A copy of the script, which has already been well over three years in the making, has been seen by *The Spectator Australia*. We can reveal, without spoiling the ending of course, that this latest drama weaves together the despicable tales of two powerful swindlers, both of whom rort the system for all it's worth for years. Their greed and brazen behaviour defies credulity. With hundred-dollar bills tossed around like confetti, eccentric habits and a byzantine trail of murky financial transactions, the scriptwriters have delved into a callous world of politics, deception, sexuality and depravity. 'How far would you go to line your own pockets?' asks the voiceover in the trailer.

As with the *Underbelly* shows, the immorality of the characters demands Australia's finest actors to portray adequately the cynical hubris of the protagonists. Industry gossip has it that Geoffrey Rush could play the starring role of the eccentric individual with a bizarre dress sense and fondness for long limousine rides, while Guy Pearce is tipped to play the beguiling character who keeps having his credit card stolen and used in brothels, all the while syphoning money from toilet cleaners and other low-paid workers. The title of the saga is a toss up between *Underbelly: The Golden Cabcharges* or *Underbelly: The Union Files*. Although the script refuses to identify the shockingly abused victims of these crime sprees, *The Spectator Australia* understands they go by the names of 'the Taxpayer' and 'the Unionist'.

In Wayne Swan's fifth budget, the Treasurer proudly announced his long-touted 'return to surplus' for the forth-coming year.
The following week was the Masterchef Finale.

Financial Review, 9 May 2012

WAYNE'S SIGNATURE DISH, BAKED TO IMPERFECTION

Viewers have reacted with alarm at the extraordinary lengths to which hopeful contenders have gone to get into this year's *MasterChef* series.

In a nail-biting audition in Canberra on Tuesday night, desperate contestant Wayne did his best to impress the judges with his unique "Baked Surplus à la Fair Go" recipe.

"My preparation for this dish has involved an awful lot of cutting to the bone, even though there wasn't much meat there to begin with," he said, as he stood up in front of a ravenous nation. "Nonetheless, my aim is to make sure everyone gets an absolute feast so that they all vote for me. Families with school kiddies, in particular, will love this dish.

"I started out by laying down a bed of 820 tasty dollar notes, which I intend to wrap the entire meal in. The idea is that people sink their teeth into it as quickly as possible, before they take a good look at what's inside."

At more than 1000 pages long, the judges were nonetheless quick to criticise the recipe for being light on detail and specifics. "Half the ingredients are missing, such as the very expensive broadbean roll-out, a pointless addition that alters the flavour of the entire dish. And there's no mention whatsoever of the 23 tonnes of greens, which we were promised we wouldn't be getting."

But Wayne, who defiantly maintained that he could walk tall in such an uncertain and fast-changing reality show, admitted that the meal had been finished off in a pressure cooker. "I've had to compete with Craig and Pete hogging the limelight all day and stealing my thunder."

He was referring to the scandal that has blighted the show, with two contestants found guilty of breaking the stringent rules and having to be sent home. Although both deny it, producers insist the pair had been caught "plating up" in suspicious circumstances, with Craig's exotic "Room Service à la Tiffany" apparently having been paid for by someone who stole his credit card, and Peter having been caught handing over blank Cabcharges for the home delivery of his dessert, an unpalatable dish called "Slippery Eel".

Responding to comments from the judges that his surplus was half-baked and not nearly big enough, Wayne denied that he had simply shoved the indigestible components into the back of the oven and left them to simmer until next year or the year after.

"It's a well-balanced meal. I've even made room for seconds, in this case $5 billion worth of new payments to households.

"Even though small businesses may go hungry, there are extra servings for those on a low income."

Claiming his concoction was good for you, Wayne said it was full of supplements for the lower paid and would improve dental health.

Tasting the dish, the judges were unanimous it was undercooked.

"We expected it to be a lot tougher," said one judge, while another questioned whether the recipe had been followed closely enough. Wayne remained defiant. "What are you on about? It's obvious I cooked the whole book."

Meanwhile, judges Tony and Rob still refuse to vote Wayne's team off the show.

Shortly after forming government in September 2011, Julia Gillard had appointed ex-Blair/Brown spin doctor John McTernan as her communications director.

Referred to as 'Gillard's Brain', McTernan was believed to be behind Labor's central media narrative of framing the Opposition, and Tony Abbott in particular, as 'negative'. Whether fairly or unfairly, he was also viewed as being behind such events as the Australia Day restaurant disturbance, installing Peter Slipper as Speaker, and Labor's 'class warfare' strategy.

Upon hearing of his appointment to the Gillard team, veteran union leader and former chairman of the Scottish Labour Party, Bob Thomson said: 'All I can say is, God help the Australian Labor Party.'

Financial Review, 12 May 2012

ACCENTUATE THE POSITIVE?
NOT LIKELY

The Tim Tams went flying as Julia picked up a glass of water from the conference table, skolled its contents, smashed the glass against the rim of the table and then thrust the jagged remnants straight towards the Scotsman. "There you go, Tony, take that!" she said, clearly pleased with herself.

There was an embarrassed silence around the room. Wayne and Penny glanced at each other, flummoxed.

"Er, I'm not sure that's exactly what I had in mind when I said 'class warfare'," said the highly paid PR man from Scotland, his thick accent difficult to understand.

Julia went white. "Oh. I thought you said 'glass warfare'," she said, in her distinctive nasal twang. "*Class* warfare? What's that? We don't have any classes in Australia. We're an egalitarian society."

"Well we better make some up then," said the dour Scotsman. "That's how I got Tony and Gordon over the line each time. Nothing fires up the working classes more than when you point out that those Tory toffs have got their snouts in the trough, swilling champagne and shagging themselves senseless in the back of their limos and living the high life, whilst the lowliest paid people in society are working their butts off and sweating away in some dead-end job paying for it all."

Penny coughed nervously. "I thought we all agreed not to mention Craig or Peter today. This is supposed to be a positive brainstorming session."

"Absolutely!" said Wayne, sitting up straight in his chair. "We've got a very positive message to sell. My budget, for example, is all about a fair go for all Australians and one that delivers a strong and prosperous future for the battlers... "

"Thank you, Wayne," said the Scotsman, wearily. "I am familiar with your pitch. I wrote it."

Wayne grinned impishly, looking around the room for approval. "Word perfect! Even Chris Uhlmann couldn't catch me out!"

Stephen tentatively put up his hand. "We had another two people sign up to the NBN in Coorabooralong this week. One was a mistake – she thought she was ordering a pizza – but the other one is really keen. I've sent them a welcome letter and explained they'll be hooked up in 2015. Haven't heard back yet, but I took it as a positive sign. Very positive."

The Scotsman slammed the palm of his hand down on the table. "How many times do I have to tell you? Keep it vague. You tell them they may, *perhaps*, be eligible to *possibly* have broadband at some point starting from 2015 or thereabouts. Never commit! It's not rocket science, you know."

Stephen nodded, his upper lip dripping sweat. "But, um, it is rocket science. I'm launching two specially built satellites..."

The Scotsman slumped back. "No! No! No!" he said, rolling his eyes in exasperation. "There are no rockets or satellites. That was just a feel-good positive story. It's all about covering our bases, plugging the gaps.

For crying out loud. It's like the schoolkids bonus thingy. Makes a great headline."

He stared around the room. He'd never seen such a hopeless bunch, even during the worst days of Tony and Gordon. "Now, back to my class warfare idea. That's our silver bullet. If we're gonna win this thing, we need to kick some heads in. Stir up some really strong, positive emotions. Like envy, greed and hatred. That's what politics is all about. What's a suburb or a place all the yuppies and billionaires hang out? C'mon! Think, guys!"

There was a nervous cough from the back of the room. The Scotsman looked up irritably. He hated being interrupted.

"The carbon tax is a positive, it will help save the planet and..."

The irascible Scotsman spun around in his chair. "And who do you think you are?" he snapped. Julia went bright red. "That's Peter. He's a pop star," she said, apologetically.

The Scotsman clenched his fists. "If I've said it once I've said it a thousand times. Don't ever *ever* mention that friggin' idiotic you-know-what tax! And if you do, call it a "pricing mechanism". Got it?"

There was an awkward silence around the room. The Scotsman glanced at his watch. "That's enough for today. Besides which, I've got an appointment with our estate agent. We're looking at a few houses in Sydney. I mean, who would want to live down here, for crying out loud? There's no friggin' beaches."

Julia smiled thinly. "Somewhere noice, I hope?"

The Scotsman shrugged. "The North shore sounds good."

In an interview with Channel 9, Craig Thomson claimed enemies within the union movement had plotted to undermine his political career. He denied making calls to prostitutes or spending money on escort agencies and said he was set up by rival union officials out to destroy his political ambitions.

Scheduled to make an address to Parliament, it was widely tipped that Thomson would suggest he was the victim of phone 'spoofing', an illegal practice in which somebody can make it seem as though they are calling from another person's phone.

Financial Review, 19 May 2012

MISSION IMPOSSIBLE

A quiet laneway behind Gosford. Wrapping his coat around his fist, the silver-haired gentleman smashes the glass panel on the council parking meter and opens a secret compartment in the machine, revealing a manila envelope and a small reel-to-reel tape recorder.

Glancing over his shoulder, the agent carefully extracts a grainy black and white photograph of a man with short-cropped hair in a shiny suit, and then presses "play".

"Good morning Jim," says the voice on the tape. "The man you are looking at is a local high-ranking union official who collects millions of dollars from lowly paid workers and toilet cleaners. Our sources suggest the money is for his personal use. Recently, he embarked upon an ambitious plot to enter Parliament, a position from which he could become a senior government minister of this country, giving him direct access to the pockets of millions of hard-working families and taxpayers. The consequences are unimaginable."

Jim flicks through to the next photo and looks puzzled. There are three men in the photo, but none of them has a face.

"In most countries, the target would normally have to go through a complicated process known as pre-selection. But we have identified this group of strange faceless men working behind the scenes to make sure he doesn't have to."

Jim frowns, as the tape hisses ominously.

"In order to stop him, you will need your very best team. On this mission, you will be accompanied by Barney Broadband, an electronics and mobile phone spoofing genius, who will be responsible for extracting the target's SIM card and credit cards, and replacing them with clones.

"This will allow you to manufacture fake 'sleeper' calls and expenses that will lie dormant for many years, then suddenly show up on his bills, causing him maximum embarrassment.

"Your second in command will be Johnny Latex, a noted actor, make-up artist, escape artist, calligrapher and master of disguise, whose job it will be to repeatedly impersonate the target, forge his signature and take his place on numerous occasions over the next three years, even fooling his wife."

Jim nods thoughtfully. It's a good team, he knows. But there's someone missing.

"We have also arranged for you the services of special agent Tiffany Legova, top fashion model, actress, beauty queen, Olympic pole dancer and burlesque performance artist.

"Tiffany's job will be to get as close to the target as is physically possible and entrap him using whatever methods she deems appropriate."

Jim smiles wryly. It's a tough gig. He hopes they can handle it.

"Your mission, Jim, should you choose to accept it, is to neutralise the target by setting him up and humiliating him so he never gets into a position of political power.

"As usual, should you or any of your team get caught, we will disavow any knowledge of you.

"Good luck, Jim. And remember, this government will self-destruct in the next six months."

Three months later. A penthouse suite in a luxury Melbourne hotel. The atmosphere is tense, as Jim surveys his team. Latex's disguise is perfect, right down to the flecks of grey hair and faint acne blemishes. Broadband stabs at his iPhone.

"Got him," he says, breathlessly. "I'm listening to his calls. He's just ordered caviar blinis and champagne cocktails."

Jim turns abruptly to Tiffany. "This is it! His room is directly adjacent to ours. Once you're in there, you're on your own. Should you get into any trouble, bang the bedhead loudly and repeatedly against the adjoining wall and we'll come and rescue you."

Tiffany swallows nervously. "Wish me luck, guys."

Five minutes later. Jim paces up and down, glancing at his watch. Months of elaborate planning have gone into this covert operation, but has he thought of everything?

Broadband is muttering to himself, frantically tapping away behind his bank of computer screens. Latex adjusts his wig and carefully practices his signature on the freshly minted credit card.

Suddenly the door bursts open. It's Tiffany. She throws her handbag down on the bed and kicks off her stilettos.

"What happened?" says Jim, startled. "What went wrong?"

Tiffany shrugs sulkily, and heads for the mini bar.

"He told me to go away. He said he's got more than enough girls in there already."

In his hour-long speech to Parliament, Craig Thomson again rejected the Fair Work Australia findings that he spent union money on prostitutes and on his election campaign, and complained to journalists that 'enough is enough'.

While some expressed concern for Thomson's mental well-being due to the extreme pressure he was under, a mysterious woman in a wig popped up on TV claiming to be a call girl who recognized him.

Financial Review, 26 May 2012

JOE BLOWS THE LID OFF A CANBERRA CONSPIRACY

In a rare public appearance, the embattled Australian voter known only as Joe Blow turned up at a hastily convened press conference on the lawns of Parliament House in Canberra.

"Look, I'm just going to make a very short statement," Blow said, as reporters rushed to gather around.

"Can I say that at the moment I'm subject to, well, we've had a bunch of new taxes – the carbon one, the mining one, there's two of them – but no company tax cuts whatsoever.

"Then there's MPs involved in ongoing scandals about misuse of taxpayers' funds and union members' expenses – there's two of them – we've had leaks from the Privileges Committee, then there's the cost overruns on the NBN, the asylum-seekers fiasco, the blowout on the deficit …

"What I'm here to say, guys, is enough is enough. Really, I mean, how many stuff-ups do we have to have before we start looking at a fresh election?

"What would be really good would be for the government to get on and do the sort of work that they need to be doing in terms of good policy issues, and let this circus kind of roll on."

With quivering lip, the distraught taxpayer claimed to be the victim of an elaborate set-up.

"Let's be realistic about this. I have consistently denied any wrong-doing in terms of voting for this hung Parliament, but we now have up to nine scandals and disasters unfolding all at once," Blow said.

He was referring to a series of events that insiders fear are threatening the sanity of the average voter. Denying he had any part in electing the current government, Blow claimed it was all lies. "There's the lie about the carbon tax, the lie about pokies reform, the lie about a tax cut for business, and so on," he said.

Addressing some of his comments specifically to an embarrassed gaggle of Labor, Greens and independents, a distraught Blow said: "We now have the completely ridiculous situation – that you guys are collectively responsible for, because it was always going to happen – where the government is paying $20 million just in interest every day.

"This defies credibility – that you would spend 20 million times higher than the alleged amount on the, er, er, original JWH credit card back in 2007.

"This is politics at its worst."

Fighting back tears, Joe Blow made an impassioned plea to the stunned onlookers.

"Let's not descend further into the gutter. What do you pollies want? Are you looking to incite the kind of terrible polls you keep getting? Is this about trying to push the taxpayer to the brink?"

Independent psychiatrists expressed concerns for Joe Blow's fragile state of mind, one saying:

"There's only so much the average taxpayer can take. But when he is put under such constant stress, there is a real risk to his mental wellbeing and his democratic health.

"The pressure on Blow's finances are becoming daily more unbearable.

His credit card has now racked up an extraordinary $300 billion of debt. Clearly, no taxpayer could survive such sustained abuse."

Earlier in the week, Joe Blow had outlined a bizarre and improbable plot where a woman he thought was the prime minister had set him up with two independents and a handful of Greens.

"Let me be totally clear about this. I had never even heard of Tony Windsor or Rob Oakeshott before all this happened."

Meanwhile, the Opposition Leader acknowledged that the taxpayer was under "enormous pressure" and said the Prime Minister should stop "clinging" to her 2010 election deal.

"The best thing for everyone – to take the pressure off Joe Blow and his family – would be for the Parliament to quit."

In a heated interview on the ABC's 7.30, a senior government minister rushed to the defence of the embattled Australian taxpayer, admitting that the stress on him had become intolerable.

"Joe Blow is being treated worse than Ivan Milat," he claimed.

On Thursday, ratings went through the roof when A Current Affair screened the first part of an investigation into the scandal in which the program claimed to have unearthed a hitherto unexplained stash of more than $36 billion that had been handed to a shelf company for an entity known simply as "Broadband Escorts".

The producers have also filmed an interview with an unidentified red-haired woman who claims to have been paid $481,000 to get into bed with the Greens.

The Spectator Australia editorial, 26 May 2012

WORLD'S GREATEST TREASURER, PART IV

Relax, sit down, put your feet up and crack open the bubbly. The Organisation for Economic Co-operation and Development — that astute and august body which so brilliantly foresaw the impending Global Financial Crisis of 2008 and so adroitly prevented the world from plunging into recession these past few years — has yet again proven its predictive skills and mastery of all matters economic.

Australia, we now learn, is set to grow at just about the fastest pace in the developed world for many years to come.

Phew! Thanks to the genius of our economic management, led by none other than the 'World's Greatest Finance Minister', we can hold our heads high, according to the OECD, and hop up on the podium alongside those other economic titans of our time: South Korea, Chile and, er, Mexico. Ignoring the fact that its prediction only last year that we would enjoy growth this year of 4 per cent was not exactly 'on the money', as it were, our learned friends in Paris have nonetheless declared the good times are here to stay, and applauded Wayne Swan's worthy determination to 'spread the boom'.

We hate to spoil the party, but it might be worth remembering that we are paying $20 million a day just to service a ballooning government debt that didn't exist five years ago. Businesses, denied their promised tax cut, are struggling to cope with ever-increasing energy prices and a high dollar. The Budget, despite pretending to be going 'back into surplus' offered nothing to reward productivity or growth. This week an aluminium smelting firm in the Hunter Valley was forced to shut its doors, citing as one of the reasons the impending carbon tax. A tax that is so unpopular the government dares not even whisper its name.

The Spectator Australia, 2/9 June 2012

HOW TO THINK LABOR – YOUR HANDY GUIDE

The battle of ideas in Australia has become bogged down in a bloody and seemingly intractable struggle between two immovable forces. Waves of carefully selected phrases are daily launched out of the trenches and straight into the incoming fire of the opposing formations of soundbites and spin. An entire generation of thought-provoking opinions is being decimated in a meaningless war. The madness has to stop. It is time to recognise that it's not a question of what you say, but rather, a question of how you think.

In this handy cut-out-and keep guide, we explain what it takes to "think Labor," to better equip you to cope in an increasingly topsy-turvy world.

Money: Money (unless it's yours) is the root of all evil. The accumulation of money (unless it's yours) is a grubby, amoral pursuit. Money (unless it's yours) represents the classes of oppression who will exploit the talents and sweat of the progressive classes before spitting them out onto the scrapheap. Anybody with money (unless it's you) is to be reviled, criticised and assumed to be of dubious moral standing. Money (unless it's yours) exists in abundance and can be lavished on whatever worthwhile cause the government sees fit. Money (unless it's yours) has no intrinsic value.

Income: Income is a bottomless pool of money that is extracted from the greedy hands of the rich and transferred via government jobs into the bank accounts of the progressive classes, from whence it can be put to productive use on kids' clothes, holidays, solar panels, entertainment systems, hybrid cars and so on.

Government bureaucracy: The primary system of employment for progressive people in a civilised society.

Business: There are many kinds of business, and most are best avoided, such as "funny business", "dirty business", "nasty business" and "big business." Most of these terms are interchangeable, and explain why the related term "businessman" is a word your children should definitely not be exposed to if you wish to bring them up to be productive and worthwhile members of society.

Small business: The one exception to the rule, this is a delightful expression that refers to the excellent Italian deli down the road and the place where you get your lattes in the marble foyer of your office.

Welfare: This is the means of ensuring that disadvantaged members of society who have been brutally oppressed by successive generations of anglo-saxons to the point where they have absolutely no ability to take care of themselves, even if they mistakenly think they can or even if they want to, are permitted to pursue a more noble and worthwhile lifestyle courtesy of a progressive society.

Entertainment: Sadly, much of what passes for entertainment these days is merely the dross fed to us by Rupert Murdoch and the ugly Hollywood machine and is best avoided. Increasingly the only source of worthwhile, insightful entertainment is to be found in abundance most Monday nights on the national broadcaster.

Free speech: This is one of the greatest gifts we enjoy in a progressive society. Free speech allows us the freedom to point out where others are going wrong, and permits us to explain to them that the measures we are taking are not only for their own good, but for the greater good of a civilised society. Free speech is to be cherished, but should not be tolerated if it is abused, such as when individuals "freely" express an opinion that contradicts what is obviously the truth.

Socialising: We live in an exciting, vibrant, colourful multicultural society full of inspiring influences and tantalising experiences, so make sure you go out with your friends to as many different types of restaurants as you can. Keep your friendships intact by avoiding people whose points of view, political opinions, cultural tastes or ideas on worthwhile matters are in any way different to your own.

Beliefs: There is much confusion surrounding this archaic term, due to its misuse over several centuries to describe offensive religious practices, which were nothing but superstitious fear-mongering and always resulted in paedophilia and child abuse. The modern expression "belief" has no such connotations, but instead refers to the perceptive recognition by right-thinking people that carbon dioxide is leading to the imminent destruction of the planet, including mass drownings, global starvation, violent crime sprees and death on an hitherto unimaginable scale.

Intelligence: This is the ability to draw on different sources of opinions in order to make up your own mind about the important issues of the day. The difference between stupidity and intelligence is in knowing what those sources should be. The stupid person will blindly open his or her mind to a multitude of perverse and discredited influences, whereas the intelligent, progressive person will stick closely to what is the consensus point of view.

Tolerance: Recognising that other countries and cultures have different ways of going about things is one of the great strengths of our democratic way of thinking. While certain ancient practices in oppressed areas of, for example, the Middle East may initially appear barbaric or even despicably cruel to, for example, women, we should not be too quick or too harsh to judge. However, there are certain actions that are clearly beyond the pale, such as anything undertaken by Israel, where condemnation must be swift and unequivocal.

Morality: Blame Tony Abbott.

The mystery call girl re-appeared on TV, claiming it was all a case of mistaken identity and she'd been duped.

In Europe, two stone age skeletons with arrow-heads in them were discovered, suggesting foul play.

Financial Review, 9 June 2012

WIGGED WOMAN SETS RECORD STRAIGHT

A mystery woman appeared on TV the other night and denied she had ever voted for Labor. "It's all a terrible mistake," she said, in a riveting interview, "and I want to apologise to everybody I've hurt."

Dressed in glasses and a wig, the woman recanted that she was ever a staunch Labor supporter.

"They flashed a photo at me of this man with blond hair and glasses," she said. "At first I was 100 per cent sure that I recognised him, but now I realise it has been a terrible case of mistaken identity. He looks nothing like the leader of the Labor Party, who has red hair and is of a different size, shape and sex altogether. In fact, they look nothing alike. I feel terrible, and that's why I want to set the record straight. A man called Swannie approached me out of the blue and offered to shower me with money if I would go on TV and say that I would vote Labor one more time. Even though I refused he insisted and kept offering me more and more handouts. I am poor, and he promised to pay the cash directly into my bank account on the first of July. I am furious that he put me under so much pressure."

Clearly upset, the woman claimed that although she was a working girl back in 2007 she had now given up that lifestyle entirely.

"I looked back at my bank statements and realised I was in the full-time employment game back then. I'm not in that line of work any longer, or any line of work," she said, fighting back the tears. "We all got laid, I mean, laid off."

The mystery woman said she had only realised her mistake when her friends pointed the blond man out on television. "He was just sitting there quietly on the back benches refusing to say a word. He isn't anybody special any more. I felt so sorry for him," she said. "They called him all these names and painted him out to be some kind of hopeless leader. It must have been terrible for his wife and family. He was supposedly bringing down the government – I had no idea about that."

The woman, fighting back tears said: "I'm really genuinely sorry for any hurt I've caused by pretending I would vote for Labor again. Particularly for the damage I've done to working families." She explained she had decided to retract her support because she was terrified she would otherwise have a Labor government following her around for the rest of her life.

In another dramatic twist to the saga, Swannie, who is the executive producer of the TV show, has gone on the offensive, saying viewers have been "hoodwinked" by the woman, and denied any payment had ever been made to her.

"This is the greatest economy in the world. We have the greatest growth of any country in the OECD. It's simply stunning," he said, several times over. "Why would I need to offer anybody any money to vote Labor again? All I said was that we would be more than happy to pay her a substantial wad of cash in order to spread the boom and compensate her for the carbon price."

Asked if the carbon price was in fact a carbon tax, Mr. Swannie refused to take any more questions.

Meanwhile, the Labor chief whip insisted the entire affair proved there needed to be far more stringent controls on the media. "It is disgraceful the way newspapers and TV shows are allowed to trawl through the gutters to find these disaffected voters," he said, describing the reporting of negative opinion polls as "extraordinary" and "unedifying." He promised new measures "in the pipeline" that would put the scandalous practice of "Fleet Street-style polling" under the strict government control of a wholly independent media watchdog led by, er, himself.

In other news this week, archaeologists on a remote hillside in Canberra were astonished to uncover the skeletons of two former Liberal leaders, dating to the middle of the past decade, pierced through the chest with iron rods to keep them from turning into leaders again.

A clearly shaken spokesperson, Mr. Hockey, explained that people believed the rods would pin the dead treasurers into their graves to prevent them from popping up midway through the term and terrorising the party.

He described the bones of Turnbull and Costello as "even scarier than Wayne Swan".

Mining magnate Nathan Tinkler announced he is leaving Australia and moving his family to Singapore.

Financial Review, 16 June 2012

TINKLER TAILOR MINER MAGNATE

Cigarette ash fell onto the crisp, freshly printed pages. Quickly, the "communications consultant" brushed it off, leaving a dirty smear on the folder's distinctive Department of Interpersonal Research Tracking logo.

"It's all here," he said. "All the dirt we could possibly want on this guy."

The Treasurer nodded, gingerly picking up the D.I.R.T file. Politics, he knew, was an ugly game. If you want to stay in the kitchen, his mum had always said, get ready to put your hands in the sink.

He flicked through the file. "Is this for real?" he said. "$13 million beach houses? Thoroughbreds? Bugattis? Stolen Ferraris?"

The consultant grinned. "Yep. Too good to be true. The ideal candidate. It's like he's been designed specially for our purposes."

The Treasurer licked his lips. "Tinkler. Sounds like a Cold War spy. I trust he's a mining magnate, as per the brief?"

"Naturally," smiled the consultant, "but not just any old mining magnate. He's into …" He hesitated, milking the drama, "…coal! He's what you might call a 'carbon magnate'."

"Coal!" cried the Treasurer, his mind racing with the possibilities. "So if I'm not mistaken this Tinkler Tailor Miner bloke is out there making gazillions from the stuff that's destroying the planet, whilst working families are stuck with the carbon tax…"

"Price," said the consultant. "It's called the carbon price now."

"Of course," said the Treasurer. "But as I was saying, he's not only rich, he's filthy rich!" He smiled at his own wit. "I can almost hear the *Q&A* audience now. They'll rip him to shreds. Don't suppose he's into any wacky CIA theories?"

The consultant forced a smile. "They call him 'The Gambler', and the '$441 million man'. Imagine the sound bites. From what I can tell, he's made his fortune out of nothing more than good luck and a massive pile of debt."

The Treasurer scratched his forehead, puzzled. "And that's bad?"

"Disastrous!" said the consultant, before noticing the startled look on his boss's face. "I mean, for a private individual, that is. Not if you're a caring, socially aware, progressive government. Then massive debt is a good thing. Obviously."

The Treasurer wiped his brow, relieved.

"Anyway," the consultant said, "play our cards right and the base will lap it up. He buys footy teams like you and I buy undies. He's only 34 and he's on the BRW Rich 200. He's everything the focus groups hate."

The Treasurer nodded slowly. The D.I.R.T. team had done well. But experience had taught him that if you're going to engage in a spot of good old-fashioned class warfare, make sure the public is left in no doubt who the bad guy really is.

"And he's, um, a generous build, if you catch my drift? Visually?"

The consultant grinned and pulled out a gigantic fold-out A2 colour photograph. "Well, let's just say 'the Big Fella' ain't exactly a pin-up for Jenny Craig."

The Treasurer took a long, hard look at the picture and smiled.

Julia Gillard attended the G20 meeting in Mexico, where she took the opportunity to lecture the assembled heads of state and to write to key global business leaders advocating they follow 'the Australian way'. She then dashed to the Rio+20 Conference, where United Nations Secretary-General Ban Ki-moon rewarded her 'vision, leadership and commitment' by appointing her co-chair to a group implementing the 'final push' to achieve the Millenium Development Goals, an initiative long-supported by Kevin Rudd. Thoughtfully, Gillard also donated 10 million tax dollars to the establishment of Korea's Global Green Growth Institute.

Back home the national press speculated that her government was 'finished'.

Financial Review, 23 June 2012

SAVING THE WORLD IS A GIFT

Dear Mr. Ki-moon, or may I call you Ban?

You may not remember me but we met last year when you popped into the Lodge expecting to see Mr. Rudd and I made you a cup of tea before you hurriedly left. We briefly discussed climate change.

I am writing regarding the vacancy for a co-chair of the Millennium Development Goals group. It concerns me greatly that such a distinguished body, which holds within its fragile grasp the future wellbeing of this precious globe we call home, should be left to complete its task chaired by an individual from Rwanda who, quite frankly, probably already has too much on his plate.

As you may not be aware, I have long been an ardent supporter of the brilliant MDG, and it is often said that as Australia's first female prime minister, I am the personification of millennium goal No. 3: gender equality and the empowerment of women.

It is in this spirit that I wish to bring to your attention a gifted candidate who would complement the skills of Mr. Geldof and others of the group, and offer the sorely needed vision, leadership and commitment to eradicate world poverty. Me.

Although I am now occupied as full-time Prime Minister of Australia, I don't expect the job to last much longer and am keen to "move forward."

I could not help but be inspired by the words of 17th century Korean poet Han Ki-moon (to whom, I believe, you are distantly related): "Only the unwise do not share their prodigious gifts with the world." As co-chair, I would bring to the role those skills recognised as recently as last February by my colleagues, who unanimously voted for me as a formidable leader, outstanding orator, visionary populist and great political mind.

Indeed, it is barely 12 months since I famously pointed out that I had no interest in foreign affairs at all and would be just as happy running a kindy, which just goes to show how quickly someone of my abilities learns on the job.

Now, of course, I am sought out by the leaders of the free world for advice in their darkest hour; teaching the merits of the economic strategy known as The Australian Way, which many people (wrongly) credit to my junior assistant without realising, of course, the World's Greatest Finance Minister was only acting on my instructions.

Among my many achievements, if I may be allowed a moment of uncharacteristic immodesty, let me single out the carbon price, which puts Australia at the forefront of nations tackling the scourge of climate change – a subject close to both our hearts.

As my Climate Change Minister pointed out this week (on my instructions), nations such as your own South Korea, and China, which are shining examples of responsible clean energy growth, are rightly aghast that Australia single-handedly continues to destroy the planet.

I imagine you already have a shortlist to fill this prestigious position. Without wishing to "dish the dirt", as it were, please allow me some candid observations.

Mr. Rudd is, I know, a close friend of yours who has talked a lot about the MDG. He is also a former colleague and friend of mine, as well as a dysfunctional psychopath incapable of performing even the most basic tasks, and unless you wish to turn the entire project into a farce I suggest you quietly recycle his CV down the nearest eco-friendly toilet.

Mr. Carr, a lightweight whose candidacy I suspect you will be receiving soon, is also a close colleague and friend of mine. Indeed, it is only through my generosity in making him Foreign Minister – a task he has sadly proven himself manifestly ill-suited to – that he has dared to think he would be "in with a beaut chance". Why have the monkey, Mr. Ban, when you can have the organ-grinder instead?

Mr. Downer is only known locally for his cross-dressing tendencies.

Please feel free to contact my friend Mr. Obama for a reference, a man with whom I have a very strong relationship built on mutual respect; so much so that he wittily refers to me in diplomatic cables as a "soft touch" and a "total pushover."

I enclose a photo of myself with Mr. Obama at the recent G20 meeting. (That's me behind his hand).

I also enclose a cheque for $10 million for the South Korean Global Green Growth Institute, an organisation close to both our hearts.

Hope to see you in Rio,

Julia x

The Spectator Australia, 23 June 2012

WORLD'S GREATEST CORRESPONDENT

It will have been heartening for many European leaders to receive a letter in the post from Julia Gillard and Wayne Swan prior to the G20 Summit in Los Cabos advising on how to fix their beleaguered economies. Offering a magical panacea for their current conundrum — "There is no need to choose" — the letter and the accompanying, earnest speeches by the Prime Minister set out what is now officially "the Australian way." "Structural reforms that lift growth also create the positive feedback loop needed to improve confidence in the sustainability of public finances," is one piece of sage advice, explaining how, for example, creating overpaid public service jobs in climate change institutions will placate people being stung more for their "renewable" energy bills. "Bringing forward investments in key infrastructure projects... can create jobs and boost demand in the short-run and add to productive capacity," is another, explaining how spending billions on Pink Batts and school halls can massively boost your workload if you happen to be on the government's preferred list of tradies and can charge pretty much whatever you like.

In a nutshell, Ms. Gillard and Mr. Swan are urging European governments to borrow more and spend more. Repeatedly referring to "reforms," they fail to spell out that the two major reforms they themselves have introduced — the punitive carbon and mining taxes — are demonstrably anti-growth.

Clearly the brainchild of one of Australia's hitherto unacknowledged great economic minds, Norman Lindsay, "the Australian way" is proof that you can have it all because there is an unlimited supply of money in the world and all you have to do is keep eating your slice of the pie until you feel full again. No doubt this will reassure Europe's leaders that they had it right all along.

On the eve of the introduction of the carbon tax she had promised not to introduce, and as her much-vaunted Malaysian solution was thrown out by the High Court, Gillard set up an 'expert panel' to resolve the asylum seeker issue she herself had promised to fix.

Faced with a six-week winter break, record numbers of politicians headed overseas on 'study tours'.

France had recently voted in a socialist president, Europe continued to fall apart, the Queen shook hands with the former head of the IRA and Obama was gearing up for the November presidential election.

Financial Review, 30 June 2012

POLLIES STUDY TOURS

Beat those Burley Griffin blues at *StudyTours-R-Us,* where you'll find a whole range of tantalising winter getaway trips. Air fares, food and accommodation thrown in. Forgot your wallet? Don't worry! The Aussie battler is picking up the tab.

Tour de France: For lovers of foie gras and fiscal follies. This study tour includes two nights at the Elysée Palace where you'll be wined and dined by 60,000 brand new public servants who've just been put back on the payroll and are keen to kick up their heels while they can-can! L'Austerite is out and La Growth is back in. Then it's off to a retirement chateau at Versailles for champagne, canapés and the official Lowering of the Pension Age ceremony.

Rediscover the Drachma: Marvel at the crumbling, faded glories of a distant epoch and imagine what life was like here in ancient times before this once-proud race succumbed to joining the euro. Highlights of the trip include not paying any taxes and a three-hour week. Here in the cradle of democracy you'll learn first-hand what it's like when a country is run by a motley crew in a hopeless minority government.

"We felt right at home" – Rob and Tony.

Obamaland: It's a non-stop roller-coaster ride as you hurtle downhill towards the next election. Why not study the tactics first-hand as both teams try every grubby trick in the book? Tour the Fox and CNN studios as the "Secret Muslim" prepares to do battle with the "Greedy Mormon." Bigger than the Superbowl, uglier than the WBA, it's the heavyweight battle of the decade. (Update: must take out health insurance!)

Sizzling Syria: Learn first-hand how to play the big powers off against each other. You'll study how to make a complete fool of Kofi and the UN, render the West impotent, and why cosying up to the Russians and the Chinese is good for your health.

"I'd give this one a miss" – B. Carr.

Boating Indonesia: Want to see first-hand how to stop the boats? Well, you won't find it here. But what you will learn are all the great possibilities for personal economic growth as local officials show you how to "turn a blind eye" to every leaky vessel that lurches out of port. Study the subtle art of baksheesh and learn the deft skill of accepting the smuggler's backhander. (Boat-building, safe maritime and naval engineering courses not available.)

Jubilee Ireland: Hone your acting skills and learn to grit your teeth behind a frozen smile as you shake hands and look pally with your sworn mortal enemy.

"Highly recommended" – Malcolm.

"Invaluable" – Kevin.

Flying Pigs Tour: Why study just one failed economy when you can pack in four? This whistle-stop tour of Europe's lowlights shows just what happens when you borrow excessively for wasteful welfare and fanciful climate-change schemes. Take in the non-spinning windmills of Portugal, the subsidised solar panels of Spain and the empty office blocks of Ireland. The tour climaxes at Italy's famed La Bunga Bunga Roman orgy.

"Count me in!" – Craig.

Brussels Bailout: A must! Under the watchful eye of a Brussels tutor you get to pick any economy, flood it with money you don't have, and then sit back and watch it spiral out of control. Weeks of fun for lovers of the fashionable euro style of economics. Will the whole show fall in a heap? Not if you just raise your debt ceiling and start all over again.

"A real eye-opener" – Wayne.

Germanic Discipline Classes: Learn the lost art of rubbing other countries' noses in the dirt, humiliating their leaders, and inflicting much-needed fiscal pain as our Prussian Hausfrau cracks the whip. Not for the faint-hearted.

Turkish Delight: Enjoy the hedonistic pleasures of the famed Istanbul nightlife as you bathe in a comforting Turkish bath of self-satisfaction, after experiencing their bustling marketplaces not seen since the glory days of the Ottoman Empire. Marvel at Turkey's lucky escape; it tried to join the EU, but the EU wouldn't have them!

Only days after the introduction of the carbon tax, scientists in Geneva announced that they'd spotted the long sought after Higgs boson, the particle that explains why all other subatomic particles have any mass at all.

Financial Review, 7 July 2012

SPIN SHOWS TRACES OF MORAL PRINCIPLES

Scientists have discovered the tiniest known object in the political universe, the hitherto elusive but highly sought after sub-atomic entity known as Moral Principle.

Moral Principle, or the Howard particle as it is sometimes known, is believed to hold even the most complex and divisive political matter in one piece, giving it mass support. "Without Moral Principle, we believe politics quickly becomes a formless soup," says one scientist. "Even though you can't actually see it, the public can always detect when it is there, and when it is not."

Recently, political experts have theorised that political power and success can be achieved without Moral Principle. "There's never been any proof that it actually exists," said one. "The nature of politics today, since the Big Bang of 2007, is that political expediency, deception, hubris and minority power-sharing deals are all that is needed to give a political party critical mass to stay in permanent orbit for as long as they like."

To test both theories and to search for the elusive Moral Principle particle, a team of scientists have constructed the world's fastest spinning machine, known as the Large McTernan Collider; a massive looping tunnel buried deep beneath Capital Hill in Canberra. Designed to recreate high-energy conditions, such as doorstop interviews, the accelerator allows words and phrases to be smashed head-on against each other at close to the speed of a normal sound bite. Over the past 12 months, billions of phrases, words, distortions, fibs, backflips, exaggerations, unfounded beliefs, voodoo theories and broken promises have been hurtled through the machine to see if any contained Moral Principle particles.

"It's been truly extraordinary," says one participant in the experiments. "We've taken such phrases as 'Real Julia', 'We Are Us' and 'Moving Forward' and exposed them to phenomenal pressure to see what could be detected. It turns out when you break them down there isn't actually anything there."

Other experiments included endlessly colliding the words "Clean Energy Future" and "Carbon Pricing" against each other, up to a billion times a second in some interviews. The astonishing breakthrough came last month, when two teams working around the clock at the McTernan Collider announced they thought they had caught a glimpse of a "previously unobserved particle" in the mass region of 89-95 per cent GaV (giga-approval-votes). "We believe what we witnessed is indeed a new particle," says a spokesperson.

"We think it must be Moral Principle because it's the heaviest swing we've ever detected in voting intentions."

"The implications are very significant and it is precisely for this reason that we must be extremely diligent. We must know that it really does exist."

The final confirmation of the existence of Moral Principle would help politicians to solve deeper mysteries. Such as how the bonds between governed and governing can be held tightly together, and the whereabouts of the mysterious invisible matter known as "popularity", which is said to make up much of the political universe but which recently even the most sophisticated telescopes have been unable to detect.

Some experts have predicted that the discovery of the Howard particle could ultimately lead to humans being relaxed and comfortable once again.

One participant in the project says the discovery data has less than a one-in-a-million chance of being mere chance. "Everybody is very excited here," she says. "This particle was lost around five years ago and we have been unable to find it ever since."

Meanwhile, a dissident group of fundamentalists known as the Church of Gaia claim to have found their own "God" particle. "When we looked into the Collider all we could see were these massive carbon particles spinning around. It's obvious to us that they are responsible for all the ills on the planet," says a spokesperson, with tears welling up in her eyes.

"Carbon is the one element that can give otherwise irrelevant and decaying bodies the most phenomenal power over the entire political universe."

The group expressed grave fears that if the Moral Principle particle escaped into the atmosphere it could wipe out their entire future.

With the introduction of the carbon tax, members of the Gillard government performed a variety of unusual stunts to celebrate that Tony Abbott's dire predictions about job losses hadn't immediately come true.

The Spectator Australia, 7 July 2012

CANBERRA'S GOT TALENT

There were fireworks, laughter, drama and high-wire action as top-rating reality TV show *Canberra's Got Talent* returned to the national broadcaster this week, with outstanding acts auditioning for a spot in the Grand Finale on the shores of Lake Burley Griffin sometime next year.

Panicked executives of rival talent shows on the commercial networks expressed their dismay that their own acts looked almost embarrassingly shoddy in contrast, and risked being outclassed by the sheer quality of talent that had been unearthed by the ABC.

"It's simply not fair," complained one insider. "These Canberra acts pretend to be amateurish, but in reality they are highly trained professionals who have been tutored by some of the world's most successful Scottish impresarios."

Canberra's Got Talent comprises a series of vaudeville acts that have been strenuously put through their paces during auditions in front of a record-breaking audience of some 25 million voters.

Rival network bosses were universal in their condemnation of the exorbitant fees paid to these so-called "taxpayer-funded acts" that dwarf anything the networks can afford to cough up.

"Their prize money is outrageous. These guys are out their earning a bloody fortune," wrote one vitriolic blogger. "They get showered with Gold passes, expenses, trips overseas, chauffeured limos and pensions for life. It's worth squillions. We simply can't compete."

One of the favourites of the show so far, Skyhooks impressionist 'Shirley' Emerson, wowed crowds with an impromptu performance of the classic hit 'Horror Movie' updated to include contemporary references to South Australian mining towns.

Afterwards, the breathless and slightly sweaty performer told a packed Parliamentary lawn of just himself and a TV cameraman why he felt inspired to re-record the song. "When I heard that Tony Abbott had said that Whyalla would be wiped off the map by the carbon tax, I was incensed," explained the craggy-featured singer. "After all, that's my line. I've been saying for years that the whole eastern seaboard would be wiped off the map by climate change and global warming."

Predicting a Skyhooks revival thanks to his re-interpretations, 'Shirley' says he already has plans to re-record smash hits 'Carbon Tax (Is Not A Dirty Word)' and his personal favourite 'All My Gay Friends Aren't Getting Married'. Asked if he had yet thought of a name for his album, due to be released around the time of the next federal election, he felt the classic Skyhooks hit 'Party To End All Parties' summed Labor's future up best.

Meanwhile, audiences were bowled over by the sheer Zen-like concentration of sit-down comedian Grog 'Way Past That Debate' Combat. As fellow *Q&A* panelists collapsed out of sheer boredom, Mr. Combat repeatedly did his knockout impression of a reasonable, sensible-sounding politician who earnestly believes that what he is doing isn't just an old-fashioned wealth redistribution scheme.

Performing one of his popular sleight-of-hand magic tricks, Mr. Combat went on to prove to a sceptical ABC crowd that you could change people's behaviour without changing their behaviour and you could stop big business polluting without causing them any financial hardship. "That's how the economy works," he explained. Warming up for the climax of his act, Mr. Combat twisted himself into knots trying to avoid saying the words "John Howard" as he performed a deadly stunt, explaining: "When I came into parliament I didn't like the idea of offshore processing. Now I think that, you know, we do need offshore processing."

Other acts include Peter G's fiery 'Batts are Burning' and impressionist Albo Albanese, a mimic who memorises scenes from Hollywood classics and regurgitates them as parliamentary speeches. His skills, however, are deemed inferior to those of Bill 'life's too short' Shorten, a talented sprinter who is desperately waiting for the starting gun to go off so he can make a dash for the top spot in the show. Insiders believe that Mr. Shorten has next to no chance of winning any contest whatsoever, although his hilarious poem "I agree with everything she says, even though I don't know what she said," has been touted as a masterpiece of contemporary absurdism in the tradition of Edward Lear or Dr. Seuss.

"There is no end to the brilliance in Canberra's own back yard. It will be a blast as we watch our last semi-finalists battle it out for the popular vote," announced one of the show's judges.

Other hopefuls are 'Swannie, the World's Greatest illusionist' who made an entire surplus disappear, and veteran hypnotist Bobby Carr, believed to be wandering around in a daze somewhere overseas, after his trite routine "look into my eyes" failed to make any impact on the votes.

A gaggle of screaming limo drivers held up gold-laced placards outside the Capitol Hill studios awaiting the arrival of the act known simply as the Slipper, an illusionist of great skill who can literally change his spots in front of your eyes.

A gasp went up from the audience when unpopular contestant The Lady in Red Hair ended up in a bloody mess after deliberately being sawn in half by the Greens and two independent members of the audience while discussing the issue of asylum-seekers. Although she said that she expects to make a full recovery in time for the finals, most experts believe she is lying.

Pundits agree that the night belonged to 'Shirley' Emerson and his sidekick 'Grey' Mr. Gray, who performed an extraordinary double act 'The Sky Isn't Falling In.' As one irate judge, Mr. A. Taxpayer, later remarked: "The sky hasn't fallen in on these clowns yet. But it's only a matter of time.

The 2012 NSW Labor Conference was held at Sydney Town Hall. As usual, there was much excitement surrounding the fringe events.

Financial Review, 14 July 2012

PARTY-GOERS, IT'S TIME
TO TALK UP LABOR AGAIN

Dear delegate or party member,

It's conference time once more and I'm delighted to welcome you to Sydney Town Hall for what promises to be two days of enlightened "light-on-the-hill" debate as we Build Towards The Future.

Best of all, the fringe events are back – so here's your guide to the most stimulating topics of the weekend.

Know your enemy (forum): Members and friends are invited to join in this cordial discussion about the greatest threat posed to the continued existence of life on this planet – namely, the Greens. In this intelligent and reasoned debate our panelists explore why these loopy, weirdo scumbags need to be wiped off the face of the earth if the planet (and indeed Labor) are to survive.

Saving the planet (drama): Concerned by the increasing attacks on science in our society? It's time to bring back evidence and reason as our interactive activists-in-the-round perform, for the first time ever, a theatrical re-enactment of Al Gore's pivotal and seminal autobiographical monologue, 'I Didn't Make It All Up, Honest'.

Know your enemy (debate): Members and friends are invited to join in this vibrant discussion about the greatest threat posed to the continued existence of democracy – namely, Tony Abbott. In this instructive debate our panel explores how Abbott's negativity has destroyed every shred of decency in the land. Learn how Abbott single-handedly botched border protection, live cattle exports, the carbon tax, the mining tax, pink batts, solar-panel rebates, green loans … (see appendix for complete list of failed government policies).

Contemporary activism (foyer): Political organisations are confronting a radical shift in the nature of contemporary engagement. The most obvious manifestation of this is the decline in membership numbers. In this lively debate we encourage fresh thinking and innovative ideas to rejuvenate our party for the next generation. (Open to senior delegates and life members only).

Know your enemy (panel): Members and friends are invited to join in this feisty discussion about the greatest threat posed to the continued existence of the union movement – namely, Mark Latham. Hear from former trade union leaders how this repellent Tory turncoat betrayed every working man and woman in the land with his disgraceful calls for Labor to abandon its very heart and soul, the great Australian workers movement. (Union membership fees must be presented at the door).

Free speech (workshop): Members and friends are invited to have their say in this free-thinking, no-holds-barred workshop about the single greatest threat posed to free speech – namely, Rupert Murdoch and Gina Rinehart.

Learn how the evil Media Magnatopoly seeks to control every aspect of our lives from shock-jocks in the morning to blogs at night. How can we stop them? (Speakers must submit all proposed material to the Free Speech Regulatory Board prior to the event).

Addressing discrimination in the LGTBI community (foyer): Recent data shows that members of the Lesbian Gay Transexual Bisexual Intersex community are more likely to discriminate in favour of the Greens over Labor on virtually any topic you can think of. Join our panel of psychologists as we try and persuade them not to.

Know your enemy (the vault): Where better than the bowels of Town Hall for us to discuss in an enlightened fashion the greatest threat posed to the modern economy – namely, the mining magnates. Delegate Wayne, armed with a comprehensive blacklist, will explain how these loathsome slugs gorge themselves on the sweat and hard labour of the impoverished and embattled slave classes of the oppressed Australian proletariat. (Comrades, er, delegates only).

A member's journey (foyer): Your chance to hear from someone who lives the Labor dream. With a must-see slide presentation, tonight's special guest Julia takes us through her personal journey of enlightenment from a humble industrial lawyer in Victoria through to the giddy heights of power and life in the Lodge with her partner, Tim. Hear how world leaders hang on her every … (cancelled due to lack of interest).

Julia Gillard and Wayne Swan announced that Brisbane would host the G20 Leaders Summit in 2014.

'It is a real honour for Australia to host the G20, and provides a vital platform to build on Australia's role in global economic decision-making,' the Prime Minister said.

'Our international standing goes from strength to strength, having fought off the global recession, achieved strong growth, low unemployment, a return to a budget surplus and key economic reforms.'

The Spectator Australia editorial, 14 July 2012

WELCOME TO BRISSIE

By the time the sun-starved members of the G20 touch down in Brisbane for their 2014 shindig, it is unlikely that Julia Gillard or Wayne Swan will be there to greet them. If current opinion polls remain an accurate reflection of Australian voting intentions, the world leaders will arrive in a nation that no longer has a carbon price, has strong and resolute border protection policies (under which economic refugees are discouraged from attempting to illegally enter the country by boat), celebrates, rather than restricts, freedom of the press, and is focused on how to increase, rather than how to greedily devour, the national pie.

Rather than lecturing the leaders of the biggest global economies on how to run their nations, we trust the new team at Australia's helm will display a degree of humility and be grateful that we have narrowly dodged the bullet of reckless borrowing, profligate spending on ideology and bureaucracy and declining productivity that are the hallmarks of the eurozone crisis, and which our former Labor masters seemed hell-bent on replicating.

Hopefully, our visitors will be able to relax in the sun and appreciate our productive way of life without being embarrassed by crooning trade ministers, harassed by hyperventilating union leaders, patronized by power-hungry politicians touting voodoo beliefs or bombarded with government advertising campaigns that attempt to "sell" wasteful government schemes to a disinterested electorate.

We also trust that our guests will be free to purchase a copy of an increasingly popular and successful Rinehart-owned Fairfax paper, and listen to whatever shock jocks take their fancy, and that our mining magnates will be introduced to the relevant officials, rather than being shunned and ridiculed as class enemies, by a government pleased to encourage investment and real jobs across our nation. They'll hardly recognise the place.

A fresh round of taxpayer-funded government advertising reminded people that it was no longer 'compensation', but a generous 'household assistance package' they were being given. The words 'climate', 'change', 'carbon' and 'tax' did not feature.

Financial Review, 21 July 2012

CARBON TAX COMPO CAN GIVE YOUR LIFE A LIFT

Confused by your household assistance package? Wondering what to do with all those spare dollars cluttering up your savings account? Our 24-hour government-affiliated help line is here to answer all your questions.

Dear Elyssia,

Of course you can use your carbon tax money to "get your breasts enhanced". This is precisely the sort of activity it was designed for – after all, it's not called a compensation package for nothing!

If you choose to spend it compensating yourself for what nature failed to give you in the first place, well, there's nothing wrong with that. We call it "spreading the boob".

Dear Jordania,

Don't believe everything you read in the newspapers.

No, Mr. Wilkie's ridiculous $1 limit does not apply to how much of your household assistance package you can spend on the pokies. The sky's the limit.

And imagine if you win – what better way to invest in your own future? Just keep a bit back to pay for a babysitter for Rhiannon (we don't want a repeat of what happened when you invested your entire stimulus package in one weekend at the RSL during that dreadful heatwave).

Dear Rheece,

Look on the bright side. Automobiles are smelly, horrible things responsible for global warming and the end of life on Mother Earth as we know it, so losing your job at Ford is good news for saving the planet.

You may not have permanent employment any more, but future generations and Gaia herself will applaud your sacrifice. At least cashflow won't be a problem, thanks to the generous carbon tax package.

Why not cheer yourself up by treating yourself to a brand new Bravia? Or taking a trip to Bali? Or buying a Mitsubishi? Or all three?

Dear Julia,

We all have to face unpleasantness at work and people saying nasty things about us behind our back. That's just the way things are these days, with so much negativity and workplace bullying going on.

The good news is that you've not only had a huge pay rise recently but your first $18,000 of it is tax free. Our advice? Spoil yourself and splurge out on getting your hair done (again).

Dear Agnes,

These sort of bureaucratic bungles happen all the time, so don't fret.

Just because you've been dead since 1923 is no reason for you not to enjoy your household assistance package today. Perhaps you could polish up your urn, or why not order some fresh flowers for the grave to cheer yourself up?

Dear Kevin,

No, you won't have to give your compensation package back when you return to your former high-paying job at the end of the year.

Dear Professor Tim,

There are many ways of investing your carbon tax dollars, but certainly waterfront properties are a safe and sensible option.

Particularly seeing as you have two or three already, why not join them all together and make an absolute killing?

Dear Mahmoud,

Yes, you will still receive the full amount of your carbon tax compensation package, even if you are temporarily detained in Malaysia, Nauru, Manus Island or some other tropical getaway. Climate change is, after all, a global problem, so we all have to do our bit.

And don't forget to apply for your home theatre DVD and iPod asylum-seeker entitlement package while you're at it.

At the NSW Labor party conference, the Greens were roundly denounced as being anathema to Labor. And Julia Gillard made a keynote speech about Labor.

The Spectator Australia, 21 July 2012

BRAND LABOR

"Labor is not a brand, it's a cause," claimed the Prime Minister to rapturous applause in her address last weekend to the NSW Labor conference. It was a neat phrase that had the desired effect and was quickly splashed all over the news bulletins. But — surprise, surprise — it was a lie. In fact, it wasn't just one lie, but two.

Whether the PM likes it or not, Labor most certainly is a brand. The definition of a brand includes political parties of all hues, and it is no more within her power to define what is and isn't a brand than it is to define what is and isn't a tuberous root vegetable.

What the Prime Minister's speech-writer meant to say was "Labor isn't only a brand, it's also a cause." But clearly Gillard felt that the inclusion of these correlative conjunctions drained the soundbite of its, well, bite.

Or perhaps, unwittingly, the Prime Minister was acknowledging a far greater truth, which goes to the heart of her term in office. The Oxford English Dictionary defines a brand as "a particular identity or image regarded as an asset." If you accept what the opinion polls clearly tell us, Labor under Gillard no longer satisfies the OED's definition of a brand because her image and the ALP's identity are no longer regarded, by more than two-thirds of the population, as an asset. So perhaps, after all, Julia Gillard broke her habit of telling porkies and came out with an honest insight.

The reason for Gillard's attempt to deny that Labor is a brand is easy to see. The most common phrase journalists reach for in these post-*Gruen Transfer* days — where everyone is a marketing expert — when describing the declining fortunes of Labor under Team Gillard's stewardship is that "they have trashed the brand." Which is true. But rather than attempt to remedy this self-evident situation, Gillard has simply decided to deny that Labor is a brand at all.

This is straight out of Sussex Street Spin 101. Don't tackle the meaning behind the words, simply change the words. Hence, if the people don't want a carbon tax, call it a carbon price. Or, if you are accused of damaging the brand, simply deny that you are a brand. Ta-dah! Job done.

So now the Labor brand had been re-branded not as a brand but as a "cause". Which is the second lie.

Labor can no more be a "cause" than the aforementioned tuberous root vegetable — say a yam – can be a cause. A cause is a principle that requires a course of action. Saving the Franklin River. Protecting old-growth forests. Keeping uranium in the ground. Stopping the boats.

Labor can facilitate, support and advocate any number of causes, as it has over the past 120 years. Some of them may even be contradictory, or some may go in and out of fashion. Even the White Australia Policy — which Labor actively supported — was a cause: to protect local jobs from cheaper imported labour.

But any one cause is mutually exclusive; it stands or falls on its own two feet, and is either achievable at a given point in time or it isn't. Gay marriage, for instance. You either support it or you don't, and you either advocate it now or you don't. You can't prioritise it or make it conditional on other causes; "Well, I support gay marriage so long as it doesn't lead to the destruction of old-growth forests." That would be nonsense.

Yet that is precisely what Gillard is suggesting by claiming that Labor is a cause.

Again, Gillard has unwittingly revealed a deeper truth. Labor can only be a cause if it supersedes all other causes. In other words, if Labor's sole purpose is the continuation of itself, the pursuit of power for power's sake. If Labor is the cause, then it follows that all the other causes it pretends to support are only there in order to perpetuate Labor's power. "Whatever it takes," as Graham Richardson admitted.

Rather than pretending that Labor is a cause, which it isn't, and denying that Labor is a brand, which it is, the Prime Minister might do better to ponder the alternative. Labor actually is a brand, and, much like many brands, it is in trouble because it has never bothered to learn how brands rise and fall. Call it Darrell Lea Syndrome. To be successful, a brand needs to have a clear identity, a clear mission and popular products.

The first mistake a brand can make is to be careless with its symbols and its mascots. So, for example, if Ronald McDonald suddenly gets overthrown by Hamburglar, and then Mayor McCheese and the McNuggets Gang all start telling anyone who will listen that Ronald

McDonald was not really a loveable clown after all but was in fact a "dysfunctional psychopath", it is reasonable to expect that the biggest loser of the stoush will not be the public, or indeed the products, but will in fact be the brand.

Similarly, if a brand goes into partnership with another brand, it needs to ensure they are compatible and that one of them doesn't end up devouring the other — unless, of course, that is the intention.

McDonald's and Coca-cola have co-existed for decades. The thought of drinking, say, carrot juice with a Big Mac is inconceivable. Maccas and Coke go hand in hand. So if little Paul the pug-faced kid behind the counter and his mate Sam in the drive-thru suddenly start slagging off Coke, claiming the fizzy drink ought to "be destroyed" because it rots your teeth and gives you diabetes, again, it is their brand, not the other one, that will suffer the most damage.

Until brand Labor redefines its values, clarifies its mission and puts out products that people actually want to buy, it will carry on marching towards oblivion.

Not so much 'game on' as 'game over'.

'Edgy' reality TV shows such as 'Being Lara Bingle' and 'The Shire' – with its colourful cast of Beckaa, Mitch et al – led to heated debate about whether or not the shows demeaned the locals in the areas they were filmed in.

Financial Review, 28 July 2012

THE 'BERRA

Canberra residents this week expressed dismay that their real estate values are being damaged through negative association with Channel Ten's "dramality" series *The 'Berra*.

The 'Berra claims to be an honest portrayal of the lives of a handful of residents in the leafy suburbs surrounding Canberra's notorious Lake Burley Griffin, but locals fear its heavy focus on wooden personalities, incessant betrayals, bitchiness and backstabbing may scare off potential home buyers.

The series, which debuted in 2010, has already had an impact on the market, said real estate pundits. Speaking on condition of anonymity, a local auctioneer said people planning on selling their lakeside homes in the near future are worried sick.

"Everyone I spoke to yesterday commented on how destructive *The 'Berra* is on the value of property in the area," they said. "Our reputation has only just recovered from the dreadful '70s reality series *The Dismissal*. That was bad enough, the way the producers focused on an extremely unpleasant group of Canberrans and how they were behaving in such a nasty way and treating each other with such contempt. But, believe it or not, this time it's far, far worse."

Filmed over the last 12 months using non-actors who have to mouth words and phrases pre-written by a highly paid Scottish scriptwriter, *The 'Berra* has been slammed by critics who are appalled by its "fatuousness". One Canberra resident said the series portrays people "who are nothing like ordinary Canberrans".

"These individuals are shallow, selfish, arrogant, insincere and relentless publicity seekers. They don't understand the value of a dollar and splash billions around that doesn't belong to them. They don't give a toss about hard-working taxpayers and they certainly don't represent what the real Canberra is all about."

Says one critic: "*The 'Berra's* hunks and babes – Wayne, Greg, Bill, Penny and so on – are far more wooden than people you meet in normal life in the streets of Manuka or Deakin. It's just not an accurate portrayal. No one on the cast appears even remotely likeable."

The main storyline, about the former couple Nicola "the girl next door" and Kev "the hottie" reuniting at a party, was, according to one critic, "contrived in its construction, pretty lame in its execution and ended really badly."

Said another: "Christine and Sarah, 'the wifeys', memorably described on twitter as the 'Green ghouls' do manage to provide a kind of gruesome fascination. They're a reason to keep watching, and would definitely liven up the party if they were ever let loose on it." Insiders believe the two were added to the series late in the day in a panic move in an attempt to shore up dwindling ratings.

The most "icky" moments of the show involve Juliaa "the party girl", she of the freshly minted nose, who is met at Canberra airport by a man who appears to be her sugar daddy but turns out to be pugnacious union boss "Howzie" who sneaks up from behind to tell her the party is already over – for her at least.

Twitter erupted over that one but where does the show take it from there, say the fans?

Rumours of dramatic in-fighting have plagued the show since its inception, with the TV network being forced to re-edit the entire "carbon tax promise" segment after it turned out the characters had been lying all along.

Other critics have slammed the clunky dialogue and unconvincing "Berra-isms," with characters being forced to mouth banalities such as "we are us" and "moving forward."

As one blogger points out: "Every time Juliaa runs into any kind of trouble she starts saying stuff like, 'I will be leading the Labor Party to the next election,' which just doesn't ring true. Nobody from around here believes that sort of crazy talk."

Meanwhile, rival reality show *Being Laura Tingle* has been receiving rave reviews.

"Everyone thought it was just a show about a typical political editor hanging around all the famous pollies," said one commentator. "But when you see the sort of boorish characters she has to listen to every day, you realise how tough her life must be."

In a major speech in Melbourne in early August, Treasurer Wayne Swan claimed Bruce Springsteen had always been a big influence on his thinking.

He cited lyrics from the 1970's Springsteen song Badlands: 'rich man wanna be king and a king ain't satisfied till he rules everything'.

'It's often the case that great artists – people like Bruce Springsteen – tend to pick up the subterranean rumblings of profound social change long before the economic statisticians notice them. Changes start long before they become statistics,' Mr. Swan said.

Financial Review, 4 August 2012

DANCING IN THE DARK

"Tramps like us . . . click… Tramps like us . . . click… Tramps like us . . ."

Sunlight streamed into the gloomy room, making patterns on the ceiling. Wayno half-closed his eyes, enjoying how the beams of light danced around his eyelids.

"Just like Go-Cart Mozart and little Early-Pearly," he thought to himself, "I'm blinded by the light!"

"Tramps like us . . . click… Tramps like us . . . click… Tramps like us . . ."

Suddenly his senses were sharply alert. He'd always had an uncanny sixth sense. Call it intuition, if you will. His razor sharp instincts were legendary among his mates at the Caloundra surf club.

"Wayno!" they'd say, "what's the swell gonna be like tomorrow?" Or "Hey Wayno, how do you stick a biro into the side of a fruit juice bottle without splitting the bottle?"

Was it his imagination, or were the beams of sunlight actually making the light bulb glow? How did that work? Light came from electricity. Everyone knew that. You switched it on, over by the wall, just next to the *Nebraska* poster, and it came on. Pow! You switched it off and it went dark.

"Darkness at the edge of the room," he muttered. But this was weird.

A thought suddenly flashed through Wayno's groggy brain. If you could make light out of electricity then it only made sense that you could make electricity out of light! There was heaps of sunlight on the Sunshine Coast! He could sell the electricity and be a billionaire! That would teach those fat rich kids like Clive and Gina a lesson!

Counting on his fingers he tried to work out how much he could earn. Did electricity have a fixed price tag or could you charge whatever you wanted?

"'Tramps like . . . click . . . tramps like . . . click . . .'"

Wayno rubbed his forehead. Maths always gave him a pounding headache, "like a freight train running through the middle of my head." Plus it had been one *hell* of a night. He grinned. Sure, the neighbours had been their usual pain-in-the-arse selves, hammering on the door and screeching about having to go to work in the morning.

"Baby this town rips the bones from your back, it's a death trap, it's a suicide rap," Wayno had told them, repeatedly, 'til they'd finally gone away. Anyway, what was the point of getting up at six in the morning and heading into Brissy in the middle of rush hour traffic just to make some other guy rich?

"Rich man want to be king," he whispered to himself, marveling at the wisdom of such insightful words, "king ain't satisfied 'til he rules everything."

If there was one thing he'd learned in life it was that all bosses – apart from The Boss, of course – were fat greedy bastards.

Wayno slowly raised his head and surveyed the empty plates on the floor. There was no pie left. All his mates had helped themselves to as many slices as they could possibly grab and now it was all gone.

Wayno eased himself to his feet – taking care not to tread on any still-smoldering ashtrays – and went to the fridge. He knew there'd be more pie in there. It wasn't up to him to create more pie. It was his job to make sure it was shared evenly.

As The Boss said: "What I've got baby I have earned." Wayno stared into the fridge for several long seconds, stunned. No pie. It was all gone. He shook his head. "In the day I sweat it out in the streets of a runaway dream," he muttered bitterly to himself, as he contemplated another crappo day at uni.

"Tramps click, tramps click, tramps click." He sighed. Life was the pits. He stared at his shiny new velour flares, crumpled on the floor. Just what were "velvet rims?" he asked himself for the thousandth time. And how do you wrap your legs round them?

"Tramps, tramps, tramps, tramps, tramps."

He spun around, startled. The record! He stared at it in dismay. It was stuck! Scratched! Ruined!

Wayno slumped down on his beanbag. He'd have to buy a new copy. But that cost money. So he'd have to get a job. He rubbed his forehead. Stuff that. If he had to go to work, then how could he fulfill his lifelong mission of becoming a hero to the working classes?

As The Boss said: "Don't try for a home run, baby, if you can get the job done with a hit." Of course! Why not just raise the debt ceiling with his mum?

Wayno smiled to himself. What did Springsteen say? "We learned more from a three-minute record, baby, than we ever learned in school." So true.

Communications minister Senator Stephen Conroy and NBNCo CEO Mike Quigley officially launched the 2012-2015 corporate plan for the National Broadband Network.

The event began with Senator Conroy disputing recent highly critical newspaper articles, including a number of pieces by the Australian Financial Review, quoting opposition communications spokesperson Malcolm Turnbull. 'I'm convinced that if Malcolm Turnbull put out a press release saying the NBN was late because the earth was flat, the AFR would run it,' Conroy asserted.

The fast-talking Conroy, who still speaks with traces of his English accent, also ran through a list of areas he called 'misreporting'.

Financial Review, 11 August 2012

NBN RUNS RINGS AROUND ITSELF AND ALL ELSE

Senator: "Cor blimey let me tell you this thing ain't easy I mean we're talking the biggest infrastructure project this country has ever seen since the Snowy Mountains scheme and the Sydney Harbour Bridge combined and let me tell you we're not playing tiddlywinks here I mean this is a national broadband network and that means three things number one it's national number two it's broadband and number three it's, er, a network and let me tell you not everything is going to go according to plan in fact I can prove that to you 'cos I've got the original plans right here on the back of this envelope see it's a bit smudgy but that squiggly bit there that's all the fibre optic cables and then those bits down the side they're all the houses and, er, hang on, it's upside down, there, that's it so you have to get the cable to every single home and it all looks fine on paper but out in the real world it's a whole new ball game I mean with the Snowy Mountains scheme – and I mean no disrespect here – but let's face it all they had to do was build a couple of dams and stick a few pipes down the side of a hill but what I'm dealing with

here is a modern technological revolution in the middle of the heartland
of working suburban families and that means you've got all sorts of
unforeseen things that you just can't predict like you can be digging a
ditch across a paddock and the shovels keep breaking 'cos some idiot
buried a load of old bricks and rubble there back in the 70's and so
it's back to Bunnings to get some pickaxes and jackhammers and those
things cost a fortune let me tell you or another time this idiot went and
stuck a brand new driveway right where our trench was supposed to
go without even telling us so we had to go the long way around up his
garden path without knocking over the flamingoes and then we had to
detour around his prizewinning hydrangeas and then by the time we'd
done all that we realised the fibre optic cable wasn't long enough to reach
so we had to go all the way back up the street and start again and as Mike
was telling me just the other day when I was screaming my head off at
him these sorts of unforeseen circumstances cost time and money and
if you look at the original budget here down the side of the envelope
where all those numbers with the noughts on them are you can see that,
er, hang on, no, sorry, I mean not those numbers they're all the postcodes
that Wayne said we had to get done before the election and let me tell
you Wayne knows a thing or two about postcodes I mean he even wrote
a book about them that's how smart he is but anyway there was another
time we were waiting for this guy to come back from his lunch break
and move his car so we could dig the trench and it was only after about
five days that the boys realised the car had been abandoned so we had
to call a tow truck and that's not cheap believe you me when you're
out in the middle of nowhere in the back of beyond and then another
time we were drilling the hole through the front wall 'cos the beauty
of our scheme unlike Tony Abbott's is ours goes right into your home
whether you want it to or not and anyway normally the drill goes straight
through but these idiots had put some stupid family heirloom in the way
without telling us so next thing you know the old duck's screaming her
head off and we had to run around and find a replacement French art

deco antique clock in Armadale which wasn't cheap believe you me plus I bought these two humungous satellites but rockets weren't included so now I've got to get them up into the sky somehow or other plus on top of that I've got to pay Telstra a couple of billion quid every year to get rid of all that copper cable and nobody knows what to do with it all so it's just going to stay stacked up in my garage until I can flog it to someone else but nobody wants copper any more 'cos like David was explaining to me the other day mobile and 4G and all that is the future 'cos everyone's going totally mobile and, er, nobody uses fixed cables any more but, er, anyway these are the sorts of indirect operating costs I have to deal with every day 'cos after all's said and done what you've got to remember is that this will revolutionise the way we do business in this country for every single working family I mean we're talking the biggest infrastructure project since the Sydney Harbour Bridge and the Snowy Mountains scheme combined let me tell you cor blimey."

The Expert Panel on Asylum Seekers released its report containing 22 key recommendations on the policy options available to prevent asylum seekers risking their lives on dangerous boat journeys to Australia.

The independent panel was appointed by Julia Gillard on 28 June 2012. It was not to be confused with other government expert panels, such as on education and press freedom.

Financial Review, 18 August 2012

THE EXPERT PANEL ON EXPERT PANELS

The government today released the findings of its Expert Panel into expert panels.

Speaking to a crowded press conference attended by senior cabinet ministers, including the Prime Minister herself, the Expert Panel – comprised of three eminent and expert panelists, all of whom have served on various expert panels – surprised journalists and commentators with the unexpected results of their six month-long inquiry.

"What we've found is that Expert Panels serve a vital and crucial role in the functioning of a dysfunctional government," said the Expert Panel's chief Panel Expert, a former expert panelist on a number of government expert panels, now retired.

"What an expert panel allows a prime minister, or indeed any minister for that matter, to do is to appear to be getting on with doing their job when they haven't actually the faintest idea about what it is they're supposed to be doing."

To approving nods from an array of government ministers, the panel went on to release some of the more detailed components of their study.

"We looked at a variety of expert panels, including some taskforces, although, to be honest, we simply didn't have the time or the resources to look into them all as the number of expert panels has mushroomed exponentially since 2007."

The key findings and recommendations of the panel have been handed to the government in a detailed report, which won't be released to the public until later in the year, allowing spin doctors ample time to remove the embarrassing bits, although some of the details have already been leaked to the media.

"We felt it necessary to leak the fact that we discovered nearly all expert panels feel it necessary to leak certain facts to make it look as if they've achieved something," said an anonymous spokesperson for the Expert Panel.

Chief among the recommendations from the Expert Panel was the suggestion that expert panels should be made compulsory for all government decision-making.

"What we found is that without an expert panel, it becomes necessary for a politician to make a decision. This is simply unrealistic in today's media-dominated environment. History shows that it is not possible for a minister to make a commitment that makes him look good on *Q&A*

but is in line with what he or she promised prior to what is known as an 'election'."

Identifying "electoral commitments" as a major stumbling block in the implementation of government policy, the Expert Panel cited numerous examples where the most effective solution had been to set up an expert panel.

"The beauty of the expert panel system is that you can perform the most outrageous backflips and nobody bats an eyelid.

"For instance, everybody has known since medieval times that any kind of supervision of the free press is unacceptable in a well-functioning democracy. But we found that the best way for a dysfunctional government to get around that fact was to set up an Expert Panel.

"In this instance, the expert panel advised the government to control what the public can read through a News Media Council, made up of a panel of experts."

Asked to nominate other areas where expert panels could prove advantageous to a collapsing government, the panel referred to areas such as education and industrial relations.

"What the Expert Panel on Education was able to do was to fantasise that if the government spent billions of dollars that it doesn't actually have on our public schools then they would be almost as good as our private and independent schools."

With thousands of jobs disappearing in manufacturing, the panel praised the government's Manufacturing Taskforce for recommending that the way to boost productivity was to set up a Manufacturing Expert Panel.

Referring to the recent Expert Panel on Asylum Seekers, the panel applauded its innovative approach to solving a tricky problem.

"The suggestion that the government scrap everything they've done and immediately return to all of John Howard's ideas and policies will resonate strongly with what are known as 'voters'."

A taped September 1995 exit interview between a senior partner of Melbourne law firm Slater & Gordon and the then-lawyer Julia Gillard was released, querying her involvement in setting up an AWU slush fund. Gillard left the firm shortly afterwards, and has maintained ever since she did nothing wrong.

Financial Review, 25 August 2012

NO MORE SNOW JOBS ABOUT SLUSH FUNDS

"Come on in Julia, sit down. Now, for the record, we are taping this interview ... and, oh, it's already on. The date is August ..."

"25th."

"25th, thank you Julia. The year is 2012. Present in the room with the Prime Minister are her two partners, Mr. Fred Bloggs, who's a voter, and Mr. Taxpayer. You have no problem, Julia, with this interview being taped?"

"No, none at all (laughs). I've done nothing wrong!"

"So you joined the firm in 2007, is that right?"

"Yes. May I point out that I began in the somewhat lowly position of deputy prime minister, which was clearly beneath my capabilities and, let's be up-front about this, I had my work cut out for me. The place was, quite frankly, chaotic and dysfunctional. My boss (name redacted) was an ear-wax munching psychopath so I had no choice other than to stab him in the back and take his job."

"That was, um, the night of June 23rd, 2010?"

"Well, it was thereabouts. I, I, I'm not sure of the specific dates. It was a long time ago. And I'd done nothing wrong."

"Then you called an election?"

"Well, I had lots to do, I had to fix the whole asylum seeker mess, then I had to save the world from climate change and I also had to tax the mining boom. I may have called an election, I can't remember. Whatever."

"But you did say to your partners, that's us, that there would be 'no carbon tax under the government I lead' – and that was immediately prior to the election?"

"Well, these things are all a long time ago now. I can't be 100 per cent sure about precisely what I did or didn't say on any one particular day; things were pretty crazy back then."

"But then after the election you did bring in a carbon tax. Without opening a file on it. Why did you do that?"

"Well, I, I, I, was young and naive back then, and I got caught up with, I now realise, a couple of shady characters who told me that I had to. But I did nothing wrong."

"So, er, who told you to?"

"Well, I can't remember all their names. There was Loopy Rob. And Tony. Window, I think his name was. A couple of hick farmers. Then there was Bob – 'the Earthling' we called him – (laughs) because he was off with the fairies most of the time. I mean pixies."

"And did you get advice from anyone else in the firm in relation to any of those matters?"

"I didn't need to. It was just a favour. But then Bob suddenly disappeared and I haven't seen him since."

"And how did you pay the others, Julia?"

"Well, I'm glad you asked me this because I looked around the Lodge over the weekend and I found all these receipts. We gave Mr. Window a brand new hospital and some roads. Loopy Rob got a …"

"OK. Julia, it would be helpful if we could have copies of those receipts. Do you have a problem with supplying them to us?"

"No, no problem at all."

"Good. So it's fair to say, as a general summary, that all of the work was paid for by you?"

"Well, actually, I borrowed the money."

"Who from?"

"The taxpayer! Where else am I going to find billions of dollars?"

"I see."

"I got Wayno the Surfie Dude to explain it to me. He's got a degree in economics from Springsteen University. It's all above board. Everybody does it. I helped him set up a special $300 billion debt ceiling which we rushed through with the budget. It's like a slush fund, or a re-election fund, or whatever. That way, Penny and Greg and Bill and everyone can dip into it whenever there's an election."

"OK. Is there anything else you think we need to know?"

"Well, it occurred to me, sorry, while I was at work Chris the Wog-stopper did a dodgy deal with some Malaysians, or Nauruans or whatever, and Pommy Conroy started building this massive, ugly broadband network that's truly hideous – I didn't ask him to – and Peter the Popstar went and bought a giant Gonski, I think that's what it's called, and he's got no idea how to pay for it and I may have accidentally promised to build an NDIS that I don't recall getting invoiced for yet."

"One more thing. Your relationship with the Australian public?"

"Oh, that's at an end."

"OK, thanks."

End of tape.

31 August 2012 was the 25th anniversary of the death of Diana, Princess of Wales.

The Spectator Australia, 1 September 2012

MY NIGHT WITH DIANA

It was one of those nights when you wake up the next morning with a distinct feeling that all is not well with the world, yourself included. So you turn to the person in bed with you and say, "Um, that was fun last night, wasn't it?" And that person groans and responds "No, it wasn't actually. My foot's killing me. Why didn't you stand up for me and biff him?"

"Er, because he's the future King of England?" you meekly respond.

To which Sarah replies, as only a newlywed can: "Or was it because you were too busy chatting up Diana?"

You glance around the room, looking for clues. There's a disheveled dinner jacket on the floor, a scrunched up white shirt, dirty socks, and a gold bow tie.

Gold! Of course. The Red and Gold Ball at the Albert Hall. Your wife's best friend Caroline has booked a box. It's in aid of Birthright, a charity that aims to reduce the number of women and babies dying during pregnancy and childbirth. Normally, of course, you are far too tight-fisted to go to such an extravagant bash, but you make an exception because Caroline is so persuasive. "They do a wonderful job raising money for medical research. It's an extremely worthwhile cause; and it's fun. Everyone wears red and gold," she says, as you mentally do the sums and inwardly wince. She senses your hesitation. "Did I mention that Princess Diana is the patron? She's bound to pop in."

The big night arrives. Sarah, of course, looks stunning as we walk up the steps to the Royal Albert Hall on a chilly November night in 1985. The champagne is flowing and I make a quip about how we all might just manage to squeeze into Caroline's box. That's the beauty of being an Aussie in London's polite society. You have a duty to behave like Barry McKenzie. It's expected of you.

Not only that, it was that very brief period in mid-Eighties London when Aussies, for the first time, were cool — a trend that I had played a tiny but not insignificant part in several years earlier by creating an ad campaign that introduced the Brits to a beer, Fosters, that they quickly developed a taste for and an actor, Paul Hogan, with whom they briefly fell in love. We'd won the America's Cup, 'Down Under' had topped the charts worldwide, and 12 months later Hoges and my mate Cornell would release *Crocodile Dundee*. Jason and Kylie were only a few short years away. Let's face it, at that point in time we Aussies could get away with pretty much whatever the hell we wanted to.

The Three Degrees were playing up on the stage, and the yuppies were cavorting across the dance floor, a shimmering sea of red and gold, when suddenly everything went quiet. The music had stopped. Walking elegantly down the steps onto the dance floor came Princess Diana on the arm of her brother, Viscount Althorp, known colloquially — and in this case quite appropriately — as Champagne Charlie. Almost as one, the sea of Sloane Rangers parted, startled, and retreated to their seats. Standing alone in the middle of the vast dance floor, Diana, wearing a sleek, figure-hugging long red dress, waved shyly to the stunned crowd. Her brother, in his regimental finery, took her hand. The band began to play. Loudly.

"C'mon!" I yelled, grabbing Sarah's hand and heading onto the dance floor. I barged straight up to Champagne Charlie, "Would you like to dance with my wife while I dance with your sister?" The Viscount's eyes lit up, and as he took my beautiful wife's hand I turned to Diana. "I'm from Australia." She grinned, and we started an awkward (is there any other kind?) of Eighties-style twitching of limbs and shoulders. She leaned forward and smiled. "I guessed as much." I slid my shoes across the floor, attempting my own cool version of the moonwalk. "Great music," I yelled. She nodded, and flashed the famous blue eyes at me. My mind was swirling. A kid from Canberra, dancing with Diana. And yes, she was even more beautiful in real life. I stared down at her shoes. "Gold!" I grinned. She glanced at my bow tie and smiled back. The music slowed. Unsure of the precise protocol of pirouetting with a princess, I gingerly put one clammy palm on her slender waist and held out the other to take her hand. Perhaps I shouldn't have.

There was a commotion from behind. I turned as a group of men in tuxedoes rushed towards us. Two of them shouldered me aside, while an angry little man, who was shouting, stomped heavily on Sarah's foot. Sarah yelled out in pain. I turned, jabbing my finger at the little man whose bald head was at my eye height and yelled out, "Oy! Listen mate! You just trod on my wife's foot! Say sorry!" But he wasn't listening. He was yelling at his own wife, the Princess of Wales. "How dare you embarrass me like this?" Prince Charles thundered at Diana. "This is the last time this happens! Get back upstairs. Now!"

Within seconds they were gone. He gave me a final, filthy look, then marched angrily off the dance floor with Diana and bodyguards in tow. Champagne Charlie disappeared, too, in search of another glass of bubbly I suspect.

Sarah was grimacing in pain. Her foot had a huge gash on the top of it, where the royal heel had left its mark. (It's still there.) We hobbled off the dance floor, to be greeted rapturously by Caroline's box and envious yuppies. Champagne all round.

By now I was busting. I scurried up into the corridors in search of the loos. Bizarrely, standing alone in a gilded alcove I saw Charles and Diana. He was berating her angrily, she was in tears.

Fifteen years ago this week, Diana died. As the funeral procession wound its way through London's streets, they showed footage of Diana visiting certain landmarks. Passing the Albert Hall, they cut to Charles and Diana arriving at the Red and Gold Ball in November 1985. She looked radiant, smiling happily at the cameras and waving at the adoring crowds, her husband by her side.

The night had just begun.

After weeks of secret talks between the government and the Greens, in a major backflip Climate Change Minister Greg Combet announced Labor were ditching their planned floor price on carbon permits, meaning the new plan resembled John Howard's ETS. Recent changes to border protection also brought Labor policies more in line with the previous government's.

A new book on Alan Turing and the codebreakers whose clandestine efforts helped win World War II was released.

Financial Review, 1 September 2012

CRACKING THE JULIA CODE

The head of Research Data Analysis gulped nervously. Up on the gigantic screens, computer-graphic images of the Prime Minister morphed seamlessly from one to the next. The hair subtly changed style from a deep red bob, to a pale orange bob, to a bob with blonde highlights. The jackets flicked from one colour to the next. White. Orange. Blue. The head tilted from left to right. The hands came up then dropped back down again.

"It's a st-stimulus input s-simulator," the chief government scientist stuttered. "Millions of images and s-soundbites in random rotation, while over here we analyse a trillion, er, tregabytes of up-to-the-minute p-polling from across the country. What we're looking for are the tiniest, imperceptible p-patterns that alert us to shifts in p-public opin. . ."

"I know all this shite," shouted the Scottish spin-doctor. "What's the code? There's always a code! A look, a phrase, and a gesture. Combine them and you've got the formula. I found it for Blair. And for Brown. For crying out loud, we're running out of time! There are thousands of livelihoods at stake. Mine for one! We gotta crack this goddam code!"

"C-certainly, s-sir, we'll. . ." But the Scotsman had already stormed out of the room.

Two floors below, in the vast maze of offices beneath Parliament House, a lone mathematician put down his slide rule, staring at the figures in his notebook. There was no mistake. It worked. Every time. Slowly, he tore the piece of paper from his pad, folded it neatly and headed for the lifts.

The Scottish spin-doctor was sitting in the back of the press room, head in hands, inwardly moaning in despair, when his mobile started vibrating. "Yes?" he hissed.

"You've g-got to come right away, sir. One... one of the b-boffins... He's..."

The Scotsman leapt to his feet and sprinted all the way back down past Central Spin and Speech Writing, past Image Control, and past Media Manipulation to the bowels of the War Room.

"The code...?" he said breathlessly, as he stared at the unassuming little man with grey strands combed over his bald patch. "You've cracked it?"

The man carefully unfolded the paper, pushing his glasses up his nose.

"Well I was puzzling over the parallel paradigm..."

"The what?"

"Quantum physics. I noticed a distinct positive reaction whenever the Prime Minister didn't do anything, as opposed to when she did. It's not about action. It's about inaction. Einstein proved moving away from an object is as effective as..."

"Einstein? Quantum? What the...?"

"I found a negative dimensional continuum between the political timeline and voter contentment. You see, we were looking at the data the wrong way around. In effect, the more the government shifts back into the past, towards 2007 or thereabouts, the more relaxed and comfortable the electorate become. For instance, reopening Nauru was a 'positive' because it restores things to how they used to be. I've analysed all sorts of decisions, and the answer's always the same. When they got rid of grocery watch, dumped fuel watch, stopped splurging on school halls, packed away the pink batts, ditched green loans, withdrew the solar rebates and so on, people responded positively.

"Every action that reverses what they have already done, or indeed any non-action by this government is seen as a 'positive'. Conversely, anything they actually do of their own volition is a disaster. They are popular when they do nothing of consequence, such as going on holidays, or when they put things back to how they were before they stuffed it all up. Simple maths, really."

"So," said the Scotsman, nodding thoughtfully, "it's not about 'moving forwards,' it's about 'moving backwards'."

"Precisely."

"It's not about 'we are us' but rather 'we are them'."

The mathematician nodded. "The formula never fails."

A slow smile spread over the Scotsman's face. "So, what if, for example, we scrapped the floor price on carbon? Just had it floating. Like Howard would have done. Does that fit the code?"

The mathematician squinted at his slide rule, nodding. "Perfectly."

The Scotsman grinned. "At last," he said, "we've cracked the code."

In a controversial speech in Perth, former Liberal leader and former head of the Australian Republican Movement Malcolm Turnbull decried the level of debate during question time, maintaining that politics in Australia had deteriorated to the point where the country was being besieged by spin, exaggeration and lies. He claimed the country suffered from 'a deficit of trust'.

He denied that the speech was in any way critical of Tony Abbott.

Financial Review, 8 September 2012

THE DEFICIT AT THE HEART OF OUR NATION'S ILLS

In a landmark speech in Perth this week, a former opposition leader bemoaned the state of discourse in Australian politics. "Forget the fiscal deficit," the Minister for Communications said to a rapt audience, "the biggest problem we all face today is a deficit of Malcolm."

"Day in, day out, an impoverished Australian polity is forced to suffer life without sufficient Malcolm. I'm not talking about Abbott or Gillard in particular, but debate in this country has become so devoid of Malcolm that we have the ludicrous situation where an unpopular PM keeps being asked questions by an unpopular Opposition Leader.

"If you love your country, have an interest in politics or policy and care deeply about our nation's future, there's nothing more certain to arouse your fury than the deficit of Malcolm. Politicians and shock jocks, scientists and coal barons, all of them can argue for as long as they like, but they cannot make up for the deficit of Malcolm."

Citing a golden age of mature, sophisticated political debate, the Minister reminded his audience of the Camelot years between 2008 and 2009, when there was a brief flowering of inspired discourse and two popular leaders conducted the nation's affairs in an atmosphere of mutual respect and civil accord.

"Today's tragic deficit of Malcolm in the national debate is only matched on the other side of the political divide by an equal deficit of Kevin," he continued. "Without these two positive forces operating in perfect unison, the harmonious nature of Australian politics has been trashed, perhaps irrevocably."

He also pointed out that it was not only Australia, but the entire world that was suffering from a deficit of Malcolm and he recalled the fleeting moment in history when the planet could have been saved from impending doom and melting ice-caps. "I won't linger on climate change – the hopeless, confused, hyper-partisan nature of the debate is clearly entirely due to a deficit of Malcolm," he said. "Call me idealistic, but a severe deficit of Malcolm lies at the heart of all the ills that plague our society. Whether it's the lack of sufficient trans-gender bike lanes in our cities, or the absurd situation where we are governed by a family of anorexics and naked billiard players frolicking around in Las Vegas, it's clear these problems are the result of a deficit of Malcolm in our public life."

Insisting that he was more than happy in his role as opposition communications spokesperson, the shadow minister for communications pointed out he was merely doing his job communicating to the public what was wrong with today's parliament.

"Basically, we have this absurd situation where Tony Abbott gets up and bangs on endlessly about all this carbon tax and boat people crap," he said. "It's not only extremely negative, it indicates a chronic deficit of Malcolm in the entire political process."

Denying that he was being disloyal to his leader, he pointed to historical precedents.

"Paul Keating, for instance, was a visionary leader of this nation with an excellent plan to replace the British monarchy with a popularly elected president ie someone such as myself," he said. "But he was stabbed in the back and disgracefully bundled out of office by those mean monarchists

John Howard and Tony Abbott who sneakily tricked people into voting for them four times in a row, then tricked them into voting against my republican movement, thereby breaking the nation's heart – mine and Lucy's in particular."

Repeating that he was extremely happy in his current position in the Liberal Party, he explained that it was the job of politicians to look beyond the daily political fray and raise the level of debate to a higher plane.

"A deficit of Malcolm doesn't just hurt the Parliament, it means every one of us suffers an unbearable loss on a daily basis," he said.

"You only have to watch popular programs on the telly such as Tony Jones's excellent and unbiased *Q&A* to realise that the entire nation is suffering from a deficit of Malcolm. Not since the assassination of Kennedy or the dismissal of Whitlam has a country been denied such a charismatic, towering intellect.

"We all remember precisely where we were on that tragic day when that despicable cur stood on the steps of Parliament House waving his infamous fake email and breaking the nation's heart.

"As I said at the time, well may we say God save the Queen, for nothing will save me from the Godwin Grech scandal."

More than 500 years after he was killed in battle, archaeologists in Britain announced that they believed they had found the skeleton of the slain hunchback King Richard III, buried deep beneath a council car park.

Meanwhile, former prime minister and current backbencher Kevin Rudd popped up on the ABC's 7.30 program, speaking from China where he was attending the world economic forum. In an unusual interview, he said that he wouldn't be silenced when it came to pushing Labor's agenda.

Leigh Sales had to extract an admission from Mr. Rudd that Julia Gillard was in fact the prime minister.

Financial Review, 15 September 2012

KEVIN VII EXHUMED

More than two years since he was slain in battle, archaeologists believe they have found the skeleton of history's most famous pretender to the Canberra throne buried above a car park in Ultimo.

Experts said an intact skeleton in ABC Studio 4 matched much of what they knew about Kevin VII, including his reputation as a "comeback".

The remains were dug up 20 minutes into an interview by a team from *7.30* led by Leigh Sales. The skeleton was an adult male with spinal abnormalities that pointed to numerous political contortions, a form of spinal curvature that can be the result of repeated and intensely painful carbon tax and mining tax backflips.

The remains showed signs of trauma to the head where a blade had cut away part of the back of the skull, an injury consistent with the so-called "faceless men" battles, and a barbed blade was found lodged between vertebrae in the upper back.

The only known account of his death is from a tearful doorstop interview with his loving wife and children where he explains how he was "poleaxed by caucus".

Lord Douglas Cameron, president of the Scottish chapter of the Kevin VII Society, who aims to restore the reputation of the deposed monarch to its former glory, and who has single-handedly driven the search for the body, said: "This will allow us to really challenge what we know about Kevin and rewrite the history of the last two years.

"We can find out how he got tricked into standing down, how he was buried, how he died – all the things that have been the subject of assumptions and misconceptions."

Kevin VII was the first of the Rudd-Gillard-Swan dynasty and his slaying was decisive in the demise of the House of Labor.

David Shakesmarr's celebrated play *War of the Rages* depicts the rise to power and subsequent short reign of Kevin VII of Canberra who is destroyed by the Machiavellian plottings of Lady Julia and the traitorous Chancellor Swan. The play portrays Kevin VII as a dysfunctional, ear wax-chewing psychopath, who craves popularity above all else.

In his opening monologue, Kevin establishes a strong connection with the audience, urging them to support his crusade for "the greatest moral challenge of our time" and introduce an emissions trading scheme.

However, after Act I, when he returns from Copenhagen empty-handed and humiliated, his reign starts to unravel as he struggles to make any decisions at all, with multiple scenes interspersed that do not include any other ministers running the show except himself.

"What do I fear? Myself? There's none else by. The people love Kevin; that is, I and I." Yet despite his ongoing popularity with the crowd, he suffers bouts of uncontrollable rage and his brief rule soon descends into chaos and confusion.

With four tragic deaths blamed on the Crusade of the Pink Batts, he quickly points the finger at his hapless court jester, the minstrel Pete. "Fool, of thyself speak well. Fool, do not flatter: my conscience hath a thousand several tongues."

When Kevin loses his bargain with the wealthy aristocratic mining moguls to give him all their gold – a scene whose form echoes the same rhythmically quick dialogue as the carbon tax backflip scene he was tricked into by Lady Julia in Act I – he has lost his vivacity and playfulness for communication. It is obvious he is not the same man, which allows the plotters to dispense with him on trumped up charges of "a good government losing its way."

The final act begins the morning after the brutal slaying of June 23, 2010, with the famous soliloquy, where the ghost of Kevin, alone and clearly upset, addresses the audience via YouTube.

"Now is the winter of my discontent,

Made glorious summer by this sunshine coast,

And all the clouds that lowr'd upon our beach house,

In Thérèse's deep bosom as I mourn my loss."

Audiences are treated to a brief dream sequence as the slain monarch reflects upon his greatest achievements, which only takes a few seconds.

Finally, as the curtain falls, a lone and forlorn Kevin faces the wrath of his enemies.

"A sauce! A sauce! My kingdom for a suck of the sauce," Kevin VII cries to no avail, as his enemies drag him down.

Despite numerous unsuccessful attempts to revive the play, historians have always viewed it as more of a comedy than a tragedy.

The Spectator Australia editorial, 15 September 2012

STEPHEN IN A SPIN

At *The Spectator Australia* we are delighted to offer our full-throated support to Communications Minister Stephen Conroy — who, let's face it, is not only an outstanding cabinet minister but also one of the brightest of the stars that make up the sparkling firmament of this progressive and morally enlightened government — for his realistic and characteristically modest acknowledgement that the NBN, although not perfect in every way, represents a milestone in the history of Australian government initiatives and will be responsible for a golden age of prosperity that awaits us provided we re-elect... er, hang on, wrong editorial. Not sure where that one came from; it was just lying on the desk here with nobody's name on it so we assumed it was one of ours. Anyway, what we meant to say was that at *The Spectator Australia* we were unimpressed to learn that public servants from the Department of Broadband, Communications and the Digital Economy were caught sending out "meticulously researched" articles spruiking the NBN to any news outlet that cared to publish them, suggesting they do so under their own journalist's names.

But when Mr. Conroy's constant advocacy of a News Media Council to monitor and restrict 'bad' reporting (i.e. opinions that his panel of experts disagree with) is combined with the fact that he himself would be the minister responsible for such a body, the warning bells start to clang. Have Labor become so enmeshed in their own media manipulation that they no longer know or care what's truth and what's spin?

The annual Australian Financial Review Magazine 'Power People' special was released at the end of September. It listed those who are deemed to be the most powerful individuals across the corporate, political and cultural spheres of the nation during 2012. And those who are not.

Financial Review Power issue, 28 September 2012

POWER PEOPLE

Kevin flicked angrily through the pages, struggling to contain his fury and his rage. This was a bloody disgrace. Fair suck of the sav and all that! Julia? Wayne? Howes? Kevin could feel his teeth grinding together behind his perfectly cool composure. Grind, grind, grind. What would

Thérèse say? He shuddered. He wasn't even on the 'covert' list! How could you get more covert than his cunning ploy to bring down the Gillard government by letting them do whatever they wanted to? Kevin growled under his breath, his teeth making strangely dysfunctional noises. "Stay cool, mate," he reminded himself, "stay cool!" Then he swore violently, tore the magazine into tiny pieces and shoved them all into a soup blender.

Stephen flicked rapidly through the pages, beads of sweat breaking out on his top lip. "F---in' fantastic," he snarled bitterly, tossing the magazine aside. "I am single-handedly responsible for building the biggest f---in' infrastructure project since the Snowy Harbour Bridge with billions of dollars literally in the palm of my hand and the future of an entire generation at my feet and at least seventeen f---in' people who have already signed up for broadband in the last twelve months even if you don't count that old duck who thought she was getting a free box-top set you'd have to say that future generations will look back on this so-called f---in' fantastic 'power list' in disbelief particularly when they download it on their 4G mobile with wi-fi I mean where's the recognition I deserve? F---in' fantastic."

Clive glanced at the list. "I could buy this entire magazine if I wanted to and in fact I could buy every magazine in the world and I could be the editor and I could even be an award-winning journalist and do a better job of taking the photos and doing the layout let me tell you and there's nobody on this list that I couldn't teach a thing or two to and on top of that I'm just an ordinary, everyday Aussie and (for the full interview see our website)."

Barnaby ripped out the pages one by one and tossed them onto the barbie. Wanker. Tosser. Loser. Commie. Nut-case. They were all there. Pooftah. Lezzo. Trotskyite. This was so typical. Wog. Fascist. Doctor's wife. Cretin. Creep. Barnaby could barely believe his eyes. What groveling bunch of self-important, nanny-state, bureaucratic, public-purse-guzzling, boofheads were responsible for this nancy-boy list? More like a

Top Thirty Losers List, he chuckled to himself. I'd rather flog myself with a horse-whip than be seen dead on this list, he snorted contemptuously. I'd rather chew razor blades. I'd rather spend a night in a Turkish prison with a sex-starved male masseur brandishing a cattle prod.

Greg flicked silently through the pages of the list, his features betraying no emotion. Carefully he pushed his glasses up his nose. It didn't make any sense, he thought. There must be some mistake. The printers must have stuffed up. He'd have a word with the shop stewards. Or perhaps some sinister Tory forces were at work behind the scenes. Tony Abbott, for example. Greg knew that deep behind his own cool and calm exterior lurked a scintillating, charismatic, fascinating and beguiling personality. He was certain of it. The embodiment of power. Born leadership material. Hawkie had told him that after about the third bottle one night. Greg stared at the list again and frowned. There must be some technical glitch.

Malcolm flicked quietly through the pages, one by one. Then he flicked to the beginning, and started again. What a rag, he thought to himself. What a petty, small-minded, irrelevant, shoddy, worthless, nonsensical piece of journalism. Didn't these people have eyes in their heads? Hadn't they watched _Q&A_? Was there a more popular, loved, adored and worshipped politician in the land than the member for Wentworth? Power? What power is there without popularity, he smirked to himself? He'd show them, he muttered to himself. One of these days, he'd show them all. He glanced at the magazine one last time, then tossed it into the bin.

In late September, former Labor minister Lindsay Tanner – who resigned when Julia Gillard overthrew Kevin Rudd – released a book called 'Politics with Purpose'. It made the headlines with its tough criticisms of the Labor party.

Meanwhile, a stomach bug forced Julia Gillard to pull out of several engagements in New York, including a reception for world leaders hosted by US president Barack Obama.

Senator Bob Carr, who accompanied her on the trip, was forced to take her place and address world leaders.

Financial Review, 29 September 2012

GILLARD STRUTTING THE WORLD STAGE WITHOUT A PORPOISE

The Foreign Minister leaned back and let his long legs stretch out in front of him. First class. He smiled to himself. The last nine months he'd racked up more frequent flyer miles than you could poke a stick at. Dubai, London, Paris, Beijing. This was the life. And now, of course, New York. He'd be sitting in the audience of the United Nations General Assembly, no less. The greatest podium on the planet.

Wasn't it Shakespeare who said: "All the world's a stage"? Every nation on the globe! That niggling little thought popped up again in the back of his mind. If only…

"Excuse me, sir," said the steward, topping up the Senator's wine glass, "will you be having the chicken or the fish?"

"Oh, the fish, I suppose," the Senator muttered impatiently. He hated it when underlings interrupted his musings. "A house divided against itself cannot stand." Lincoln. Again that thought. If only…

Suddenly he felt a tap on his shoulder. It was Julia. "Bob, I need to pick your brines," she said. Even over the pleasant, purring hum of the

Rolls-Royce engines and the Dvorak symphony in his headphones, her accent instantly set his teeth on edge.

"What's our porpoise?" she said, sliding uninvited into the empty seat next to his.

"Our porpoise? I, er, its, um an indigenous species of sea mammal, like a dolphin."

"I said purpose, not porpoise."

"Oh I, er, I don't know. To live a good life? Why do you ask?"

"Mr. McToyernan says I've got to include a porpoise in my speech to the General Assembly. Tanner's releasing some stupid book called 'How they Stabbed Kevin in the Back for No Porpoise' just to spoil my foinest moment stroiding the world stage and the journos are going feral. He's saying Labor's got no porpoise. So I have to announce one at the UN."

The Senator nodded slowly. "I see. I'm pretty certain we had a very good purpose when I was premier of NSW. Maybe you can use that one. Buggered if I can remember what it was, though."

He took another sip of his wine. That niggling thought again. He tried to suppress it, but it wouldn't go away.

He felt his jaw tightening. Why, oh why, did this ill-educated trade union hack lawyer from South Australia not only get to be PM but also get to make all the speeches to the UN while he, the greatest orator since Gough, the Cicero of Canberra, had to sit in the audience twiddling his thumbs? It was so unfair. If only . . .

"Madam, the boiled chicken, as requested. And for you sir, the fish head curry with stewed sambal cabbage."

The Senator stared aghast at the slop on the plate as it was gently placed in front of him. What on earth had he been thinking of? The memories came flooding back of that week holed up in Dubai spewing his guts out into a dunny that looked like the Wivenhoe Dam had burst again. Hadn't that been the fish head curry? With sambal vegetables? He shuddered at the memory.

Julia looked down at her plain, boiled chicken, clearly regretting her choice. Bob couldn't help notice her glancing enviously at his own dish.

"Plus, Wayne says I've gotta put in a bit about how Australia's booming and it's not just miners but teachers and health workers and social workers and council workers. There's heaps more of them since we took over so that proves the economy's going gangbusters. Maybe that's our porpoise? Creating prosperity for all!"

The Foreign Minister frowned. Economics had never been his strong suit – that's what he'd had Michael Egan for – but he was pretty certain that public servants didn't count as wealth creation. But try telling that to that surfing bogan from Queensland with the dreadful taste in music.

He sighed irritably. The leaders of 140 nations. Prime ministers, presidents, kings and emperors. What an audience! If only it was he, rather than her, mounting the podium. He closed his eyes and smiled at the thought.

His mellifluous tones, rather than her grating strine. His mesmerising baritone, rather than her fingernails-on-the-blackboard shriek. His chiseled, masculine, authoritative looks, rather than her...

He glanced down at the fish in front of him. And a cunning thought crossed his mind. He turned to the PM.

"Julia, I must say your chicken looks a little dry. From previous experience, I know the curry is quite exceptional. Packs quite a punch, you might say." He smiled at her. "Why don't we swap?"

On Oct 8, Julia Gillard stood up in parliament and hit back at Opposition Leader Tony Abbott's call for Peter Slipper to be removed as Speaker, based on Slipper's texts equating female genitalia to 'salty mussels'. Gillard refused to be 'lectured' about such matters by Abbott, whom she attacked for relentlessly promoting 'sexism' and 'misogyny'. When the YouTube video of the speech became a global hit, the Prime Minister, basking in her newfound fame, maintained that when it comes to sexism or misogyny 'I'll call it whenever I see it.' It was claimed Mr. Abbott looked at his watch when the Prime Minister was speaking during question time and had made reference to women ironing, among other sexist activities and statements. Mr. Abbott later referred to the Prime Minister as 'a piece of work'.

Financial Review, 13 October 2012

PM CALLS IT AS SHE SEES IT – WHEREVER SHE LOOKS

"Good evening, Prime Minister. Thank you for joining us."

"My pleasure."

"Our first question, Prime Minister, is from a Fred Smith of Manly, who asks you to name the major achievements of your government over the past two years."

"Well, I'm sorry but I've had enough of this. As I said, from now on I'm calling out sexism whenever I see it, and I'm seeing it right now. What a vile, sexist and misogynistic question to be asking of a woman! Fred is obviously a man, he sneakily identifies himself as being particularly manly, and he seeks to belittle my achievements by labeling them 'major.' 'Major' is a typically aggressive masculine word which has ugly military and chauvinistic overtones. I won't stand for it."

"Um, I see. Ah, well, our next question relates to the carbon tax, and the fact that we now learn that the AWU opposed it all along. . ."

"I'm sorry, but here you go again. As I've said many times, my government has a duty to protect our planet from being attacked by misogynists and sexist nut-jobs who despise Mother Earth simply because she's a woman. Those who deny that climate change is real are denigrating the nurturing, caring role that women like Mother Nature play in our everyday lives and, as a woman, I won't stand for it. And allow me to point out that 'carbon' is a dirty, filthy thing that comes out of tall, phallic chimneys in the most aggressive misogynistic and sexist ways and I've had enough of it."

"Er, um, yes, OK. About asylum seekers, and I'm referring specifically to the billions being wasted due to the complete failure of your policy to achieve. . ."

"There you go again. I'm sorry, but when I see it, I'll call it. Many boat people are women, and that's why Tony Abbott wants to stop them because he doesn't want any more women in our country. He hates their femininity and the fact that these are extremely capable women who have travelled halfway around the world all by themselves despite losing their passports and he has a problem with that. On top of which Tony Abbott keeps saying 'stop the boats' but, as everybody knows, boats are women, too. This is just another sickening example of his sexism and misogyny that we see. . ."

"Oh, er, thank you. I also wanted to ask about the billions being squandered on the national broadband. . ."

"I'm sorry, but I must stop you right there. The term 'broad' is a nasty, sexist term that denotes a hatred of all women and treats them as sex objects to be sneered at and suggests they have a large bottom or large breasts and I won't be a party to it. I know I speak for all the women of Australia when I say we've had enough of these misogynistic insults."

"Yes, I, er, I see. Moving right along, how do you intend to pay for the billions of dollars you have committed to things like Gonski and the national disability insurance scheme, when our terms of trade have been declining dramatically as China slows down faster than anyone predicted, when the mining tax and GST aren't raising nearly enough and, as Tony Abbott pointed out, even the head of the IMF has warned of the possibility of another global recession, yet we. . ."

"Even?"

"I'm sorry?"

"You said Tony Abbott said: 'even the head of the IMF . . .'"

"I did, yes. That's the question."

"No it's not. The real question is why Tony Abbott would say 'even' when he is referring to the head of the International Monetary Fund? Well let me tell you why. Because the head of the IMF is Christine Lagarde and she happens to be a woman. And Tony Abbott clearly has a problem with that fact. No doubt he would far prefer that horrible, disgusting sexist misogynist Dominique Strauss Kahn, that bloke who jumped on top of a hotel maid in New York. I'd bet Tony Abbott would rather he was still in charge of the IMF because he's a man! What my government will focus on is the big tough questions of the day, like: 'Has Tony Abbott ever been to New York? And did he order room service?'"

"Yes, yes, thank you Prime Minister. Unfortunately, that's all we've got time for. But join us next week as our special guest the Treasurer explains how misogynistic mining magnates like Gina Rinehart are ruining our economy."

Following the Prime Minister's speech, the Macquarie Dictionary decided to expand the recognized definition of 'misogyny' from 'hatred of women' to also include 'entrenched prejudices against women'.

Financial Review, 20 October 2012

POLITICAL SPEAK DECIPHERED

Following the Macquarie Dictionary's decision to redefine "misogynist", this column has revised certain words and phrases in line with current progressive political standards.

Mussels (n, pl): non-sexist, humorous, colloquial everyday descriptive terminology for female genitalia.

Salty c--ts (n, pl): see above.

That man! (expletive): a horrible person, a male political leader with a deep-seated hatred of women.

Piece of work (n): sexist terminology designed to demean a successful and popular female national leader.

Abbott 1 (n): a weird kind of priest (see also vicar, Catholic, pope, church warden, monk, choir master).

Abbott 2 (n): an odious creature (see also misogynist, sexist, coward, bully, abortion, ironing housewives, climate denier, speedos).

Abortion (n): sexist, derogatory term that when coupled with expressions such as "easy way out" is clear evidence of a deep-seated hatred of women.

Ironing (n): sexist, derogatory term that when coupled with expressions such as "housewives" is clear evidence of deep-seated hatred of women.

Watch (n): a wrist piece used by aggressive males to denote a deep-seated hatred of women.

Ditch (v): obscene and offensive sexist slur.

Witch (n): ditto.

Bitch (n): ditto.

Sniveling grub (n): humorous, non-sexist, inoffensive terminology used to describe a person who has a deep-seated hatred of women (see misogynist, Abbott, 'that man').

Unflushable turd (n): humorous, non-sexist, inoffensive colloquial term of endearment for a politician with bushy eyebrows who won't go away.

Skanky ho (n): non-sexist, inoffensive, colloquial term of endearment for right-wing female journos.

Prostitute 1 (n): a victim of male sexism and misogyny.

Prostitute 2 (n): a legitimate credit card expense for overworked and underpaid union officials.

Slipper 1 (n): enlightened, non-sexist but tragically doomed Speaker of the House.

Slipper 2 (n): night-time footwear.

Jenkins (n): deleted.

Swan 1 (n) a great financial brain at work, also the world's greatest finance minister, the envy of world.

Swan 2 (n): a goose.

Swansong (n): progressive musical ditty by economically inspired balladeer Bruce Springsteen such as We Take Care of Our Own, Deficit at the Edge of Town, etc.

Up the Swanee (coll): see "up creek without paddle".

Surplus (n): fictitious amount of non-existent funds that will never actually materialise (see also National Disability Insurance Scheme, Gonski, NBN).

Carbon tax (n): usage deleted.

Carbon price (n): nothing to do with a carbon tax.

Climate change (n): deleted as problem now solved by carbon price (see above).

Border protection (n): enlightened policy designed to encourage paperless maritime immigration.

Trip (n): taxpayer-funded journey around the world.

Trip (v): to fall flat on your face.

We've got to lift ourselves above the ruck (coll): when a deposed dysfunctional psychopath desperately wants his job back.

Twitter (n): popular social media platform wholly representative of enlightened individuals (see Kevin Rudd, Malcolm Turnbull).

Talkback (n): sexist media platform wholly representative of lowest elements of society (see Alan Jones, Ray Hadley).

Moving forward (v): where a select group of individuals heads in one direction while the nation goes in the opposite.

We are (coll): meaningless (see also 'us').

Slush fund 1 (n, West Australian usage): legitimate corporate entity designed to advance the health and safety of workers.

Slush fund 2 (n, Victorian usage): deposit on a house.

Election (n): see day of reckoning, bloodbath, doomsday, wipeout, Armageddon, end of days, baseball bats, oblivion.

Deputy Prime Minister and Treasurer Wayne Swan released his Mid-Year Economic and Fiscal Outlook, updating the budget for 2012-13, and requiring big business to pay corporate tax in monthly instalments.

"The 2012-13 MYEFO released today shows the fundamentals of the Australian economy remain strong, with the budget returning to surplus this financial year as scheduled,' he said.

Financial Review, 27 October 2012

'IT'S ONLY FAIR' SAYS SWAN, AS HE EMPTIES THE TILLS

The Treasurer, Wayne Swan, this morning unveiled his highly anticipated updated Update of the Mid Mid-Year Mid-week Mid-morning Economical and Fiscal Outlook, which reveals a dramatic downturn in the forward estimates since yesterday morning's MMYMWMMEFO update.

"This micro-mini-budget is firmly in line with Labor values and yet again shows that we have world-beating public finances," Mr. Swan said.

The Treasurer proudly announced that the government is still on target to deliver a surplus of $346.73 despite an unexpected collapse in government revenue, thanks to the deteriorating global economic outlook. The chief pillar of the update, designed to free up billions of dollars of dormant revenue, requires all registered businesses to empty their tills at the end of each day and send half of it straight to the Tax Office.

"It's simply ridiculous that all this money is left lying around in cash registers overnight," the Treasurer said. "This way, businesses pay their fair share as they go along."

Other budget savings announced in the update require bus stations, department stores, schools, cafes and kindergartens to return any lost property to the government the same day they find it.

"It's simply unacceptable that thousands of perfectly productive mobile phones, iPads, umbrellas, lunch boxes, hats and bits of shopping are left lying around contributing nothing whatsoever to our economic outlook. This way we can maintain a healthy surplus by taking the lot straight down to Cash Converters," he said.

Mr. Swan reiterated that Australia's public finances are the envy of the developed world.

Citing documented evidence, the Treasurer maintained other nations were doing it far tougher: "I'm reliably informed that in New Jersey, for instance – and I'm quoting directly from a highly respected social economics commentator known as 'the Boss' – they're closing down the textile mill across the railroad tracks. The foreman says 'these jobs are going boys, and they ain't coming back'."

Mr. Swan announced a raft of measures designed to maintain a healthy surplus in line with Labor values, including scrapping the controversial "baby bonus".

"This was a sexist, misogynistic scheme introduced by Tony Abbott and Peter Costello in order to reflect their hatred of unmarried, childless women in the workforce. From now on, the baby bonus will only be given to people who don't have any babies," he said.

Questioned as to why there were no tax cuts for business in order to help stimulate growth, the World's Greatest Treasurer pointed out that the disbanded Business Working Group had decided there was no need. "We told them they could have as many tax cuts as they wanted so long as they paid for them out of their own pockets. What could be fairer than that?"

Refuting the criticism that his mining tax was an abysmal failure and a laughing stock because none of the mining companies had paid a brass razoo of it, Mr. Swan pointed out that both he and the Prime Minister Julia Gillard were personally involved in the complex negotiations with three global mining corporations that led to the unique revenue-raising design of the tax.

"The whole point of the mining tax, as Julia and I made clear to the mining companies, was to 'spread the boom.' As all three of their accountants astutely pointed out to us, the best and fairest way to share the profits of the boom was if there weren't any. That way, everyone got an equal slice. Of zero."

Bruce Springsteen was unavailable for comment.

On October 28, Julia Gillard released the 'Australia in the Asian Century White Paper', a roadmap showing how Australia can be a winner in the Asian century.

'The White Paper lays out an ambitious plan to ensure Australia will emerge stronger over the decades ahead, by taking advantage of the opportunities offered by the Asian century,' she claimed.

Financial Review, 3 November 2013

IT'LL TAKE A CENTURY TO BECOME AN AUSSIE BLUDGER

The Asian Productivity Commission today released its long anticipated *Asia In The Australian Century White Paper.*

The paper's "Road Map for Navigating the Australian Century" sets out ambitious goals for all Asian nations to achieve to fully benefit from deeper engagement with Australia.

By 2025 every business in Asia will have on their board a fixed quota of at least one "Aussie bludger" who can instruct his fellow board members in such crucial cross-cultural skills as "chucking a sickie," "pay increases", "unfair dismissal", "slush funds", "penalty rates" and "misogyny and sexism: calling it whenever you see it". Asian business studies will include specific "water-cooler conversations" to instruct students in the requisite skills of "slagging off your colleagues" and "sucking up to the boss."

Courses will be available focusing on the themes of football players, favourite television and radio programs and the direction of local house prices. Students will be expected to complete the conversations with a severe hangover on a Monday morning.

Asian students have been promised the opportunity to pursue one of several "Aussie" language skills.

Male teenage students will be able to specialise in courses devoted to mastering the intricate system of monosyllabic grunts and four-letter expletives, along with subtle hand gestures known as "giving the finger", while female students will be taught the complex phonetic nuances of the words "like" and "hello".

Asian preschools will be encouraged to teach Australian Culture from an early age, including such quaint practices as "making sure everyone gets a prize regardless of talent or skill", "receiving excessive praise for doing the minimum amount of work", and "removing stressful and barbaric examination techniques such as exams".

Students wishing to progress further in Australian studies will be given special tutorials in "taking offence at the drop of a hat", "blaming others for personal failings" and "insisting on individual rights and entitlements". Optional courses will include "avoiding all responsibility".

The White Paper envisages that exposure to the unique work practices and values of the Australian way of life will see a massive increase in personal wealth across all strata of Asian society.

Explaining the benefits of this approach, the paper's author, renowned Asian economist Dr. Ken Hen-Lee, pointed out that Asians would be mad not to take advantage of their geographical proximity to the Australian economy, blessed with natural resources like the World's Greatest Treasurer.

"Clearly, if we in Asia adopt the same approach as the Australians, we'll be in a position to kid ourselves that we can have it all: higher wages, higher living standards, and endless entitlements."

When questioned about Australia's rapid decline in productivity, excessive red tape, and bloated bureaucracy, Dr. Hen-Lee pointed out that an Expert Panel of Australian government bureaucrats had concluded that lack of productivity was unrelated to the money wasted on government bureaucrats.

Admitting that huge challenges lie ahead, the White Paper makes several critical recommendations, among them the establishment of an Australian-style industrial relations body to be known as Fair Wok Asia. "For too long, hospital workers and other lowly paid members of society have been forced to go without. But by 2025 we envisage a situation where engagement with Australian workplace relationships and practices leads to Asian workers' representatives and their family members achieving a superior lifestyle that includes unlimited credit cards, high-class prostitutes, fast cars and other such well-earned cultural benefits."

The paper is confident that the Australian boom can be shared by everyone in the region, and can boost the average Asian wage from around $5 a week to a minimum of around $100,000 per annum, plus super.

"It is simply not enough to talk about hard work, tough economic decisions and sound financial management," said Dr. Hen-Lee. "We need to do what the Australians do, and just rely on good luck."

At a rally on November 7 in his hometown of Chicago, the newly re-elected Barack Obama delivered his victory speech, widely regarded as one of his most generous and statesman-like after the vitriol and unpleasantness of the election campaign.

A campaign many had expected Mitt Romney to win.

Financial Review, 10 November 2012

GILLARD'S VICTORY SPEECH

Julia Gillard returned to the Lodge last night following her election victory against Tony Abbott, "more determined and more inspired than ever before" to reach out and divide the nation.

Promising to pick up the phone in the next few weeks and tell Mr. Abbott he's a vile woman-hating North Shore-dwelling wall-smasher, Ms. Gillard pledged to do everything within her power to keep blaming the opposition for everything the government got wrong.

"Tonight, more than two years after a group of faceless men won the right to choose who gets the top job, the task of perfecting my grip on power moves forward." In her rousing speech, Ms. Gillard reaffirmed that the things that divided Australians were more important than the things they had in common.

"Let us all embrace the spirit of class envy, the lust for class warfare, and the burning sense of entitlement and victimhood that can only be understood by single, childless, atheist women in this great country of ours," she said to rapturous applause.

After a lengthy and bitter campaign, the Prime Minister reached out to her opponent.

"I just spoke with Tony Abbott and I congratulated him on losing the unlosable election.

"In the weeks ahead, I look forward to sitting down opposite him and daring him to ever call me a 'piece of work' again."

Ms. Gillard was also quick to recognise the efforts of her team.

"I thank my friend and partner of the last four years, Canberra's happy highlighter, the best hairdresser anybody could hope for.

"And I wouldn't be the woman I am today without the man who agreed to step down for me three years ago, not that he had any choice.

"Let me say this publicly: Kevin, I have never loved you more. I have never been prouder to watch the rest of Australia give you the finger once and for all.

"I also want to say thank you to the best spin doctors in the history of politics. The best ever. Some of you were new, like Mr. McTernan, and some of you have been by my side since the very beginning when I skedaddled from Slater and Gordon."

Ms. Gillard said she had triumphed by listening to ordinary people.

"You hear the determination in the voice of a young Indonesian skipper navigating his way to Christmas Island. You hear the pride in the voice of a Treasury official who has just leaked some fabricated Coalition costings. You hear the deep gratitude in the voice of a roofing contractor charging a fortune for pink batts. You hear the whoosh of a union boss's credit card being swiped at Tiffany's House of Pleasure. That's why we do this. That's what politics can be.

"To the young union worker who works on the south side of Fitzroy and sees a house he wants to buy with somebody else's money. To the mortgage broker who wants a deposit, so long as it's in cash. That's the vision we share. That's where we need to go – forward.

"Whether I earned your vote or got it by promising the independents stuff they'll never get, I have learned from you. Tonight you voted for politics as usual. In the coming months, I will commission dozens more white papers promising loads more stuff we can't afford.

"This country has more wealth than any other nation, but that's not what makes us rich. Compensation packages do. We have the biggest military cuts in history, but that's not what keeps us strong. The Americans do. We are the most isolated place on the planet, but that's not what keeps the world coming to our shores. Our border protection policies do.

"Just the other day a father told the story of his eight-year-old daughter whose long battle with misogynists in her playground nearly ruined her lunch break. Every politician in that room had tears in their eyes, because we knew that little girl could be Julia, or Tanya, or Nicola or Kate.

"Tonight, despite all I've been through as a single, childless, atheist woman, I've never been more hopeful about my future. Hope is that stubborn thing inside us that insists, despite all the evidence of slush funds, despite all the failed policies, despite all the broken promises and backflips and wasted billions, that something better awaits us so long as we have the courage to keep on calling misogyny wherever we see it.

"God bless the Labor Party. Not that He actually exists."

Throughout November the 'Slushgate' scandal surrounding Julia Gillard's activities as a lawyer for the AWU in the 1990's intensified, with deputy Liberal leader Julie Bishop leading the numerous attacks inside and outside of Parliament. The allegations concerned the Prime Minister, her ex-boyfriend Bruce Wilson and self-confessed bagman Ralph Blewitt

As a lawyer in Slater & Gordon Julia Gillard helped establish the AWU Workplace Reform Association for her then-boyfriend Bruce Wilson, an entity which the WA Corporate Affairs Commission initially ruled ineligible for registration because they deemed it to be a union. Gillard drew up a constitution and rules that emphasised the purpose of the fund was to promote workplace safety, and she successfully argued this in a letter to the WA Corporate Affairs Commissioner. This letter, which has never been found, supposedly led to the association being established.

Gillard was also involved in providing legal services in relation to the purchase of a property in Fitzroy by Wilson and Blewitt. Renovations on Gillard's home also occurred around the same time.

When questioned in a taped interview about the affair, Julia Gillard told her partners

at Slater & Gordon that the true purpose of the association and its bank account
was to be a 'slush fund' to help the re-election of a select group of union officials
committed to workplace safety. Shortly after, Gillard left the firm.
At all times Julia Gillard maintained she 'did nothing wrong'.

Financial Review, 1 December 2012

IF THERE'S NO NOTE, THERE'S REALLY NO PROOF

Yet again, the freckle-faced little girl with red hair and ponytails glared at her headmistress and pursed her wafer-thin lips. One sock lower than the other, as usual, and a grazed knee and telltale smudge of chocolate on the side of her mouth.

The headmistress shook her head wearily. "Not again, young lady. Can't you stay out of trouble? Just for once?"

The little girl stared defiantly back, the familiar steely glint in her pale green eyes. "I did nothing wrong, Miss."

The older woman sighed. She'd heard it all a thousand times before. "I'm sorry, dear, but Miss Bishop says you were caught standing on top of the ladder in the staff kitchen in the middle of lunch break with your hand inside the cookie jar."

The little girl sneered aggressively. "Miss Bishop is a stuck-up lying cow and she's so, like, scraping the bottom of the barrel, Miss."

"Language, please. Nonetheless, it must have been you up the …"

The little girl grinned mischievously.

"Where's her proof but?"

"We don't put 'but' at the end of a sentence."

"Whatever."

"Well, for starters, this is your handwriting, isn't it? It's on the lunch monitor's logbook. Purpose of visit? 'To refill the milk crates.' Yet the milk crates were empty. So what were you doing in the staff kitchen?"

"Never was. I just wrote that 'coz Bruce said he wanted to help the povos."

"Povos?"

"Poor kids. Bruce gives them leftovers and makes sure nobody in the Gang ever beats them up and then they donate their pocket money to him."

The headmistress frowned. "Really? That sounds a bit odd …"

"Nup. That's the rules. Gang's Rules. I should know 'coz I made them up, Miss."

"Well, where does all the pocket money go?"

"Little Ralphie hides it. Bruce made him Gang Treasurer. He buries it in his backyard for emergencies."

"Emergencies?"

"Like if we need to get some extra treats from the tuck shop. Or if we need to fix things up." The little girl smiled triumphantly. "We fixed my cubby house!"

"Well, it all sounds very confusing. But the question I was actually asking was what were you doing in the staff kitchen? Ralph says …"

"Little Ralphie's a spaz and a thicko and besides he looks at naughty magazines, Miss. Even his sister says so. Who you gonna believe, Miss? Some sicko perve or the lunch monitor?"

"Um …"

"I did nothing wrong. I fill in thousands of lunch monitor logbooks every year. So it must've been Little Ralphie! It was him all along with his hand in the cookie jar. You ask Bruce. He says so, too!"

"But Bruce is your sweetheart, isn't he?"

"No way! He's got boy germs so I dropped him. Even he says I did nothing wrong, so there!"

"Well, perhaps you can explain how Miss Bishop found five bags of hundreds and thousands in your lunch box? Who put them there?"

"Dunno. Don't care. I did nothin' wrong. And anyway, all this stuff is from ages ago. It all happened last term."

The headmistress sat down on the edge of her desk, exhausted. When did kids get so impertinent, she thought to herself as she rubbed her eyes. So cocky. So convinced normal rules didn't apply to them.

"But Miss Bishop says you wrote a note to the kitchen staff saying that you had permission to let your friends into the kitchen because they were collecting leftovers to give to charity and it had nothing to do with the Gang, so they let you in to the kitchen unsupervised during lunch break. And when they came back there was a ladder up against the back wall and the cookie jar and all the cake tins were empty and there was a trail of cookie crumbs that led all the way to ..."

"I've never seen a note like that, Miss. Have you got it?"

"Well no, but ..."

"Got no proof then."

"No, but you haven't answered ..."

"Suck rocks then, Miss. I gotta go," said the little girl, leaping defiantly to her feet. "The bell's ringing."

As the little girl merrily skipped away one more time, the headmistress slumped back down in her chair.

"Indeed it is," she muttered to herself. "But for whom, I wonder?"

Labor's elder statesman John Faulkner made a plea for the ALP to abolish its factional system. And in New South Wales the Independent Commission Against Corruption began a lengthy investigation into allegations against a former minister in the New South Wales Labor government, Eddie Obeid, and how ministers in that government awarded lucrative coal mining contracts.

In his opening address, counsel assisting the ICAC claimed a level of corruption not seen since the days of the Rum Corps – a reference to the wildly corrupt troopers who policed the early white settlers more than two centuries ago.

Julia Gillard released a spoof video warning that zombies were coming and the end of the world was approaching, according to the Mayan calendar.

Financial Review, 8 December 2012

DEMOCRACY SURPLUS TO LABOR'S REQUIREMENTS

A party elder has called for widespread internal reform of the Labor Party, saying the only way to substantially strengthen the power of the factions is to get rid of politicians altogether.

Demanding that the ALP abolish its old-fashioned system of "democratically elected MPs" in the wake of a cavalcade of backflips, broken promises, failed policy implementations and disastrous decision-making, he has reignited calls to overhaul the party's internal rules to force it to become more union-based.

"We need a fundamental root-and-branch set of reforms so that the system works like it used to, where the pollies do whatever we tell them to."

But a senior minister, speaking off the record, defended the right of politicians to exist within the ALP. "So long as we are well rewarded with freebies and travel and other perks, I see no reason why we shouldn't just do whatever the factions tell us to," he said. "One thing is certain – the guiding principle must be greater factional empowerment in and across the party."

Labor's reform challenge includes addressing its structure, rules, pre-selections and patronage to eliminate "the stunted perspectives of a few backbenchers and members of the cabinet."

Citing such critical matters as drawing up boundaries for new mining leases, the minister maintained that the power of persuasion should always prevail over "petty, poll-driven so-called political promises and election commitments." He added: "If it's left to some idiotic politician, nobody would ever make a buck. There's nothing like a serious bit of factional arm-twisting to concentrate the mind and improve the ability of an overworked MP to make the correct decisions."

But a former cabinet minister argued that while Labor should "improve its processes" it would be impossible to do away with politicians altogether.

"Politicians play a vital and pivotal role within the Labor movement," he said. "They are the public face of the party, without which we would all be, er, faceless."

Speaking from the misty highlands of Papua New Guinea where he is single-handedly solving the Middle East crisis, Foreign Minister Bob Carp strenuously denied that elected politicians played a significant role in today's Labor party.

"It's simply not a problem. The idea that some halfwit who spends most of his or her time schlepping around the suburbs handing out how-to-vote cards should have any say in the political process is quite absurd," he said. "That is simply not the way we do things nowadays."

Senator Carp, a member of the party's reform committee set up in the wake of last year's ALP national conference, said he was confidant of seizing the leadership without having to bother with an election.

"I've made it perfectly clear, on a number of occasions now, that

Tony Abbott is a complete charlatan and the only way to defeat him is if I take over the reins from Ms. Wots-her-name asap."

Calling for the Israeli ambassador, Mr. Seth Tel-Mentz, to be publicly horse-whipped and daubed in chocolate in front of Max Brenner's in Marrickville for his government's decision to build a block of time-share units on the outskirts of Jerusalem, Senator Carp explained: "The Syrians may well be about to murder half their citizens with mustard gas, the Iranians about to nuke the joint and the Egyptians start a civil war, but what the Israelis have done with Project El Retirement Villa is the gravest threat we face to world peace, and I let them know it."

Meanwhile, Treasurer Wayne Swan refused to comment on the ructions within the party. "I'm far too busy getting ready for the next election to worry about all that," he told the ABC.

"As Mr. McTernan told me to say, there is no emergency whatsoever and just because we said when interest rates were at 3 per cent it was because the economy was cactus, it doesn't mean that just because interest rates are now at 3 per cent the economy is cactus."

In other news, Prime Minister Julia Gillard has been involved in a bizarre "end of the world" video stunt which has been widely praised by world leaders from Barack Obama to Aung San Suu Kyi, in which she screeches at the Leader of the Opposition, calling him a "sexist, misogynist, flesh-eating zombie".

Attorney-General Nicola Roxon released draft legislation for new anti-discrimination laws in late November, which made it an offence to cause offence. 'Making protections and obligations clearer for individuals and organisations will help everyone understand what behaviour is expected,' she said.

Many saw the proposed laws as an unacceptable attack on free speech.

Financial Review, 15 December 2012

SWAGMAN AND JUMBUCK VINDICATED AT LAST

In a landmark court decision today, the late Australian poet Mr. Banjo was found guilty under Section 19(2)(b) of the Human Rights and Anti-Discrimination Bill recently introduced to Parliament by Attorney-General Nicola Roxoff for causing "offence in extremis" with his poem *Waltzing Matilda*. Under the new laws the disgraced poet is guilty of "behaving improperly" for failing to prove beyond any doubt that had not deliberately intended to cause maximum offence.

The court further ordered that bookshops, libraries and kindergartens destroy all copies of the publication. Speaking on behalf of the plaintiffs, a jubilant spokesperson shed tears of joy on the courtroom steps while speaking to the waiting media throng. "There is not a single progressive individual in Australia who has not been deeply offended by *Waltzing Matilda's* vile, disgusting, elitist, racist, sexist, misogynist, animalist overtones," the spokesperson said. In particular, the judges singled out such divisive terminology as "swagman" and "squatter" as referring to social origins in a derogatory context.

"This court believes that the publication deliberately seeks to promote class-based conflict in our enlightened, progressive society," the judges said. "The depiction of the swagman – clearly a recently unemployed welfare recipient – as a thief who treats animals cruelly is an unimaginable slur on all unemployed welfare recipients. Furthermore, the assumption by the 'squatter' that both the land and the animal in question automatically belong to him is hugely offensive to all first home buyers and pet owners."

The judges cited the grievous offence taken by an indigenous billabong collective that Mr. Banjo was clearly encouraging non-indigenous trespassers to ride across their spiritual homeland without paying due respect, in the form of a welcome to country, to the billabong's original owners.

Feminist groups have long taken exception to the poem's failure to condemn the misogynist, patriarchal society in which the sole function of women is to dance, or waltz, for the perverse sexual gratification of men.

An association that offers support to the victims of police brutality also welcomed the judgment. "Mr. Banjo is clearly advocating the use of three heavily armed police officers to brutally subdue a desperate, starving man, who clearly fears for his life," an association spokesperson said. "To make light of such brutality is a cruel insult to the growing number of taser victims."

Charitable welfare groups also praised the verdict. "The idea that the only way to escape life's problems is to jump into a pond and drown yourself is hugely insulting to the relatives of suicide victims," they said. "Depression is a serious illness. Boasting 'you'll never catch me alive' is not only irresponsible, but also factually incorrect."

A key plank in the defendants' argument was the question of haste and speed, with a spokesperson for Mr. Banjo arguing that the actions he described were clearly spontaneous and so any consequences – including causing offence – were not intended. With the aid of a kettle and a stopwatch, he went on to prove beyond doubt that the entire saga occurred in the time it takes "to watch a billy boil".

The question of animal dignity loomed large in the lengthy trial, with the defendants attempting to prove via a re-enactment in the courtroom that there's nothing degrading about gently placing a sheep in a large hessian bag. However, lawyers for the prosecution were able to demonstrate that in the event of the sheep being of a sturdy build, the likely result of "shoving" it into a "tucker bag" would not only be undignified, but could lead to bone and ligament damage, or asphyxiation. In a setback for the Banjo case, the judges determined the phrase "jolly jumbuck" denigrated overweight sheep.

Reacting to the verdict, a delighted Ms. Roxoff told *The Australian Financial Review:* "Tony Abbott and the nay-sayers have been proved wrong. The legislation works as intended – to help everyone understand precisely what behaviour I expect of them."

On December 20 Treasurer Wayne Swan admitted that although it was nothing to do with him or his economic management, a surplus was now 'unlikely'.
According to the ancient Mayan calendar, the world came to an end the next day.

Financial Review, 21 December 2012

WHIP OUT A WHIPPING BOY
AND THE BLAME IS ON

As another influx of asylum seekers landed on Australian shores, members of the government were quick to point the finger at Tony Abbott. "Clearly, Tony Abbott is to blame for the fact that it's now open slather for people smugglers, and any Tom, Dick or Hari who fancies coming to Oz just has to hop onto the nearest leaky boat," a spokesperson said.

Asked why it was the Opposition Leader's fault, the spokesperson was unequivocal.

"If Tony Abbott had had the balls to tell John Howard to stand down in favour of Peter Costello in 2006, then that dysfunctional psychopath Kevin Rudd wouldn't have been elected and we'd still have perfectly good border protection policies in place.

"This is just one more classic example of how Tony Abbott is to blame for the endless problems that beset the Australian people. Take the economy. It's clear that despite all the brilliant work Wayne Swan has done to put us on a sound footing after the global financial crisis there is now no way we can deliver a surplus. Thanks to Tony Abbott."

Asked to explain how the Opposition Leader was responsible for the government being unable to deliver the surplus it had promised, the spokesperson was quick to apportion the blame.

"It's obvious! Tony Abbott was a member of the very same government that left this country with a stupid $20 billion surplus that nobody ever asked for. How utterly irresponsible, and he should apologise immediately. Now any old fool thinks you can have a bloody surplus whenever you feel like it!"

When questioned about how much the carbon tax was to blame for soaring energy costs, the spokesperson was again unequivocal.

"How many times do I have to say it? The carbon tax has nothing whatsoever to do with rising energy prices. The main culprit behind soaring electricity bills, as every household in Australia knows, is Tony Abbott. Every time Tony Abbott rides around on his bike, or goes surfing, or traipses around in his fluoro vest some idiot films it and sticks it on the news! During peak electricity time! It's a disgrace. The government's new energy price reduction plan makes it clear: people should simply switch off their televisions every time Tony Abbott comes on and your bills will come down."

Asked whether the plans of the Attorney-General, Nicola Roxoff, to make causing offence an offence was a threat to free speech, the spokesperson was deeply affronted. "I take offence at the very suggestion, and suggest you withdraw it quick smart. The only threat to our freedom of expression is Tony Abbott."

When asked to elaborate on how the Leader of the Opposition was a threat to free speech, the spokesperson explained that any freedom-loving people should be entitled to hear their government tell them what to do without being contradicted by Tony Abbott. "Clearly, if free speech includes the right of Mr. Abbott to criticise decisions taken by the Labor government of the day then that offends our democracy."

Responding to reports that starving Africans were being robbed of Australian aid in order to pay for flat-screen TVs for Nauru, the spokesperson said it was clear Tony Abbott was to blame. "Asylum seekers require decent access to the ABC and *Lateline* so they can be properly warned about Tony Abbott."

The spokesperson also blamed cost blow-outs and poor uptake of the NBN on Mr. Abbott.

"If Tony Abbott didn't keep pointing out that the whole shemozzle could have been done cheaper by the private sector, then we wouldn't be forced to spend millions of taxpayers' dollars running ads saying the NBN thing's nearly ready, when clearly it isn't."

Tony Abbott also came in for heavy criticism regarding the poor performance of school children during the past five years, when compared with overseas.

"If school kiddies could be left alone to get on with their studies rather than having to turn up to listen to Tony Abbott read them a story every time he rocks into town and wants a photo op, then clearly they'd be able to devote themselves more seriously to their studies. On top of that, we've had reports from teachers that vulnerable, innocent children can't sleep at night because they're so terrified of the 'Tony Abbott is an evil monster' poster kindly donated to us by the union movement that is now obligatory in all government classrooms."

The spokesperson was also asked whether the world would end on December 21. "If it does, the Mayans make it abundantly clear who's to blame," he said.

*One of the most famous editorials ever written – 'Yes Virginia, there is a Santa' –
came about when a little girl wrote a letter to the editor of the New York Sun in 1897
to enquire if Santa Claus really existed.*

Financial Review, 27 December 2012

YES WAYNIA, THERE IS A SURPLUS

At this time of year, when it is tempting to decry the jaded cynicism of
our age and the shallowness of our politics, it is an opportune moment
to remember the tale of the world's most famous newspaper editorial,
written in response to a young girl's question.

"It was a habit in our family that whenever any doubts came up as
to how to pronounce a word or some question of historical fact was in
doubt, we wrote to the Question and Answer column in *The Fin*. Father
would always say, 'If you see it in the *The Fin*, it's so,' and that settled the
matter.

"'Well, I'm just going to write to *The Fin* and find out the real truth,' I
said to father. He said, 'Go ahead, Waynia. I'm sure *The Fin* will give you
the right answer, as it always does.'"

And so Waynia sat down and wrote to her parents' favourite
newspaper.

Dear Editor,

I am 58 years old. Some of my little friends say there is no such thing
as a Surplus. Papa says, "If you see it in *The Fin*, it's so." Please tell me the
truth, is there a Surplus?

Waynia O'Swan,

115 Boulevard of Broken Promises,

Gold Coast

Dear Waynia,

Your little friends are wrong. They have been affected by the scepticism of a sceptical age. They do not believe except when they spin. They think that nothing can be which is not comprehensible by their little minds or told to them by mendacious Scottish communications directors, pollsters and public relations peoples of little talent. All minds, Waynia, whether they be of this faction or that other faction, are little.

In this great Party of ours man is a mere insect, an ant, an irritating flea in his intellect, as compared with the boundless world of union bosses and party officials about him, as measured by the inner-city intelligentsia capable of grasping the whole of truth and knowledge every time they express the shallowest thought in the merest tweet.

Yes, Waynia, there is a Surplus. It exists as certainly as trend growth and quantitative easing and the euro zone exist, and you know that they abound and give to your life its highest beauty and joy.

Alas! How dreary would be the world if there were no Surplus! It would be as dreary as if there were no Waynias. There would be no ideological faith, then, no Labor values, no stimulus spending, no increased deficit ceilings to make tolerable this existence.

We should have no enjoyment, except in bickering and backstabbing. The eternal light on the hill with which Labor fills the world would be extinguished.

Not believe in a Surplus! You might as well not believe in fairies! You might get men and put them in a lock-up to watch over all the forward estimates on Budget Eve to catch the Surplus, but even if they did not see the Surplus written down in any of the columns, what would that prove?

Nobody sees the Surplus, but that is no sign that there is no Surplus. For we live in most very unusual times and happenstance, what with tumbling commodity prices and tax receipts that have fallen well below that which was in all of our wisdom foretold and foreseen. The most real things in the world are those that neither treasurers nor bureaucrats can see.

Did you ever see fairies dancing on the lawns of Parliament House? Of course not, but that's no proof that they are not there. They are there a-plenty in both texting and deed if you only pull back the covers of your deepest fantasies. Nobody can conceive or imagine all the wonders there are unseen and unseeable in the dim corridors beneath the grounds of Capitol Hill.

You tear apart the baby's rattle and see what makes the noise inside, but there is a veil covering the fiscal world of which not the most faceless man, not even the united strength of all the faceless men that ever lived, could tear apart. Only the underlying fundamentals, jobs growth, low unemployment, strong GDP, poetry, love, romance, hope and trust can push aside that curtain and view – and picture the heavenly beauty and glory of fiscal certitude that lies beyond the next election.

Is it all real? Ah, Waynia, in all this world there is nothing else real and abiding.

No Surplus! Thank God it lives, and it lives forever in our minds. A thousand years from now, Waynia, nay, 10 times ten thousand years from now it will continue to make glad the hearts of caucus and enlighten true believers everywhere.

Merry Christmas and a Happy New Year!

Editorial page, *The Fin*, 1897

For the first time in 27 years the Woodford Folk Festival welcomed a current Prime Minister through the gates.

On December 29, joined by former PM Bob Hawke, Julia Gillard took to the stage and was overtly optimistic in addressing topics including the environment, the economy, gender politics and the future of parliament.

Financial Review, 2 January 2013

REASONS TO BE INCREDIBLY OPTIMISTIC, PART 2013

Thousands of hippies, peaceniks and music lovers descended unexpectedly on a small farm in upstate Queensland last weekend to attend a little-known event called the Woodstock folk festival, billed as "3 days of Optimism and Spin".

"Man, it was unbelievable," said festival organiser "Spin" McTurn-on. "We were expecting, like, hardly anybody, but then word got out and they just kept pouring in, all these cool pollies and groovy PR dudes and TV cameras. There must have been half a million of them at least. Man, the vibe was unreal. We'll never see anything like it again in my lifetime."

An epoch-defining list of celebrities and politicians took to the stage over the course of the weekend, and it is hoped that a film and a 3-CD set of the event will be released in time for the upcoming federal election.

Flame-haired blues singer Julia Joplin wowed the audiences with her stunning solo rendition of her self-penned ballad, 'Oh Lord won't you buy me an NDIS', which music insiders tip will be a major hit for her later this year.

Speaking from the stage, the singer, who is rumoured to be battling a severe addiction to opinion pills, addressed the adoring audience in a rambling and at times incoherent monologue.

"I'm an incredible optimist and everything about our nation should instill a sense of optimism in us," she said, to wild applause from an ecstatic crowd. "Which is why I'm so optimistic."

Drawing on her background, the unmarried singer drew cheers and applause as she talked about her journey to the heights of success.

"What a story. I mean, far out man! You can migrate to Australia at the age of four with nothing but a nasal, whining voice and go on to become the nation's first female blues singer," she said. "How can you not be an optimist?"

Ms. Joplin explained how a new era was dawning, the Age of Entitlements, and a new consciousness was changing the world for the better.

"I'm optimistic about the future of optimism," she said, to wild applause from the excited crowd.

The singer was briefly interrupted on stage by former *Keating and the True Believers* roadie Bob "Silverhair" Hawkwind, who had to be dragged away from the microphone after repeatedly insisting, to boos and jeers from the crowd: "If you look at the world ... there hasn't been a single outstanding political leader since me."

When asked to explain the meaning behind her provocative lyrics, in which she implores the states to give her sufficient funding for her national disability insurance scheme in time for the next election, Ms. Joplin outlined her alternative economic world philosophy.

"It's not about the money, man. What is money, anyway? It's just these numbers and bits of paper, dude. And big words.

"Money isn't real. Nothing is real. So if we all just hold hands and say 'yes, we have the money', then the money will appear.

"I'm an optimist, and we optimists believe in positive things, like being optimistic that we'll have the money."

The singer also reiterated her faith in her mysterious guru, the Maharishi Mahesh Gonski, at whose feet she often sits, espousing his controversial philosophy of Transcendental Education.

"Gonski teaches us something that can be defined as a means to do what one wants in a better way for maximum results. It's not about the money. Money's just a drag. It's about Optimism and Spin."

Also surprising audiences at the festival was legendary rock band *Malcolm and the Muddles*, who took to the stage early on in the weekend, where they performed in its entirety their psychedelic concept album, *Q&A*, a tragic rock opera about a young man who passionately believes he is destined to be prime minister or president of the republic but gets caught fiddling about with his wicked uncle Godwin.

Lead singer Malcolm Muddle is known for his passionate opposition to the Opposition.

"All they do is tell lies all day long and it's all everybody else's fault that I'm not their leader. In particular, I blame the media," he explained to puzzled reporters.

The festival wasn't all peace and love, however. Complained folk singer Ms. J Baez: "I came for the music, but suddenly all these pollies turned up, and what should have been a beautiful event turned into three days of rolling around in the mud."

A hoax press statement was released by environmental activist Jonathan Moylan saying that ANZ had withdrawn a $1.2 billion loan facility intended to be used to develop the Maules Creek coal project.

The hoax briefly wiped over $300 million off the market value of Whitehaven Coal shares.

Financial Review, 12 January 2013

WAYNE, OUT OF HIS TREE, ON HOAXES

The man behind the devastating hoax that wiped billions of dollars off the Australian economy today was adamant that he would "do it all again" if re-elected.

Speaking from his pole house in the wooded hinterlands of the Sunshine Coast, Wayne Swanlon, a proud tree-hugging, anti-mining activist, maintained that his stunt was a deliberate attempt to wreak economic havoc.

Earlier in the week, Mr. Swanlon had sent a fake email purporting to be from the Australian Treasury which claimed there would no longer be a surplus of $1.1 billion.

"It was a hoax all along," he said. "There never was such a thing as a surplus. I made the whole thing up."

Asked if he had qualms about lying to the public, Mr. Swanlon compared himself to practical jokers such as *The Chaser* team to support his actions. Mr. Swanlon has long been known for his anti-capitalist views and his vehement objection to the mining industry.

A founding member of the radical protest group Federal Labor in Action, he has admitted to sending out hundreds of fake press releases in the past, claiming "we have one of the best economies in the world."

Asked to justify his extreme actions, Mr. Swanlon was defiant: "These coalmining magnates are wandering around the Pilbara offering jobs to unemployed people and indigenous Australians and somebody has to put a stop to it. The long-term damage they are doing to the credibility of the Australian Labor Party is enormous."

"Misery, deprivation and victimhood are our crucial resources. Once these people start earning money and looking after themselves and becoming productive members of society, the next thing you know is you find them voting for right-wing nut jobs and then the whole show's over. We can never get them back."

Mr. Swanlon said he had tried a lot of other tricks in the past to get his message across, including a fake "stimulus" package and sending large amounts of taxpayers' money to dead people.

"I've attempted to start a class war, I've ridiculed wealth creators as vested interests and I've made fun of them as individuals and what postcode they live in," he said. "And I have no intention of stopping now.

"I went into this with my eyes wide open. I realise there are consequences, and I also realise that any change throughout history has never been made without taking risks."

To loud cheers from a dwindling throng of starry-eyed supporters, to whom he is known as "the world's greatest hoaxer," Mr. Swanlon explained how he wouldn't stop until the Australian economy had been driven into the ground.

"I'll just keep promising to spend more and more on Gonski and the NBN and the NDIS and all that touchy-feely stuff and at the same time I'll just keep borrowing billions more that we don't have by raising our debt ceiling. It's as simple as that. Whatever it takes."

Mr. Swanlon also complained that the powerful mining lobby had an unfair advantage over him because they paid no tax under the new mining tax that he himself had designed. "We really want to show people what the world could be like if it was governed by a bunch of undergraduate uni students who've never held a proper job and just sit around all day listening to Bruce Springsteen records. And we've succeeded."

A leading Greens senator was quick to offer her support, describing Mr. Swanlon's "no surplus" stunt as being "part of a long and proud history of Labor hoaxes, going right back to Bob Hawke's promise that "no child will live in poverty", Paul Keating's "recession we had to have" and Julia Gillard's promise that "there will be no carbon tax under the government I lead".

Her comments followed a tweet by a Greens colleague who invited Mr. Swanlon to join her for a nutritious coffee and chocolate waffle on a pavement in Sydney's Marrickville.

"He's been living up that tree for so long he's probably starving, the poor thing," she added. "He's clearly delusional."

Meanwhile, there are calls for appropriate action to be taken against the hoaxer before he does any more damage. In Australia, anyone convicted of disseminating false information to the electorate that could affect people's livelihoods faces savage retribution at the polling booths, often accompanied by a severe beating by baseball bats and a potential sentence of being exiled to years in the wilderness.

Throughout the summer, bushfires ravaged large parts of southern Australia.

Financial Review, 19 January 2013

CLIMATE CHANGE EXPERTS CONTINUE TO TREND
AUTOCUE TRANSCRIPT:

Jacinta: Good evening. I'm Jacinta and this is the 7 o'clock news. As catastrophic bushfires continue to rage across our ravaged, blackened country, leaving devastation and catastrophic destruction in their paths, we cross live to an emergency panel of leading climate change experts who predict "we ain't seen nothing yet".

(Insert interview with frowning Indian Bloke)

Frowning Indian Bloke: To me it's clear you Aussies ain't seen nothing yet. In the very near future, as global warming trends continue to, er, trend, what we have seen this week in Australia, which is unprecedented in the history of the world, is a series of catastrophic fires that make Dante's Inferno look like a kid's birthday party.

(Insert stock shot of cute kid blowing out candles on a cake)

(Match dissolve to shot of fires raging, kids screaming, running for cover etc.)

Jacinta: Experts predict that if global warming trends continue trending at these alarming levels, such catastrophic bushfires will become a regular occurrence, threatening lives and devastating communities and wildlife on a daily basis.

(Insert stock shot of smoldering koala)

(Insert interview with bloke stroking beard)

Beard-Stroking Bloke: Although it's impossible to blame any one single event on climate change (cut to shot of ice floes collapsing) it's clear that according to our extensive modeling (cut to pie chart or column graph or whatever it was we used yesterday) catastrophic climate change will lead to catastrophic bushfires, as we are seeing in Australia.

(Insert shot of bushfire sign. Zoom in on word "catastrophic")

(Insert shot of Julia Gillard wandering through bushfire zone comforting kids, holding a singed koala, etc.)

Jacinta: As climate change continues to devastate communities across the country, another expert predicts that the intensity and frequency of the fires will only get worse, and could lead to widespread panic and mass evacuations of coastal communities in the near future.

(Insert interview with bloke with egg-stain on shirt)

Shirt-Stained Bloke: As the climate heats up by up to six degrees over the next 50 years, the potential for catastrophes is, er, catastrophic.

(Insert clip of tsunami hitting Japanese village)

(Insert shot of beachfront home for sale)

(Insert interview with Byron Bay real estate agent)

Byron Bay Estate agent: Already we're seeing people who live on dangerously eroding beaches happy to take whatever offer they can get before it's too late. If you, too, are thinking of selling your beachfront home you can contact me on . . . (cut it here)

Jacinta: Meanwhile, a catastrophic wave of drive-by shootings has devastated Sydney's western suburbs. I spoke earlier to a leading member of the government who explained that the unprecedented heat, er, I mean crime wave, is directly linked to catastrophic climate change.

(Insert interview with federal minister who looks like Clark Kent)

Kent: Well, it's pretty clear that as the planet heats up by up to six degrees in the next 50 years, and that's what the experts are telling us, well what happens is you get these catastrophic heatwaves that lead directly to kids getting all hot under the collar and smuggling illegal weapons into western Sydney from places like Campbell Newman's corrupt Queensland where hundreds of workers have been laid . . . (cut it here)

Jacinta: (off camera) Thanks honey, that was great.

Jacinta: And now to world news, where unprecedented flooding has devastated Jakarta. I spoke earlier to an expert who warned that such flooding was a direct result of catastrophic climate change.

(Insert interview with frowning Indian bloke)

Frowning Indian Bloke: To me, it's clear you Indonesians ain't seen nothing yet. As global warming trends continue to, er, trend, what we have seen this week in Jakarta, which is unprecedented in the history of the world, is a series of catastrophic monsoon rains that make Noah's Ark look like a kid's birthday party.

(Insert clip of kids splashing in a plastic pool)

(Match dissolve to cars floating down street)

Jacinta: And that's the news tonight. We'll be back tomorrow where I'll be joined by a government minister who explains how today's catastrophic rise in unemployment figures is clearly linked to a catastrophic rise in sea levels. Until then, good night.

The Prime Minister's partner caused a minor controversy when he made a joke about prostate examinations being carried out by "small, female Asian doctors".

At her address to the National Press Club, Julia Gillard announced the election would be held on September 14.

The next day NSW police arrested Craig Thomson and charged him with 149 fraud offences. He was released on bail.

Financial Review, 2 February 2013

JULIA AND ALL THE OTHER MCTERNANS

The Prime Minister of Australia, Ms. Julia McTernan, shocked a stunned and startled nation with her surprise announcement that this year's federal election would be held on September 14, explaining that her decision was necessary in order to send an unambiguous signal that it's "business as usual" to a Mr. K. Rudd of Nambour Heads, Queensland.

"I do so not to start the nation's longest election campaign, quite the opposite," Ms. McTernan told a packed National Press Club in Canberra as she announced the start of the nation's longest election campaign.

The Prime Minister appeared as a guest at the lunch in front of the nation's top political journalists and commentators, where she wowed the excited crowd by sporting a fashionable new look, including designer hipster glasses and slimline black-and-white "Audrey Hepburn" jacket designed especially for the occasion by international fashion guru Coco McTernan (no relation).

Explaining the surprise absence of her normal stylist, Mr. Tim McMathieson, the Prime Minister noted that he was "taking a break" in Canberra Hospital's intensive care unit following a freak accident at the Lodge which had resulted in him finding himself tragically impaled on the end of a red-hot poker.

A spokesperson for the hospital confirmed he was being cared for by an elite team of small female Asian doctors.

When pressed by reporters to explain the processes behind her decision to call an election, Ms. McTernan explained that she had consulted widely with all her colleagues within other political parties and the Scottish bloke in the next room before springing the surprise announcement upon her own stunned cabinet and startled caucus.

"It's none of the ALP's bloody business when I call an election," said the feisty PM. "Besides, if I'd told cabinet what I was up to, Bob would have used it as an excuse to roll me, just like he did on that Palestinian thingy, and I'd've been cactus in caucus."

Asked for his opinion on the abrupt announcement, Foreign Minister Bob McTernan (no relation) was typically lost for words.

"This is wonderful news. I was just saying to my good friends here in the League of Arab Despots over a long liquid lunch in Geneva that I am completely ready for this campaign. I have done all the groundwork and I have been eagerly anticipating the starter's gun. 'Game on!' as my opponent so colourfully puts it in her appallingly lower-class nasal twang. This election will be good for all Australians and I intend to fight it vigorously and with all means at my disposal so that Julia's out by the end of March and I get four months as PM." Also announcing they were "totally prepared" for the opportunity to fight tooth and nail were half the cabinet and most of caucus. "What this (election announcement) does is provide us with the certainty that, if she's still the leader in eight months' time, then it's actually 'game over' for most of us," said a minister who offered the PM his unqualified support.

However the Treasurer, Mr. Wayne McTernan (no relation) denied that the announcement of an election campaign had anything to do with an election campaign.

"This is a battle of ideas. What we are doing is getting on with the job of governing by putting out properly funded and costed policy ideas every single day, while all we get from our opponents are meaningless platitudes and singalong clichés."

When asked to elaborate on how he intended to pay for his Gonski and NDIS ideas, the Treasurer responded: "Money, money, money it's a rich man's world. What we are all about here is Labor values such as helping the poor and the sick and bringing the little children up in a world free of the burden of, er, burdens, and what I think to myself is what a, er, wonderful world that would be."

Asked how Labor intends to deliver a surplus, the Treasurer pointed to compulsory superannuation. "We'll make it compulsory that you give all your super to us."

In other unrelated news, an elite crime-fighting squad from the NSW and Victorian police forces announced they had finally caught the nation's No. 1 wanted man, the fugitive former union official Mr. Craig McThomson who had eluded them for many long months by hiding out in bushes in the backyard of his home on the central coast.

"Mr. McThomson's arrest is a matter for the police and has nothing whatsoever to do with my announcement of an election campaign which, as I have made clear, isn't an election campaign," explained the Prime Minister.

At the ICAC hearings, it was alleged NSW Labor factional player Eddie Obeid offered free accommodation at his family's Perisher Valley ski lodge to Labor members.

Financial Review, 9 February 2013

PERISH THE THOUGHT

Heading off on your first skiing weekend with your work pals to Perisher? Here's a handy cut out and keep guide to the local lingo to stick in your wallet. Not that you'll actually need your wallet.

Light on the hill – the gorgeous log fire roaring at the all-expenses paid luxury resort that awaits you at the end of each day.

Slippery slope – a cup of coffee with Eddie, Moses or Paul.

Treacherous conditions – what you agree to in return.

Accommodation – using your ministerial position in later years to reward those who picked up the tab.

Frosty reception – what to expect if you don't.

Snow job – pretending it's all above board and you had no idea what you were getting yourself into.

Eddy – a flurry of swirling water underneath the snow, fatal to skiers who pretend not to see it and then get sucked in.

Slush – a brown murky substance (often found in back gardens) and a good place to hide the cash.

Perishing – the values of Ben Chifley's Labor party.

Hard pack – a group of union officials and faceless men who actually run the country, er, the resort.

Out-of-bounds – this refers to discussions within the ski lodge about how they all got so rich.

Grooming – being befriended by Sussex Street power brokers.

Binding – any agreement struck with the owner of the resort.

Feel the heat – after-effects of excessive exposure to Eddie, Moses or Paul.

In too deep – see above.

Shovel – keep one handy for digging yourself out at a later date.

Maps – all skiers should make sure they leave a spare copy of the latest maps lying around, particularly if they show where coal is buried.

Après ski – redistributing mining leases.

Hand in glove – the cosy relationship between union bosses, party powerbrokers and government ministers, see also Sussex Street, NSW Labor Inc, HSU, AWU, etc.

Sharing the hot tub – after a hard day on the slopes you may find yourself in hot water, along with any number of Labor heavy hitters.

Excessive glare – don't be surprised if you need dark glasses to protect yourself from the unwanted glare of sudden media exposure.

Snow boarding – a form of extreme torture that requires sleep-deprived subjects to stay awake during hours and hours of John McTernan's power point presentations on "how we're going to win the next election."

Light and fluffy – Mr. McTernan's policy prescriptions.

Limited traction – Mr. McTernan's policy prescriptions.

Depression – the result of listening to Mr. McTernan's policy prescriptions.

Black run – why not live dangerously and choose your very own indigenous female candidate for pre-selection in order to make your mark on history? It's downhill all the way.

Fresh dumps – see also Trish Crossin, Nicola Roxon, Chris Evans, the surplus.

Polls apart – you and the Coalition on a two-party preferred basis.

Below zero – the amount of money in the national coffers.

Backflips, One Eighties, U-Turns – highly skilled manoeuvres designed to deflect attention from unpopular policies and regular stuff-ups.

Break a leg – recruitment technique to encourage voluntary union membership.

Boots – what you can expect to be given in September.

Hypothermia – the result of being left out in the cold, also known as "feeling like Kevin".

Planned ascent – also known as "doing a Kevin".

Gon-ski – Uphill race with no money.

Slow zone – see the economy.

Getting rid of moguls – denigrating wealth creators and industry leaders by labeling them as class enemies.

Fakie – making a world-famous speech pretending you're the victim of sexism and misogyny.

Indy grab – mandatory if you want to win, also known as doing an "Oakeshott" or a "Windsor".

Liftie – New Zealand Labor colleague.

Vertical drop – your current trajectory in western Sydney.

Lost in the wilderness – where you'll probably be spending the rest of the decade.

Avalanche – see also landslide, whiteout, disaster, Abbott victory on September 14, etc.

Federal Minister for Justice Jason Clare and Sports Minister Kate Lundy called a press conference to claim that the nation's top sporting codes were under a cloud following a yearlong investigation revealing widespread doping and links to organised crime.

They maintained the Australian Crime Commission had uncovered the use of banned drugs by "multiple athletes across a number of codes", and that orchestrated doping programs of entire teams had been facilitated by coaches, sports scientists, support staff, doctors and pharmacists.

No specific evidence was provided. Those responsible were encouraged to hand themselves in.

A former head of the Australian Sports Anti-Doping Authority said: "This is not a black day in Australian sport, this is the blackest day."

Quentin Tarantino released his thriller-western Django Unchained.

Financial Review, 16 February 2013

DJASON UNHINGED

"And now for the latest McTarantino film. There's been a lot of anticipation, Margaret."

"Indeed there has, David. And I, for one, was really looking forward to seeing it."

"Tell us about it. Plenty of blood and lots of action, I imagine."

"Well, you would hope so. It's called *Djason Unhinged*, and it tells the story of Djason – the D is silent, he explains to us early on in the film – who goes from being a slave to the Labor spin machine to becoming a federal justice marshal and ends up on the front page of every newspaper as the greatest crime fighter in the land."

"I see. It's a western then."

"Well, the action all takes place in the western suburbs, and of course we already know there are plenty of guns and drive-by shootings and drug lords and Middle Eastern crime gangs and all of that out there but, well, the odd thing is Djason isn't worried about any of that."

"No? So what happens?"

"Well, that's the problem. A huge build-up, and then … nothing."

"Let's take a look."

Cut to scene of Djason surrounded by group of bulky men in grey suits.

Djason (threateningly): Don't underestimate how much we know and if you are involved in this, come forward before you get a knock at the door.

Official (menacingly): We will leave no stone unturned.

Second official (grimacing): This is not a black day in Australian sport, this is the blackest day.

Cut back to studio.

"Oh dear. That dialogue is pretty clunky."

"Isn't it dreadful! Djason has been sent in by Wild John McTalltale – played by McTarantino himself, incidentally – to win back the west, which is being terrorised by all these terrible stories about corrupt politicians and so on. But Djason panics and decides to clean up the entire town of Sportsville instead. He comes charging in on his high horse with a whole posse behind him, and also with his pretty little sidekick Kate, who he hopes to rescue from political obscurity. Then he gets up on a special media platform and announces that the entire town is riddled with drug cheats and organised crime and illegal betting, and everyone has to give themselves up."

"Hmm. I see."

"But the town's just full of normal sporting types. Mums taking their kids to basketball practice. Cricketers at the local park. Professional tennis players. A few footy boofheads. Saturday morning soccer dads and so on. No one's got the faintest idea what Djason's banging on about. Hence the film's title: *Djason Unhinged.*"

"So what happens?"

"Well, Djason tells anyone who's still listening that 'they know who they are' and they've got to hand themselves in. Or else."

"Or else what?"

"Well, er, nothing. That's it. That's all that happens."

"That's the entire film?"

"Yep."

"So what about all the drugs?"

"There aren't any. Which is a bit of a problem from a plot construction point of view. It's certainly not up to McTarantino's normal standards. Unfortunately, the whole script is contrived. We learn that Djason's surname is Clare – he's obviously supposed to be the Angel Clare pretty boy hero type. Then there's the lawman whose name is – wait for it – Lawler. And another bloke who's busy riding off into the sunset as fast as he can is called Gallop."

"Hmm. Not very credible."

"Worse, the back story is nothing but hackneyed clichés; corrupt politicians selling mining leases and some secret map that shows where all the gold is buried, and turns up mysteriously on Moses's desk, but no one can explain how or why. Then there's the mysterious mining taxes that have gone missing and Old Swanny is being hung out to dry. So with all this bad news McTalltale wants to get the stories off the front pages before the county elections, which for some reason that is never properly explained are months and months away."

"Oh dear. Bit of an anti-climax then?"

"Yep. Certainly not a patch on McTarantino's earlier efforts. Nowhere near as imaginative as *Australia Day Restaurant Massacre* or *Misogyny Dogs.*"

"I always liked *Surplus Fiction* myself. Particularly the scene where the money disappears into thin air."

"Yes, that was a classic. And I particularly loved *Kill Kev*. Both the original and the sequel."

"So let me guess. This one ends in a bloodbath?"

"Only for Labor."

"I'll give it one and a half stars."

"I'm giving it a miss altogether."

As the polls continued to worsen for Labor, there was much speculation that behind the scenes the numbers were firming for a leadership change.

'I support the Prime Minister … that remains my position,' Kevin Rudd said. 'Everyone should take a long, cold shower.'

Financial Review, 23 February 2013

SOAPIE

Johnte leans forward and thumps the table. "*Think*, you motherf---kers! *Think!* How in God's name do we bring the pr---k back into the goddam show?"

Around the table the group of writers all shift uneasily in their chairs. As head writer of the country's longest-running soap opera, Johnte is terrifying enough, even without the outbursts of anger and his expletive-laden Scottish brogue.

"These ratings suck!" says one of the younger writers, flicking through the latest figures. "Where did we go so wrong?"

An older writer puts his hands behind his head, his eyes fixed on the ceiling.

"Killing off Kevin. That really was a dumb idea."

"That was nearly three years ago already!" protests another. "Can't have been that bad an idea – we picked up the Emmy in 2010."

"No thanks to you, Howzie. You even went on some stupid chat show and boasted that you wrote the whole scene yourself! Talk about knuckle-headed. Completely blew the audience's suspension of disbelief."

Another writer interrupts: "We got the Emmy coz I wrote in Tony and Rob, those two crazy farmers from *The Bald and the Beautiful*. Brilliant!"

"Oh man," chimes in another. "I had to write the dialogue for Rob's big scene. 17 minutes worth. 'It's gonna be ugly but it's gonna be beautiful in it's ugliness.' Still can't forgive myself."

A grizzled, grey-haired writer looks up from stirring his pencil in his styrofoam coffee cup. "It was the Big Lie episode that killed us. And we all know it."

Johnte slams his hand down on the table. "It wasn't a lie! What Julia said at the end of season 1 was in character for that series. Who knew the plot would get so screwy in season 2? It was the only way we could write the Greenies into the script. "S---t happens. Audiences accept that stuff."

The young writer glances down at the ratings. "Not any more."

Johnte stares menacingly around the room. "Gimme a break here, guys. It's not like I haven't tried. The Restaurant Riot scene. That was effing genius, even if I say so myself! And let's not forget my Misogyny episode, eh? Two million hits on YouTube! You can't beat that."

One of the freelance writers nods. "Johnte's right, he's a brilliant writer, guys. He's got us through some really tricky sub-plots. Like, that whole surplus cock-up. Or when we forgot the mining tax was supposed to make money? The way Johnte twisted the dialogue was awesome. Wayne may not be the world's greatest actor, but Johnte always gets him out of a tight spot."

The door slides open, and unannounced, one of the show's producers slips quietly into the room.

"Here come the faceless ones," mutters the styrofoam stirrer under his breath.

Johnte stares aggressively at the newcomer. "Well?"

The producer smiles, like a wolf having freshly devoured a lamb. "Word from upstairs. Julia's out. Kevin's back in. Get writing."

The room erupts. "But he's dead, we finished him off last season!"

"We said he's a dysfunctional psycho! Now he's the hero again? You gotta be kidding me!"

"The viewers won't buy it."

"This is even dumber than knifing him in the first place!"

"How many people get killed off in this joint? It's mental!"

"Whoah, guys! Hold yer effin' horses," says Johnte. "We're professionals. We'll figure it out. Let's brainstorm it. Thought starters, anyone?"

"Maybe we say Kevin's got a twin brother and they were separated at birth?"

"Maybe Kevin never really died? Maybe he faked his own death and disappeared but now he wants his old life back?"

"Maybe Kevin was locked away in a Tibetan monastery by mandarin-speaking monks but he's escaped?"

Johnte frowns. "Hmm. I like it, but . . ."

The styrofoam stirrer looks up. "We do what Dallas did. Bobby never died. It was all just a dream."

A slow smile spreads across Johnte's rugged features.

"Now you're talking. We say the last two seasons never happened. There was no Julia. So no Big Lie. No Wayne, either. No mining tax, no vanishing surplus, no boat people, no live cattle exports and all the other rubbish. None of it ever happened! It was all just a bad dream.

"Do you think people will buy it?"

The producer smiles. "That the last three years has just been one long nightmare? You bet."

Police charged a 21-year-old Sri Lankan on a bridging visa over the alleged indecent assault of a university student, as it emerged the federal government, through the Red Cross, was housing large groups of male asylum seekers adjacent to girls-only campus accommodation at Macquarie University in Sydney's west.

The Prime Minister Julia Gillard moved the entire cabinet out to Rooty Hill for a week to re-connect with the voters of the western suburbs.

Financial Review, 2 March 2013

ILLEGAL VOTE PEOPLE
TERRORISING OUR SUBURBS

Residents in Sydney's west were horrified to learn this week of large groups of Labor politicians being housed among them in temporary accommodation in hitherto unreported numbers.

"It's a disgrace," said one startled father. "Nobody warned us! A whole bunch of them moved in right next door, and apparently there are dozens more being housed down the street. What about our kids? What about our daughters? It's completely unacceptable."

"They don't belong here," said a furious grandmother, who refused to give her name for fear of reprisals. "They've just been dumped on us, without any thought for how they fit in. They don't understand our customs, and most of them barely even speak our language."

Irate residents are demanding that the group of Labor politicians seeking a safe haven in the western suburbs be sent away as soon as possible. "When you get an invasion of unprocessed publicity seekers, it's not surprising the locals feel threatened."

"The problem is that these aren't your normal blow-ins," said the owner of one local pub. "These are economic refugees from Canberra who have turned up here without any proper permission. It's out of control. They've literally just landed on our doorstep and there's nothing we can do about it. You see them wandering around the shopping malls and hanging around the schools and kindergartens. Dozens of them at a time. They pester you and try to get you to talk to them in front of the TV cameras but we just want them to go away and leave us alone. My kids were terrified!"

Authorities admitted they had no idea what the so-called "pollies" did with themselves on a day-to-day basis or where they went. "They're basically free to roam wherever they want," said one bureaucrat, speaking on condition of anonymity. However, the owner of a large Novotel admitted he was secretly housing "dozens" of Labor politicians – in fact, the entire cabinet – at Rooty Hill, and that it wasn't unusual for other "hangers-on" such as media advisers and publicists to be sleeping under the one roof. "It's just a contract, like any other," he said. "OK, they make a fair bit of noise but other than that they're no different to any other bunch of people."

Others begged to differ. "For a start, they stand out like sore thumbs around here. They dress funny and speak funny. I don't understand a word they're saying," a local small businessman said. "I've learned to keep an eye on my wallet whenever they're around. I can't tell you how often I've caught them with their hands in my till."

"I know I'll be accused of pollie bashing, but they're not the same as us," said a local cafe owner. "They've never done an honest day's work in their lives. Most of 'em wouldn't know an electricity bill if it bit them on the bum. And the joke is, it's my hard-earned taxes that pay for them to sit around gas-bagging all day long."

Other residents were concerned that many of the customs the pollies brought with them were completely alien to the local culture. "They worship different gods – climate change and carbon pricing and stuff."

Officials admitted that some of those being housed in Rooty Hill didn't adhere to "mandatory behaviour protocols" and were rumoured to be connected to unsavoury elements back home in Canberra. "But it would be unfair to demonise the lot of them due to unproven stories of prostitution rings, credit card embezzlement, Cabcharge fraud, slush funds, dodgy renovations, police investigations and so on."

The group had been smuggled into the region by a well-organised network of spin doctors to whom they paid millions of dollars.

"They haven't come through the proper channels – most of them watch the ABC or SBS – and they threw away all their papers during the voyage," claimed one official. "Particularly the Murdoch ones."

An unemployed drinker at the local pub, who would only give his name as Kev, spoke bitterly about the newcomers. "These people stole my job. I've been coming to these parts for years and everybody around here knows and loves me. Someone should tell this mob to zip off. Fair suck of the sav! But don't worry, I plan to get my own back one of these days."

The Spectator Australia, 2 March 2013

HOW LABOR CAN WIN

It is clear from most opinion polls that Labor in all likelihood faces defeat at the forthcoming federal election. Of crushing proportions. Within Labor circles, the despair is palpable. The Gillard-Rudd death roll drags the party deeper and deeper into swirling, muddy waters from which many will never return.

Yet, ironically, Labor could easily win the next election. Here's how:

Give McTernan the flick. 'Spin' is the Party Immune Virus from which all of Labor's other fatal diseases are born. In the heyday of Bob Carr's NSW premiership, spin was an art in its infancy, akin to advertising in the 1950s; a shiny, new way of using mass communications to mesmerise the public. As master of the art, Carr had more in common with Don Draper than his illustrious Macquarie Street predecessors, but by the time spin arrived in a major way in Canberra, post-2007, its tricks and prestidigitations were become more easily recognisable. With the arrival of John McTernan after Gillard's narrow 2010 victory, the artform began to become a parody of itself. McTernan cut his teeth under Tony Blair, a practitioner who surpassed even Carr. By the time the irascible Scotsman arrived in Australia, his ilk (and possibly he himself) were already being parodied in the TV sit-com *The Thick of It* — although even that show's Malcolm Tucker might have thought twice about the wisdom of stirring up a race riot on Australia Day. Weirdly, McTernan has allowed himself to become the story, thereby shining unnecessary illumination upon his supposed dark arts. When the Prime Minister's chief spin doctor gets lampooned on the highest-rating radio station in the battleground seats of western Sydney for inviting the show's presenter out for a beer, the game is up.

Nowadays, Labor's 'talking points' and daily synchronised soundbites on everything from the flailing economy to the evils of Tony Abbott are about as plausible and persuasive as your typical 1950s Playtex Miracle Bra ad. In all likelihood, Gillard's supposedly spontaneous misogyny outburst emerged from McTernan's febrile imagination as part of his self-confessed practice of "killing your opponents".

Wayne Swan's loathsome class warfare twaddle and anti-mining mogul shtick, too.

The sorry truth of the matter is that the harder McTernan tries to find a "circuit- breaker" or to "change the narrative" the lower Labor sink in the polls.

When learning of McTernan's appointment to Team Julia, veteran union leader and former chairman of the Scottish Labour Party Bob Thomson reportedly said: 'All I can say is, God help the Australian Labor Party.' Indeed.

Stop doing things — anything! In marketing meetings, strategic planners play a game where they try to distil the essence of a brand down to one single word. Often, this involves a lengthy process of tearing words and pictures out of magazines, cutting up headlines, choosing relevant song titles and so on and plonking them up on a whiteboard before eliminating them one by one. Eventually, after many hours, one single word emerges. That becomes the brand essence. In the case of Labor, I shall save them the bother. That word is "incompetent." From the horrors of boat people lost at sea to the cumbersome carbon tax, from the fantasies of "spreading the boom" via a nonexistent mining tax to the vanished surplus, from the anti-discrimination proposals to the calling of the election (surely there isn't an easier task for a PM to get right?), incompetent execution of thought-bubble schemes is the hallmark of pretty much everything this government attempts.

Ironically, apologists for the government cite its frenetic workload as justification for its continued existence, excitedly pointing to the unprecedented number of bills it has put through parliament. Sadly, "doing something" is not the same as "doing something well," or even "doing something worthwhile." Thus, four years on we find the head of the NBN musing aloud as to whether there is a better way to implement his squillion dollar scheme. (Perhaps a detailed cost-benefit analysis around the time of conception mightn't have been such a bad idea — just saying). We find taxes that threaten to lose more money than they raise. We find a hurriedly re-thought Gonski and a ream of unfunded, and unfundable, schemes and promises.

The solution is simple. Labor, don't touch anything between now and September. By all means, turn up to parliament on the appropriate days and answer the appropriate questions, but don't actually do anything. That is the only way to prevent more untold damage being inflicted upon our economy and our way of life, billions being needlessly wasted, promises being made that inevitably will have to be broken and more importantly, will stop you being all over the media day and night for stuffing stuff up. Indeed, so grateful would the electorate be for a total absence of news for six months about anything whatsoever to do with

Swan, Combet, Albanese, Rudd, Shorten, Carr, Garrett, Gillard, Wong and Plibersek that they may actually forget how much they dislike them. After all, Belgium didn't have a government for 541 days. The joint was never better run.

Don't change leaders. It's so tempting. I know. The opinion polls love him. The TV shows adore him. Schoolgirls go all gooey whenever he's around. But don't be fooled. We Aussies always root for the underdog. We love a loser, particularly when they were "unfairly" done in. Ned Kelly, Gallipoli, Phar Lap. But we only love them so long as they are the underdog. Imagine if, despite the dastardly poms stitching us up, we'd actually won at Lone Pine? Or if Phar Lap, having recovered from his mafia poisoning, ended up his days coming third-last at Flemington? Or Ned Kelly rode off into the sunset?

Bring back Kevin and the public will go off him faster than you can say "fair suck of the sav." Or "programmatic specificity," if you're that way inclined.

Ditch the unions. Mark Latham was right.

Carry on with your one successful policy — stopping the boats. The way things are going, with our borders now wide open to any old boatperson who feels like wandering in and taking up residence wherever he fancies (dormitories adjacent to single female dorms are proving particularly popular), Sydney's western suburbs will soon be chockers with legalised illegal immigrants. All of whom will obviously want to say "thank you" by voting Labor!

The Gillard cabinet's week-long sojourn in Rooty Hill failed to inspire the voters.

Financial Review, 9 March 2013

ROLL UP! ROLL UP!

Beatles fans across the country expressed dismay and bewilderment at the band's latest effort; a confusing, ad hoc road trip specially made for TV called *Marginal Mystery Tour.*

In the show, the band and a group of hangers-on hire a bus and head off to the west country with only a vague script written on the back of an envelope and no idea where they are going. Viewers are taken on an aimless trip around marginal electorates of the western suburbs, during which the band try to engage with locals in staged encounters.

Although some of the songs will please die-hard fans, critics were quick to point out that such ditties as 'The Fool on Rooty Hill' and 'Your Mother Should Vote' are no more than rehashes of previous hits.

The film and soundtrack are largely the brainchild of lead singer and bass player Paul McTernan, who has increasingly provided creative inspiration since the band's "svengali" Brian Ruddstein abruptly died of a publicity overdose earlier this year.

Band leader Julia Lennon, who has begun wearing small round glasses and a variety of colourful outfits as part of her new image, only contributes one song to the new album; a bizarre and chaotic piece of post-modernism called 'I Am The Elephant (in the room)', which has been relegated to a B-side. Meaningless ramblings such as "I am he as you are he and we are us" are interspersed with perplexing phrases such as: "Misogynistic sexist, boy you've been a naughty girl, you let your poll ratings drop."

Viewers complain that the dialogue is barely comprehensible; much of the road trip is filmed with the band standing beside a busy motorway as trucks roar past.

In one typically oddball scene, the band attempts to persuade local bus driver Barry O'Farrell to build a new road for them to drive on, but O'Farrell claims he has no cash left. When Julia attempts to seduce him with her rendition of 'Barry, You're A Rich Man', the scene descends into farce.

The group is rumoured to have experimented with new instruments on the soundtrack including high-pitched dog whistles only audible to trade unionists, xenophobes and protectionists.

Perhaps the most telling song is by the band's so-called "quiet one," Wayne Harriswan, who was nominated recently by Eurorocker magazine as "the world's greatest guitarist".

In a dreary and uninspired dirge, Harriswan, whose last successful song was the powerful hit 'Taxman', laments that he "doesn't belong" because his "friends have lost their way". Indeed, many critics fear that this latest outing may signal the final demise of the once popular band, with gossip circulating of endless friction, poor decision-making and splits at the top. Tensions remain high, driven by an obvious lack of fresh ideas.

Perhaps highlighting deeper problems, in one scene a girl known only as "Little Nicola" abruptly hops off the bus and disappears without explanation.

Even drummer Ringo Shorten, the least talented member of the group, appears to be working on a solo project.

Invariably, the group's latest effort suffers from comparison to its predecessor, the extraordinary *Sergeant Psychopath's Lonely Hearts Club Band*, an album that defined 2007's "summer of Kev" and topped charts across the country.

With a plethora of great songs, such as 'Fixing a Hole (where the pink batts go in)', and 'Being for the Benefit of Mr. Rudd', the album was best known for its tantalising cover, which drove fans into a frenzy of despair with its strange clues that "Kev Isn't Dead."

Conspiracy theorists interpret the song 'A Day in the Life', with its haunting opening "I read the news today, oh boy" and symphonic crescendo, to be a clue that Kevin isn't really dead and buried and plans to make a dramatic comeback.

(In the final groove of the record, a voice can be heard endlessly repeating a mantra that sounds like "I will not challenge her" over and over again. Fans dispute what this means).

Although it's too early to write off the group entirely, critics point to the tragic symbolism of the final scene of *Marginal Mystery Tour*, where the band, arm in arm, descends the glittering staircase of the Rooty Hill RSL.

As one, they optimistically chant: "I say hello …" while a chorus of westies wearily reply: "… and we say goodbye."

Senator Stephen Conroy proposed legislation for a government-appointed Public Media Interest Advocate to scrutinize and oversee all media, including blogs, as part of his response to the Finkelstein media inquiry and his desired media reform package.

Again, Labor's proposals were seen by many as an unacceptable attack on freedom of expression.

Financial Review, 16 March 2013

BIG BROTHER

It was a bright cold day in April, and the clocks were striking 13. Winston Smith slipped quickly through the doors of "Sweetest Victory" McMansions.

The hallway smelt of boiled cabbage. At one end a large coloured poster had been tacked to the wall. It depicted an enormous face, more than a metre wide: the face of a man of about 50, with glasses, black hair with streaks of grey and an excessively protruding top lip. Winston made for the stairs. It was no use trying the lift; the electricity was cut off whenever there was insufficient wind for the giant turbines.

On each landing, the poster with the enormous face gazed from the wall. "PUBLIC INTEREST MEDIA ADVOCATE is watching you," the caption said. The eyes in the photo seemed to follow you around.

Inside his flat, Winston heard a fruity voice saying something about the long-promised surplus. The instrument (the flatscreen, it was called) could be dimmed, but never shut off completely.

Down in the street the face with the protruding top lip gazed at him from every corner. "PIMA is watching you." The dark eyes behind the glasses looked deep into Winston's own.

Another poster, torn at one corner, flapped fitfully in the breeze, alternately covering and uncovering the single word, LABOR. In the far distance a helicopter skimmed between the roofs, hovered for an instant like a bluebottle, and darted away. It was the pollies, heading to Canberra.

Behind Winston, the flatscreen was still babbling away about the bountiful revenue from the mining tax. The flatscreen received and transmitted simultaneously, so there was no way of knowing when you were being watched by the Public Interest Media Advocate, plugged in as he was to the national broadband network. You lived in the assumption that even in darkness your every tweet or Facebook update was being scrutinised.

A kilometre away, the Ministry of Surplus towered above the leafy landscape. This, he thought with vague disquiet, was Canberra. He tried to squeeze out some childhood memory to tell him whether Canberra had always been like this. But it was no use. From where Winston stood it was just possible to read, picked out on the building's white face in elegant lettering, the slogans of the Labor Party: "REGULATION IS DIVERSITY, TAXES ARE SAVINGS, UNIONS ARE PRODUCTIVITY, DEFICIT IS SURPLUS."

Not far away were the other ministries upon which the apparatus of government rested. The Ministry of Communications, which regulated all news and entertainment. The Ministry of Border Security, which mainly released boat people into the community. The Ministry of Justice, which hunted down drug-cheating sports people. And the Ministry of Energy, responsible for power cuts and pricing carbon.

Mini-Comms was the really frightening one. There was no transparency to it at all. It was a place impossible to enter except on Labor Party business, and then only by penetrating a maze of red tape, closed shops, and faceless factions.

Winston crossed into his tiny kitchen and took a cigarette from a crumpled plain olive-green packet marked "cigarette", and a burger from a plain olive-green packet marked "burger". He took down from the shelf a bottle in plain olive-green packaging marked "beer" and poured out a glass, nerved himself for a shock, and gulped it down.

Feeling emboldened, he took out a pen, ink, and a blank piece of smooth creamy paper, yellowed by age. He had carried it guiltily home in his briefcase. The thing that he was about to do was to write a letter criticising the Public Interest Media Advocate for the opinion pages. This was not illegal, but if detected it was reasonably certain it would be punished by instant career death, or 25 years in a forced-Labor camp.

He dipped the pen into the ink and then faltered for just a second. A tremor had gone through his bowels. This was the decisive act.

In clumsy letters he wrote: April 4th, 2013. Dear Sir …

On the morning of 21 March, Julia Gillard and Tony Abbott formally apologised to thousands of parents and children affected by the practice of forced adoption that occurred in Australian hospitals in the 1950's, 60's and 70's.

Later, following intense media speculation and a surprise press conference by Simon Crean, in which the minister switched his support to Kevin Rudd, Julia Gillard called a ballot for the Leadership and Deputy Leadership of the Labor Party that afternoon at 4.30pm. Just 10 minutes prior to the scheduled ballot, Rudd announced that he would not challenge and so Gillard and Swan were re-elected unopposed. Mr. Crean was subsequently sacked.

Financial Review, 23 March 2013

THE RUDD STOLEN GENERATION KEEPS HURTING

Prime Minister Julia Gillard has delivered a heartfelt apology to the voters of Australia for grievous harm done to them by the forced adoption of a Labor government.

"No words can undo the damage," Ms. Gillard told thousands of voters gathered around their television screens for the formal apology from Parliament House. "By saying sorry we cannot undo the terrible wrong done to them.

"These voters themselves are utterly blameless. Their lives have been blighted by the profound sense of loss and tragedy that each one of them carries throughout their lives thanks to those dreadful events that occurred so long ago on the night of June 23, 2010."

Ms. Gillard was referring to the so-called "Rudd Stolen Generation," who lost their beautiful, blond, blue-eyed cherub when he was needlessly snatched from their arms by a callous group of bureaucrats known as the "faceless men."

"These voters were tricked out of the chance to be governed by their own natural leader, sometimes forced to sign ballot papers that didn't even have his name on it."

The formal apology follows a lengthy campaign in the opinion polls to force the Prime Minister to recognise that a cruel government machine cannot go around separating voters from their natural-born leader.

Ms. Gillard spoke of young women in the Greens shackled to ideology and naïve Independents drugged on power being tricked into signing a formal power-sharing agreement to keep her government afloat. She spoke of voters across the nation being ignored and their children who grew up thinking Mr. Rudd had never loved them.

"Tragically, my government has suffered ever since from a debilitating sense of illegitimacy."

Members of the Rudd Stolen Generation recounted harrowing tales of depression, disillusionment and despair.

"I'll never forget that night. I woke up and he'd vanished. They wouldn't tell me why or where he had gone or what I'd done wrong. I never stop dreaming we'll get him back. Wherever I go, I see his face. On the TV screen, in shopping malls, and at the local church. I recognise his smile. And the cute way he pats down his hair. I know it must be him."

Many survivors have never been able to grieve properly for their loss.

"It's not only Ms. Gillard that we've been forced to adopt. We've had to adopt all her policies as well."

Some lashed out at the relentless sense of betrayal. "It's been nothing but constant lies. They said there wouldn't be a carbon tax and then there was one. Then they promised a surplus. No ifs, no buts. They lied about that, too. Then they said they'd pay us lots of money out of the mining tax, but we haven't seen a brass razoo."

Other victims tearfully explained how they'd been constantly disappointed by false hope that their beloved one might some day be returned to them.

"I remember last February when I finally thought he was coming back to us. We were so excited. We got out all our old Kevin '07 tee shirts and flags and decorated the living room. But at the last moment they wouldn't let him. It was such a cruel blow, to get our hopes up like that and then dash them all over again."

One gentleman, who would only give his name as Simon, described the confusion and loss of purpose that had blighted his career since last Thursday when he finally plucked up the courage to make contact with his long-lost leader Mr. Rudd.

"I desperately urged him to challenge so that the two of us could be together again. But he didn't want to know me. He refused to even put his hand up. That one simple gesture would have made all the difference, yet he's so damaged by his experiences that he couldn't bring himself to do it. Now I know we'll never see him again."

Meanwhile, Mr. Abbott admitted he had shown insufficient sensitivity to the Rudd Stolen Generation when he described the Labor caucus as "a bunch of bastards".

Australia's Climate Commission published a report called 'Angry Summer'. It catalogued the spate of extreme weather events such as floods and bushfires over the previous summer, concluding that they were definitively tied to climate change.

Financial Review, 6 April 2013

MAD AS A MAPLE

In startling news today, a report by a team of highly qualified climate change experts warns Australia is in the grip of a terrifying cycle of climate-induced events they have dubbed the "Angry Autumn". Bizarre changes within nature – due entirely to the ravaging effects of catastrophic climate change upon the continent's fragile ecosystem – are now being felt on a daily basis.

"This is unprecedented in the history of mankind and indeed the history of autumns," a spokesperson for activist online group Get Off! said. "The devastating impact of the Angry Autumn is already upon us and is being felt by thousands of people."

"What we are seeing is the death of trillions of irreplaceable ecosystems – known as leaves – as their life support systems fail," announced Professor Torn Flannel-Shirt from his home in the Blue Mountains. "These fragile ecosystems are now dying before our eyes, withering on the branches – a clear symptom of the ravages of global warming – before turning strange colours and collapsing to the ground."

The professor recently moved to the mountains to escape rising sea levels that have decimated his waterfront property portfolio.

"Thanks to the ABC and taxpayers I've travelled all over, even to the most amazing places like the outback," he said, "but I've never seen nature as angry as this. Some of the leaves have gone bright red, as if Gaia herself was bleeding before our eyes. Others have gone fluoro orange and yellow – the exact same colours as a safety vest! – which is nature's way of screaming 'Rescue me'!"

But the professor held out little chance of any species of *folium arborum* actually surviving the horror autumn. "Once these so-called leaves start changing colour, they're doomed," he said.

He indicated a man sweeping up a pile of rotting leaves by the side of the road. "This scene is being played out everywhere," he said. "Millions of once verdant nature strips are covered with dead and decaying matter. It's a catastrophe."

The professor blames human-induced anthropogenic warming for the extreme weather conditions. "We've had gusts of wind literally powerful enough to strip the trees bare," he said. "And of course the destruction is exacerbated by unprecedented heavy rainfall that pushes the dead leaves to the ground and makes them go all mushy. Plus the air is much colder than normal which is a clear sign that the planet is so traumatised by global warming that it's actually cooling itself down as we head towards what will be a Very Angry Winter indeed."

The professor said there would be an increase in dead crops and loss of food types as the Angry Autumn progresses. "I wouldn't be at all surprised if, for instance, we saw whole fields or orchards dropping their fruit altogether and becoming nothing more than stick-like skeletons dotting a catastrophically barren landscape."

Experts expect future autumns to get angrier and angrier to the point of blind rage or unbridled fury.

The new report comes only weeks after the government Climate Commission's earlier devastating review of recent extreme weather events, entitled the 'Angry Summer'.

According to an explosive documentary on the ABC: "There's never been an Australian summer like it. Bushfires! Floods! Thunderstorms! And, er, other stuff too."

Experts claim that during Australia's horror summer entire species were seen behaving in ways never before seen. One witness claims to have observed a swarm of flies congregating on the back of a man walking down a street in Dubbo. "There were literally millions of them," the clearly-shaken witness said. "All over his back. And he didn't even notice them. It was terrifying."

Another witness recounted how the sand on a beach had become blisteringly hot under her feet. "I felt like I was walking on red hot coals," she said. "This is nature's way of saying she's furious. She's punishing each and every one of us the only way she knows how."

Meanwhile, in London, climate change experts were baffled by a strange phenomenon of small yellow bulbs – known as daffodils – suddenly sprouting up through the snow, in what they claim foreshadows a "Furious Spring."

Margaret Thatcher, the controversial 'Iron Lady' who dominated a generation of British politics and won international acclaim for helping to end the Cold War, died following a stroke on April 8 aged 87.

Politicians and commentators from around the world rushed to heap praise – and scorn – on her legacy in equal measures.

Foreign Minister Bob Carr claimed Baroness Thatcher made an 'unabashedly racist' comment when visiting Australia during her retirement.

Financial Review, 13 April 2013

THE IRONING LADY

Startling claims by Australia's foreign minister, Senator Bob Carp, have ignited debate over the legacy of Britain's first female prime minister, Baroness Thatcher, who died this week.

"I couldn't believe it," Senator Carp declared to an equally amazed Emma Alberquirky on the ABC's flagship propaganda program, *Laborline*.

"We'd invited her over for tea and my wife had cooked a bowl of Maggi Asian Beef Cup 2 Minute Noodles in her honour. Yet this despicable woman hardly ate any of it. I've never seen such a disgraceful display of racist and sexist behaviour in my life."

The senator explained that this in no way diminished his professional respect for the political qualities of the woman he dubbed "The World's Most Unabashed Racist."

The debate has seen politicians of all persuasions keen to put forward their own recollections about the woman known as the most divisive human being to ever walk the planet. "You either loved her or loathed her," said Senator Doug Camer-rouge.

"Personally, I loathed her. This is the woman who put thousands of people out of work, including me. Thanks to her, I lost my job as General Under-Secretary of the Associated Union of Yorkshire Union

Officials Revolutionary Fund for the Equality of Distribution of Union Committee Positions and had to come out to Australia and join the Labor Party instead."

The senator went on to explain that this in no way diminished his professional respect for the political qualities of the woman he dubbed "The World's Most Loathsome Tory".

State Minister David O'Burninhell was equally critical of the woman known to many as "Adolf Hitler". "This woman was a Nazi war criminal who should have died swinging from a lamp post. The way she invaded Poland and put her puppet master Lech 'the Drunkard' Walesa in power and invaded the Soviet Union and stuck her puppet master, Mikhail 'the Traitor' Gorbachev, in charge was a disgrace. On top of which, she used chemical weapons against her own people by sending them down the Yorkshire mines to work in slave labour camps where millions died horrible deaths."

In Britain, opinions of Margaret Thatcher's legacy were hotly debated.

"I, er, yeah, well, I kind of might have bumped into her once. It was a while ago, not really sure what year it was; maybe it was someone else to be honest, now that I think about it. What did you say her name was? Maggie? No doesn't ring a bell. I thought you said my 'ironing lady'. No, sorry, can't help you with that one," said British Prime Minister David Cameron only moments before learning the news of Mrs. Thatcher's death.

He instantly clarified that what he had meant to say was that he was deeply saddened to learn of the passing of the woman he described as undoubtedly "The World's Greatest Human Being".

Leading feminist and author Getoffyer Gear told a panel of women on the ABC's alternative propaganda program, *Q&ALP*, that the Thatcher legacy is in need of re-appraisal. "Basically, she was this batty grey-haired old woman who didn't recognise that she was no longer of any relevance to anybody and spent her days wandering around the place spouting all sorts of rubbish just to get herself onto TV shows like this one."

Ms. Gear explained that although Margaret Thatcher was the planet's major arms dealer, No. 1 war criminal, and founding member of al-Qaeda, this in no way diminished her professional respect for the feminist qualities of the woman she dubbed "Nowhere Near As Important In World History As Me".

Speaking from China, where she is struggling to remember the names of the new mob in charge, Julia Gillard was unequivocal in her praise for the woman who, like herself, was the first female prime minister of her country.

"As a very tough woman, I admire her for being a woman. The difference, of course, is that I've had to fight endless sexism and misogyny, whereas Mrs. Thatcher wasn't even tough enough to win a ballot against that blond-haired idiot, Kevin – I mean, Michael Heseltine."

The prime minister went on to explain that this in no way diminished her professional respect for herself.

Polls showed the Labor Party dropping to an unprecedented 29%, as racing legend Black Caviar is retired by its owners.

Financial Review, 20 April 2013

RED JULIA FINALLY PUT OUT TO PASTURE

The racing world was stunned to learn of the sudden retirement of Australia's greatest thoroughbred racehorse, the sprinter Red Julia.

"We thought long and hard about racing on but believe she has done everything we asked of her and felt it was the right time to put her out to pasture," her trainer, colourful Canberra identity Jock "Moody" McTernan, said on Friday.

"Her owners at the AWU and myself have had a long chat for the past couple of weeks and collectively we decided that although the mare's in great shape, it's time for her to bow out. We got a few more furlongs out of her than we ever thought we were going to get," he admitted. "We thought she would be retired post-Ruddscot."

McTernan was referring to the sprinter's triumphant win in late March when against all odds, she won a convincing victory in a one-horse race. The race became famous after an extraordinary sequence of events that saw the late scratching of local front runner, Kevin Diva, as well as skittish behaviour from false favourite Phar Left, who was found to be carrying not enough weight.

"It was the race that stopped the nation. For good," declared popular racing billionairess Thérèse "Reins" Rein.

Said McTernan: "We were very fortunate to bring Red Julia home that time. It took a very heavy toll on her and I think the owners are to be congratulated on allowing me to race her on and give the Australian public three more opportunities to see her: last week in China, yesterday at COAG and, of course, sitting around with school kids flogging a dead Gonski.

"She's in such great shape at the moment but that's always been the way we wanted her to bow out," McTernan added. "Red Julia's done everything she was asked to do; she's given her owners in the union movement more than they could ever have imagined, even in their wildest dreams. Fair Workhorse Australia. Penalty rates for racing on weekends. Unbridled access to recruit members in the mounting yards. No foreign horses allowed to compete."

The mare's distinctive style of racing, wearing blinkers and refusing to be distracted by external factors, led to her being given the affectionate nickname of "Tin Ears" by her closest supporters. Always the first out of the barriers with half-baked ideas scribbled on the back of a form guide, Red Julia mesmerised the punters with her phenomenal ability to tangle herself up in red tape and her inability to rein in galloping spending. Time after time, hare-brained schemes would coming crashing down before she got anywhere near the finishing line.

Red Julia first attracted the eye of her owners when she successfully ran as a two-year old in the West Australian Slush Fund Stakes – although one of the jockeys was later disqualified after race-fixing allegations from a bagman, which remain unproven. Controversy has often followed the mare, with her strapper once famously promising before a race that "there will be no carbon hoof-prints under a horse that I lead" and then immediately afterwards denying he ever said it.

Punters have long since become used to the feisty filly always winning by a nose.

The sprinter's trainer admitted that they wanted Red Julia to quit while she was still on the bottom of her game.

"We decided 29 was an unbelievable number and her polling figures couldn't go any lower than that, so we decided to call time. Nobody's seen a number like that in nearly 100 years."

Red Julia's racing career took off at Canberra's notorious Poisoned Cup on June 23, 2010, and in less than four years, she has twice been crowned Australian Prime Minister. Despite 27 bad polls on the trot, she retires with a pension roughly equal to $7,953,936 in the bank.

Jockey Craigie "Horrormovie" Emerfield fought back tears as he remembered the early days of riding the champion to victory. "Those were the glory days. There was no stopping her. She couldn't have possibly done any more. But I think she deserves a break now," he reflected. Commentators noted that the public think they, too, need a break.

Speaking from the Gold Coast, home of the Magic Millions, bookmaker Wayne "the Treasurer" Swallivan boasted: "No horse has cost the country more money. It's magic how she makes the millions disappear.

"We've taken a total of $45 million worth of deficits on Red Julia across each budget and the Independents and Greens have won billions of dollars worth of promises backing her," Swallivan said. "She's been phenomenal for bleeding hearts and she's an absolute champion, but I won't be shedding a tear over her retirement.

"No other horse has attracted as many six-figure and seven-figure deficits as what she has," Swallivan maintained.

Red Julia will now begin a lucrative media and book-touring career, with her appearances potentially worth hundreds of dollars.

The Spectator Australia, 27 April 2013

EPIC FAIL

Fresh from the wild scenes of jubilation, champagne-popping and pavements strewn with red and black streamers that accompanied the street parade thrown by Parramatta City Council last Tuesday to celebrate the fact the Western Sydney Wanderers had, er, lost the Grand Final, it's increasingly obvious Australians no longer need to 'win' in order to celebrate.

Any humiliating loss, or indeed any bloody disaster, will suffice. After all, the nation's biggest party — which grows more popular, more extravagant, and more festive every year — is in honour not of some extraordinary, against-all-odds military victory but rather, in memory of an unfortunate wartime manoeuvre that saw thousands of brave young men needlessly perish in order to achieve little of strategic value.

"For god's sake, don't glorify Gallipoli — it was a terrible fiasco, a total failure and best forgotten," said the last surviving Anzac soldier, according to his biographer, who lamented in *the Age* recently that Anzac Day was turning into the Big Day Out, "packed with excitable fans instead of mourners".

But perhaps it is simply that the great Aussie traditions of celebrating the underdog and paying tribute to doomed acts of heroism are what give us the greatest thrill. Or, at least, a good excuse to party.

Either way, here's a list of upcoming celebrations for fun-loving Aussies to jot down in their party planners.

Gonski Week: Future generations of schoolkids will eagerly anticipate this much-needed week-long escape from the harsh rigours of modern schooling, in which gallant battalions of teachers' unions across the land take time out to remember those dark days of struggle and despair when class sizes were above double figures and monthly salaries below.

Highlights include a televised parade of what remains of the army of 4,000 brave DEEWR bureaucrats who soldiered on in the face of terrible adversity (i.e. no money) to implement the Great Gonski Reforms of 2013. Popular celebrations include Street Spelling Bees (in which members of the public are asked if they can spell, um, anything) and Two Up, a hugely popular game only permitted on Gonski Day in which children win a prize every time they can add up two primary numbers. Bonus prizes are awarded if the answer is actually correct.

Surplus Sunday: Originally designed to commemorate the most humiliating and decisive defeat by any Australian government since the war against the Turks, Surplus Sunday is a quiet day of reflection on which the elderly and the infirm recall the Last Great Surplus of 2006-7. (Not to be confused with an event most historians now agree never actually occurred, the four year period of Phony Surplus Promises leading up to 2012-13).

Nonetheless, the public are encouraged to celebrate, rather than feel regret over, an epoch-defining and character-building moment in the history of this great nation: the demise of the so-called "Commitment to Surplus". Free of the artificial and outmoded concept of "living within your means" and by embracing rather than fighting against ever-greater deficits, Australians found themselves able to indulge in higher wages, better jobs, better health and disability care, higher unemployment benefits, greater maternity and paternity leave, larger schoolkids bonuses, more sick leave, fewer working hours, earlier retirement and all the other wondrous benefits of what is now loosely termed our "Euro-lifestyle".

Carbon Hour: To replace the increasingly barbaric and old-fashioned celebration that was previously known as Earth Hour (in which the entire nation celebrated by switching off their lights for one hour every year), Carbon Hour was recently introduced by popular demand.

Only once a year, for up to 60 minutes but no more, members of the public are permitted to switch on all the lights in their home, which is pretty much all they can afford.

Mining Tax Monday: To celebrate one of the greatest failures in Australian history since Malcolm Turnbull tried to overthrow the monarchy, Mining Tax Monday is a uniquely antipodean event that encourages us to laugh at our own ineptitude.

Celebrations are ushered in with the hugely popular "Big Fizzer" fiasco which always attracts tiny crowds; a fireworks display over Sydney Harbour in which none of the fireworks actually explode, much to the delight of the three mining CFO's who drew up the original design of the event. This is typically followed by a "Big Breakfast at Bondi" at which a huge banquet is promised to everyone who attends, but at which no food is ever served up, in honour of the quaint historical practice known as "spreading the boom".

Super Saturday: Once a year, dressed up as old or retired people, ordinary Australians take to the streets clutching their colostomy bags and knock on their neighbour's door and say "not one jot, not one tittle" while asking for money, or food, or medical supplies. This delightful custom harks back to the quirky historical event known as All Budget's Eve in which a succession of Labor politicians pretended that they wouldn't tamper with the superannuation of the nation's retirees but tricked them into handing over the lot anyway via taxes aimed "only at the fabulously wealthy".

Many participants love to dress up as scary figures from the past, by donning large noses and red wigs or by terrifying people by pretending to be a Bruce Springsteen fan in charge of the nation's finances.

Boat Race Weekend: Undeniably the most popular event of Australia's now permanent year-long "Festival of Failure". During this riotous celebration, all-comers from around the world are invited to descend upon any part of the Australian coastline they see fit in any variety of makeshift craft or leaky vessel, each crammed with as many women and children as can possibly fit in before the boat capsizes and they all drown.

Anything goes in this "no rules, no borders" festivity, and participants are rewarded with a large bowl of sugar sitting on a table on the beach, provided they burn their papers first. Alternatively, winners may prefer to choose from a list of other prizes, including a Bravia TV, an iPad or a furnished room adjacent to an all-female university dormitory.

As the Australian government's debt continued to head towards $300 billion, the economic theories of Reinhart and Rogoff came under scrutiny.

Financial Review, 27 April 2013

GILLHART AND SWANOFF

Banks, financiers and economists around the world greeted with unabashed excitement the release today of the long-awaited research paper by two hugely influential Australian academics into the dangers of fiscal "rebalancing" in an era of supposed austerity.

Entitled *This Time It's Over,* the groundbreaking paper is already being hailed as a masterpiece, and its authors, professors Gillhart and Swanoff, are being lauded as two of the greatest financial visionaries of our age.

Their work explodes the doctrine of "mindless prosperity", which the authors describe as the pointless quest by individuals working outside the public sector to generate wealth of their own accord.

Built upon the work of several obscure and hitherto unrecognised economic thinkers of the 20th century such as Germany's Professor Weimar von Wheel-Barrow and the American folk-singer Idaho Dustbowl, the brilliant new theory explains how governments can repay spiraling debts through the simple but effective expedient of borrowing more money.

Speaking as the guest of honour at the Bruce Springsteen Foundation's annual financial think tank in Washington last week, Professor Swanoff lectured an enraptured crowd of European leaders and bureaucrats on the innovative design of his minerals resource rent tax, which was designed to raise as little money as possible. And succeeded spectacularly.

"Furthermore, Professor Gillhart and I have demonstrated through extensive experimentation with a complex working model we call 'the Australian economy' that it is impossible to pay off your debts if you don't actually have any money. So why bother?" he said.

"In any advanced economy, the choice these days is between printing more money on the one hand, or on the other, simply pretending you've printed more money."

In their seminal work, Gillhart and Swanoff explain through the use of pie charts and column graphs how soaring public debt can lead to soaring political confidence by generating soaring promises leading to a soaring sense of entitlement.

Their conclusion is that "growth" – which the pair define as "a debt that keeps on growing" – is the only means to resolve the perennial problem of how to pay for commitments you can't afford.

Nor do they rule out two-way causality. "Sometimes making promises you can't afford allows you to grow your debt, other times growing your debt allows you to make promises you can't afford," they claim. Speaking against the backdrop of a large poster of a sweaty man clutching a guitar with a handkerchief hanging out of his pocket, Professor Swanoff drew attention to the outmoded concept of living within your means.

"They're just four random words, dude. How can you live within a 'means'? What is a 'means'? And why is it 'your' means? Why isn't it somebody else's? 'Living within your means' should mean living by whatever means we want it to mean. That's what 'means' means."

NSW Premier Flabby O'Barrell, a recent convert to the pair's radical teachings, was effusive in his praise.

"After all these years of strict abstinence, I suddenly realised I can eat whatever I want!" he excitedly told reporters as he loosened his belt and undid the top button of his trousers over a large meal at popular Canberra "eat-as-much-as-you-want" eatery Gastro Gonski's.

Critics, such as Australia's opposition leader Tony Luddite – dismissed by Professor Gillhart as an 'economic cretin' – struggled to grasp the intellectual significance of the new theories. To see the enormous influence Gillhart and Swanoff have had on the European debate, it is worth quoting from last year's speech by Olli Outofcash, the European Commission's economic chief, to the Council of Indebted Nations: "Gillhart and Swanoff have coined the '90 per cent rule'," he said. "That is, 90 per cent of what a given government says they own, somebody else actually owns. The Chinese, normally."

Other converts to the groundbreaking theories include many of the world's top finance ministers, foremost among them Australia's highly respected Wayne Goose.

"To cut to the bone – as our political opponents advocate – would drive our economy back into the black and mean people would no longer feel entitled to our, I mean their, entitlements," he said. "Why would we do that?"

Professors Gillhart and Swanoff are rumoured shortly to both be taking an extended sabbatical.

Julia Gillard announced an increase to the Medicare levy to fund the National Disability Insurance Scheme, saying she would put the legislation before parliament if the Opposition agreed to it.

Interviewing Treasurer Wayne Swan on the ABC, Leigh Sales pointed out that the government had the numbers and didn't need the Coalition to legislate the increase.

Financial Review, 4 May 2013

WAYNE SCORES AN OWN GOAL AT POLITICAL FOOTBALL

"Oh my goodness! Wayne! What a mess! You're all grubby and covered in mud. And all these bruises! And a black eye! My goodness! What on earth's been going on?"

"I ... I ... (sob) ... I wasn't allowed to ... to... to play..."

"Don't cry! Come in and sit down! And tell Mummy all about it."

"But they... wouldn't... let... me... (sniff) play."

"It's OK. Don't blub. Here's a tissue. Who said you couldn't play?"

"And Leigh c... c... caught me out, Mum."

"Leigh? But she's just a little girl, Wayne... you're way too clever for her!"

"I was trying to... to play... but Tony... wouldn't... he... (sob)."

"It's OK. Have an Iced VoVo. We'll wipe away all these tears and you can tell me exactly what happened from the beginning. Leigh caught you out but Tony didn't want to play? Is that it?"

"I... I... just... (sob)... wanted... to... play... foot... (sniff)... football... "

"Football? That's nice, Wayne. You just wanted to play football with Leigh and Tony?"

"No... with... (sob) the dis... disabled kids. But... but..."

"You wanted to play football with the disabled kids? Well there's nothing wrong with that, Wayne. What sort of football?"

"P... p... political football."

"Political football? I haven't heard of that one before. Here, blow your nose. How do you play political football, Wayne?"

"(Sniff) You... you... have to do a W... Wedge. I... I... w... wanted to get the dis... disabled kids to... be the Wedge."

"Well, there's nothing wrong with that, is there? If it's all part of the game? It sounds like fun. But I don't understand how you got so roughed up and covered in all this mud! Where on earth were you playing political football? In the park?"

"In... in... in the gutter, Mum."

"In the gutter? No wonder you got so filthy! So... um... how did Leigh catch you out? I always thought she was on your side. Normally she catches Tony out, if I remember correctly. Have another VoVo."

"She... she said... that we didn't need Tony anyway. That we had enough numbers on... on... the floor... of... of the house... and we didn't need him. She said... I was... making it all up... and... just using the disabled kids as a (sniff)... W... W... Wedge."

"Well, surely there's nothing wrong with that, is there? So long as you explained to the disabled kids the rules of the game first. You did, didn't you, Wayne? Were the disabled kids happy to be a Wedge against Tony?"

"We... we... didn't tell them (sniff)."

"Try not to wipe your nose on your sleeve. You didn't tell them? Well, that's not really fair. Still, I'm sure they didn't mind."

"We... we... just wanted to... score points against Tony..."

"Of course you did. Who's we? You and Leigh? Or you and the disabled kids?"

"Ju... Ju... Julia."

"Julia? She was there too? My goodness. It does sound very

complicated. I do hope she didn't tell the disabled kids fibs now, did she? You know what she can be like! Promising them the earth. No doubt she's gone home smelling of roses while you get covered in all the muck as per usual."

"It… it… was all… (sniff)… it was all mister… mister… Mac… Mac… Turner's idea."

"Him again? That Scottish so-and-so! Why does that not surprise me? Put him and Julia together and all hell breaks loose. Remember that punch-up with Tony and the indigenous kids on Australia Day last year? Those two were in it up to their eyeballs, I'm certain of it."

"L… L… Leigh was really… (sniff)… mean to me, Mum… on TV… in front of the whole world… I thought she… was… one of us…"

"Try not to worry about it. Have another cup of cordial and let me get this straight. You and Julia wanted the disabled kids to play a Wedge – even though you didn't tell them so – in a game of political football you were playing in the gutter to score points against Tony but Tony refused to play along and instead you got caught out by Leigh who knew precisely what you were up to? Is that what happened, Wayne?"

"(Sniff) … yes."

"Well, look, let's just forget all about it. It'll all work out in the end and the disabled kids will be happy and you and Tony can find some other grubby games to play. Anyway, you should be concentrating on your homework. Only five more weeks 'til the end of term and then we're going away on a very, very long holiday."

"(Sniff)… OK, thanks, Mum."

"But before then you've got a very big maths assignment due in next week! And let's face it, Wayne, pluses and minuses have never been your strong point."

The Spectator Australia editorial, 11 May 2013

CLIMATE CHANGE WAGS OFF

"As a Prime Minister, she makes a very good education minister" was one of the more amusing – and accurate – tweets during Julia Gillard's lengthy "High School Showdown" on *Q&A* recently. Almost certainly Ms. Gillard would have made a more effective and successful schoolteacher than she has a Prime Minister. There was much to admire about the way she communicated with the kids; prepared to admit to her own moments of self-doubt, and offering inspiration and encouragement. Her obvious rapport and ability to get on the same wavelength as some of her more unusual interlocutors was impressive.

Needless to say, "sexism" got a good run, morphing into rape culture, violence against women, "sauntering down the road in the middle of the night" and other topics. Slightly disingenuously, Ms. Gillard allowed the assertion to go unchallenged that "women (in politics) are faced with sexism every day in every way." Really?

Tellingly, her famed bête noire Tony Abbott, once the convenient excuse for every ill in the world, didn't rate a single mention. Even more noticeable by its absence was the one topic that until recently was guaranteed to fire up any idealistic school student: the "greatest moral challenge of our time," climate change. After all the pain of the carbon tax, soaring energy bills, jobs lost or pushed overseas, floor prices abandoned, tax cuts cancelled, global gabfests collapsed and economic activity stymied in the name of saving the planet for future generations, how disappointing that those future generations themselves seem to have lost all interest in what was so recently a matter of such vital national importance.

Tony Abbott and Eric Abetz launched their long-awaited Industrial Relations policy, a two-term plan designed to head off a scare campaign by Labor and the unions that a Coalition government would reintroduce elements of Work Choices.

Financial Review, 12 May 2013

DEAD WORKCHOICES SKETCH

This week opposition leader Tony Abbott unveiled his tough new industrial relations policy – designed to curb the power of corrupt union bosses – in a highly anticipated document, entitled *It's OK Fellas, It's Business As Usual.*

The Coalition's workplace relations plan contains a plethora of aggressive measures that aim to "swing the pendulum" back to exactly where it is at the moment.

"Make no mistake, I mean every word of what I say," declared a fiery Mr. Abbott, as he defiantly threw down the gauntlet and declared he would not rest until the entire union movement had woken up to the fact that nothing whatsoever would change.

"The only people with anything to worry about from this policy are dodgy members of the Labor movement, in particular those known as the 'government'."

Mr. Abbott vowed to toughen up the right of entry laws, by which he meant he was determined to guarantee the Coalition the right of entry to parliament via the little door marked "Govt" for the next six years at the very least.

Mr. Abbott is adamant that his industrial relations policy will protect the pay and conditions of nearly every single member of the Coalition.

"We want to maximise the opportunities to get ourselves elected as often as we can," Mr. Abbott told a packed news conference. "It is my firm and unequivocal commitment that I intend to fight to the last breath in my body to overhaul and improve the Fair Work Act so it stays exactly as it is now."

Mr. Abbott vowed that he was determined to protect unfair dismissal laws, declaring that the last thing on earth he wanted was for Australians to dismiss him and his government, unfairly or otherwise.

Mr. Abbott pointed out that "under our plan, no Australian worker will be worse off unless of course they are foolish enough to run a business or worse still actually own one."

"Make no mistake. Work Choices is dead, buried, cremated, no longer of this earth, shaking off the mortal coil, departed to the heavenly choir and six feet under," said Mr. Abbott, parroting his own popular "Dead Work Choices" YouTube sketch.

Mr. Abbott was backed by his formidable IR spokesman, fellow comedian Eric Idle, who sported a bright yellow tie and a silly grin as he sang his signature theme song: 'Every Perk is Sacred. Nudge nudge wink wink.'

"We've been very careful in designing this policy to ensure there's nothing in here that could actually be construed as being in any way like what it is we really want to do. Say no more! Say no more!" he joked, to loud applause from the audience.

Mr. Abbott explained he was one of the few cabinet ministers who had argued against the hated Work Choices reforms of the Howard government. "Nup, nup, nup, nup, nothing whatsoever to do with me," he maintained. Pressed for further details, he shook his head ruefully. "As I recall, it was all because of this funny little bloke in a tracksuit with bushy eyebrows," he sighed, before holding up a copy of his latest book to the cameras, a recently revised version of his autobiography, entitled *Union Days, the Happiest Time of My Life.*

Mr. Abbott claims to have been a member of the Wall-punchers and Speedo Packers Union when he worked as a journalist in the 1980's.

"We were always striking. Walls, mostly," he recalled fondly.

"I understand unions, I respect well-run unions. I understand and respect unionists. But I also understand and respect the 87 per cent of MPs in my party who will turf me out if I even mutter the words work and choices in the same sentence," he said.

The policy was immediately attacked by a defiant Bill Shortensweet, who declared it "should send a shiver up the spine of every member of the Labor Party who thought all we had to do was rerun the old Work Choices ads and Tony would be cactus."

Interviewed on the ABC's late night news, a clearly distraught Mr. Shortfuse angrily defended the views of the ACTU president: "I agree 100 per cent with whatever she says, even though I have absolutely no idea what it is she said."

The Greens immediately jumped on the announcement, angrily describing Mr. Abbott as "a wolf in sheep's clothing."

"If there's one thing we won't stand for in the Greens, it's when politicians say one thing just before an election and then do the complete opposite as soon as we tell them to straight afterwards," said fiery Greens MP Adam Ant.

Mr. Ant was adamant that the Greens would use their numbers in parliament to stop any attempt by Mr. Abbott to do anything whatsoever.

Baz Luhrmann premiered 'The Great Gatsby' at Cannes.
Treasurer Wayne Swan delivered his sixth and final budget, confirming the country would remain in deficit for many years to come.

Financial Review, 15 May 2013

THE GREAT GONSKI

Undaunted by bad reviews and a massively overblown budget, Australia's most flamboyant movie director, Baz Swansong, last night premiered his long-awaited masterpiece *The Great Gonski.*

Crowds of delighted fans lined the red carpet on the opening night of the glittering Festival de Cannes-berra for what critics are dubbing the most overblown extravaganza yet from this highly talented master of illusion.

Filmed to the thumping beat of a Bruce Springsteen soundtrack, it was shot in 3-D, as opposed to AAA. It's best viewed wearing rose-tinted glasses.

Critics were quick to pour scorn on the laughable dialogue and risibly constructed plot, which takes place over the next 10 years. "While certainly ambitious – and every bit as visually dazzling as one might expect – Baz Swansong's *The Great Gonski* emphasises visual splendour and flights of pure fantasy at the expense of its source material's bottom line."

The film deals with lies, broken promises and endless deception set against a backdrop of the three parallel worlds of the Roaring 2013's: Old Money, New Money and No Money. The latter, mainly.

In the original novel, regarded by many as a flawed classic, the mysterious Jay Gonski tries to seduce the flame-haired girl from the wrong side of the tracks, the beguiling Julia, with his promise of a better education for all. But when the narrator finds out that Gonski has lied about his wealth, and has in fact stolen about $2.8 billion from his own university, the plot takes a turn for the worse. When one character reveals that Gonski is having an affair with a mistress known only as "the voter" who lives in the "valley of ashes", a wasteland located between West Egg and Rooty Hill, Julia insists that she has to go and visit. Sadly, she doesn't survive the encounter.

The film has been plagued with financial problems from the outset. Swansong was forced to mortgage the entire nation's future in order to complete the final few scenes. The first trailer, released almost exactly a year ago, hinted at a very different ending from the one released tonight. In the original script, the opening scenes feature a dazzling, spectacular sequence entitled "return to surplus" which was cut for budgetary reasons. "It's such a shame," admitted one critic, "because now none of the movie really adds up."

A recurring visual motif throughout the film is the giant billboard on an anonymous roundabout in Canberra, featuring the Eyes of J. B. Hockey, who gazes down in despair at the disaster he sees unraveling before him but can do nothing to prevent.

The Great Gonski also explores themes of national disability, profligacy, resistance to climate change, social welfare upheaval and financial excess, creating a portrait of the Age of Entitlement that has been described as a cautionary tale regarding voting for Labor.

Meanwhile, there were calls today for a resumption of the F. Scott Fitzgerald inquiry into hopelessly incompetent politicians.

Researchers successfully converted human skin cells into embryonic stem cells – via a technique called nuclear transfer.

Tony Abbott's 'Budget Reply Speech' was widely praised, including by former Treasurer Peter Costello, who called it 'the best in decades'.

Financial Review, 18 May 2013

BUSHY EYEBROW STEM CELLS

Australian researchers have reported an extraordinary breakthrough in stem cell research, describing how they have cloned a future national leader from human bushy eyebrow cells alone.

The technique involves transplanting a retired political leader's DNA into a budget reply speech that has been stripped of monetary material, a variation of a method called somatic cell prime ministerial transfer.

"We demonstrated our ability to convert a relentlessly negative opposition leader into an inspirational and visionary leader of the future offering hope, reward and opportunity," said a leading political scientist. "The results have been outstanding. From one bushy eyebrow cell extracted from the appropriate donor we can reproduce several different cell types, including nerve cells and ticker cells."

"The study has significant implications for potentially treating a range of budgetary diseases," said the head of the Neurodegeneration Research Program at the Canberra Institute of Medical Research.

"Our finding offers new ways of generating poll results for patients with damaged fists and completely eradicates any trace of diseases such as sexism and misogyny," said the study leader. "Bushy eyebrow stem cells can replace those damaged issues and alleviate political suffering for the entire front bench."

Experts claim cloning bushy eyebrows could even help restore damaged spines without actually having to cut to the bone.

The technique, known as Bennelong cloning, is ethically controversial because in order to guarantee maximum efficacy and positive results it involves the production, and subsequent destruction, of an aborted budget speech, also known as a "swan song".

"We were extremely lucky," said one scientist. "It was a unique opportunity that presented itself. We had a Treasurer dying on his feet and a potential national leader waiting in the wings. We grabbed the moment and haven't looked back."

The chairman of stem cell sciences at the University of Canberra said this new method also offered a unique approach to preventing inherited deficit diseases, which cause debilitating degeneration in the brain and heart of affected individuals. "We've seen patients with such distorted frontal political lobes that they can't even perform the most basic arithmetic operations such as recognising the difference between plus and minus," said one startled scientist. "Obviously, there's no hope for those experiments and we plan to abort the lot of them in about four months' time."

In 2007 scientists developed a method to reprogram normal bushy eyebrow cells into induced pluripotent blond-haired stem cells, a process that won its inventors the 2007 federal election.

In that instance, to obtain stem cells from a human bushy eyebrow, the team transferred the votes of several key marginal electorates into a human egg cell whose political nucleus had been entirely removed and replaced with nothing whatsoever.

The cells grew into early-stage eyebrows, or conservo-cysts, that gave rise to the idea that you could clone a prime minister into a younger, friendlier, gentler, kinder, more telegenic version without doing any long term damage to border protection or the economy.

"We were fully aware that it was a procedure that carried both inherent risks and its own socio-ethical concerns," a scientist said. That particular experiment, alas, ended in complete disaster, with Klone '07 increasingly exhibiting erratic characteristics of extreme dysfunction verging on psychopathy, before abruptly expiring on the night of 23 June 2010. Subsequent attempts to revive the experiment all failed.

Other teams have produced cloned human bushy eyebrows, but have failed to obtain any popular support from them.

In 2010 a South Yarra research team of faceless scientists led by Paul Howzat published claims they had overcome the donor problem by using high quality eyebrows, derived from a silver budgie, grown in a solution containing pure alcohol, and transplanted them into a female body.

However, their experiment was later found to be built on fake polling data. Bill Shortang, an associate professor at the West Australian University of Slush Funds, said the method relied on a strong woman being willing to undergo radical hair and clothing makeovers in order to make her appear "real."

"The only resemblance between the silver budgie donor and the 'real' fake clone was that they both tended to keep bursting into tears."

As the Gillard government continued to implode, carmaker Ford announced they would cease to manufacture in Australia, with the loss of hundreds of jobs, despite the millions in subsidies they had received.
A bill to legalise euthanasia failed in the NSW parliament.

Financial Review, 25 May 2013

VICTORIAN CABINET-MAKER TOPPLES AFTER LEANING TOO FAR TO THE LEFT

Victorian cabinet-maker FRORD on Thursday announced it would cease all local manufacturing and production of federal cabinets and their component parts from September 14 onwards.

For decades, the Victorian arm of FRORD has been responsible for churning out high-spending, left-wing, union-based federal cabinets in a variety of popular styles and shades of red, pink and green, whilst being entirely beholden to the unions. But a spokesperson last night announced that "we can't go on. Quite simply, the public is no longer buying it."

"It's a combination of factors. With debts of around $300 billion and the fact that we can't seem to sell anything any more to the public, it's time to call it quits."

Successive Australian governments have poured literally billions of taxpayers' dollars into trying to keep Victorian-based federal cabinets and their union masters viable, but most of the money has disappeared into what critics have labeled a "spiraling black hole".

Said an expert: "The problem with Victorian-manufactured cabinets is they are entirely dominated by union hacks, union lawyers, union officials and invariably lean heavily towards the left. No matter how much money is spent propping them up, they always topple over in the end."

Key components in the manufacturing of Victorian cabinets are also expected to be ditched in mid-September, having long outlived any reasonable purpose. These are rumoured to include the Combet, which is made entirely of carbon and is disintegrating rapidly, the Conroy, a piece of ludicrously expensive optical technology that will be obsolete before it is even operational, and the unreliable Short One, known for repeatedly blowing a fuse.

Earlier this year, production of the incredibly durable and long-lasting Crean component was abruptly discontinued when it started malfunctioning and performing erratically, whilst the equally pragmatic Ferguson bit part had to be retired early.

The latest cabinet model, designed especially to appeal to women, trade unions and inner-city elites, has been a spectacular flop, with experts pointing to the heavy weight of union-based scandal that is inherent in the design and was manufactured out of company slush funds in the early 1990's. This has made it extremely heavy in the rear end and means certain members of the cabinet keep getting dragged back into their murky past.

Others pointed to the ugly compromises the cabinet makers decided to make to the basic design in 2010 in order to stay in business. "They painted themselves bright green but that was a huge mistake," claimed one dissatisfied customer. Others complain the latest federal cabinet has no idea which way it faces or where it actually stands on anything.

Recently, the manufacturer has valiantly tried to revive the popularity of the Ford Fairworkact, Victoria's most popular model for many years, but businesses that have bought into the model have found their productivity keeps stalling and they end up going backwards very fast.

Nonetheless, a spokesperson insisted that the company would remain viable in Australia for many years despite the imminent redundancies, with future programs such as the NBN, the NDIS, Gonski and so on continuing to be marketed under the slogan "Remember, it's still a Frord".

Despite it's amazing pulling-power, the manufacturers have so far avoided the temptation to re-issue the briefly popular but extraordinarily dysfunctional 2007 Queensland model.

The head of Australia's only other major federal cabinet maker, HOLD-ON (I'm A Comin'), Mr. Tony Abbott, announced he fully intends to be manufacturing cabinets in Victoria, NSW, Western Australia, Queensland and the rest of the country for decades to come.

"Basically, I intend to replicate our most famous model, the Statesman."

Meanwhile, in NSW, supporters of a bill to legalise the controversial procedure known as "pollie-nasia" vowed to carry on the fight, even thought their bill failed to pass parliament this week.

Proponents of the bill believe it is time society recognised that politicians whose careers are in their final, terminal stages should be allowed to "move on" without further suffering. "For too long, we have witnessed pollies who are clearly on their last legs lingering on and on. Not only is this incredibly painful for them, it's even more painful for us."

Advocates of the bill believe that politicians facing certain annihilation at the ballot box should be able to quietly slip away without facing the interminable suffering of another four months of electioneering.

"It's all so pointless. They know they're goners. There's nothing anyone can do to avoid the inevitable outcome. Why prolong the agony a day longer than is strictly necessary?"

TV and radio personality Eddie McGuire was forced to apologise after a bizarre on-air joke linking a popular AFL star to the opening of the musical King Kong. Two days earlier, a 13 year old girl had called the player an 'ape.'

Financial Review, 1 June 2013

KING KONG APOLOGISES FOR AFL RAMPAGE

The city of Melbourne was in complete shock on Friday, as one of the town's biggest stars broke down and offered a tearful apology live on national TV.

"I…I…don't know what…what I was thinking…it…it all came out wrong…" sobbed a tearful King Kong, blubbing into his handkerchief. "I was…kind of zoned out…I guess…I just…completely lost it…"

Mr. Kong was referring to a recent episode in which he went on an early morning rampage on top of the towering Triple-M radio station building, pulling airplanes out of the sky and tossing one-liners and unfunny gags up and down the street like kids' toys.

"I…I just kind of snapped. When they compared me to an AFL player…well, that was the final straw," said Mr. Kong, a well-known and much-loved Hollywood movie star. "I've been called all sorts of things in my life. A 'gorilla'. An 'overgrown chimpanzee with anger-management issues'. But an 'AFL star'? That was the final insult. It's hard to be portrayed as the opposite of what you are, you know. Besides which, I'm NRL through and through. Everybody knows Aussie Rules players are all pansies and fairies."

Mr. Kong fought back tears as he attempted to justify his devastating rampage, which brought Melbourne's central business district to a grinding halt when the star smashed his way through several layers of poor taste and political correctness with his bare fists as crowds of terrified theatre-goers ran for cover. Police were forced to cordon off the entire downtown district while Mr. Kong ran up the side of a building and hurled himself headlong into a major PR disaster.

"I know I made that blue yesterday and I've explained the whole situation and all the rest of it, but it's, you know, it's really hard. I was trying to be witty and think of a clever joke. That's what they pay me for. But it's a jungle out there in radio land.

"I was once the biggest act in town," Mr. Kong continued, fighting back the tears. "Once I had my own blockbuster show called *Who Wants To Be A Silverback?* The kids were all terrified of me. Then . . . it all started to go horribly wrong. I got the sack from the TV network even though I was running it. Then I made some stupid gaffe about 'chickpea-eating falafel monkeys' so they kicked me out of western Sydney. Next thing you know, they've turned me into a giant puppet and stuck me in the hot seat in this song and dance routine at the Regent. Like I'm some pathetic circus act. But then to insult me by calling me an 'AFL mid-fielder'? That brought it all back. The humiliation. The bullying when I was growing up. 'Hey, you AFL-er!' the Sydney kids would yell at me, 'show us yer ballet moves'. Now all my mates think I'm an absolute laughing-stock."

Mr. Kong, who began his meteoric rise to fame playing scrum-half in a popular Sydney rugby team, has always denied reports that his unique appearance and superhuman strength is in any way connected with his daily diet of anti-ageing medicine and nutritional supplements.

As stunned Melbourne residents surveyed the scenes of devastation, Mr. Kong was asked what he intended to do to repair the extensive damage.

"It's absolutely abhorrent, but I'm not going to sit here today and cry into my cornflakes. I've got the best image consultants and PR people working out how they can clean up this awful mess.

"I was probably a bit too tired yesterday. I'm tired this morning as well. I'm probably more tired today, to be honest, and I'll be just as tired tomorrow," he said.

Mr. Kong admitted people were also getting pretty tired of him.

But Mr. Kong's co-star, Fade Wray, offered her full support to the embattled primate: "I love him. I've always loved him. Whatever happens, we can't let this one incident spoil the entire opening weekend," she said, wiping away the tears.

In other news, a 51-year-old red-haired girl was ejected from the stands during a violent and aggressive sporting match in Canberra for yelling abuse at a player.

The girl, identified only as Julia, apparently screamed out "Misogynist!" at the top of her voice halfway through the match. "I was just sitting there doing nothing except making snide comments under my breath about people dying of shame when all of a sudden this crazed woman leaps to her feet and starts shrieking these terrible insults at me in this hysterical nasal twang. It was the worst day of my life," said a mortified Mr. Abbott.

Julia was promptly escorted from the grounds by a group of faceless men.

Fresh opinion polls saw Julia Gillard and Labor plunge in popularity, leading many commentators – including Bill Shorten – to predict a 'landslide' against the government at the forthcoming election.

Kevin Rudd continued to dominate speculation of a leadership change.

The roll-out of the National Broadband Network was interrupted by asbestos, and boat people continued arriving at over 100 a day. Many deaths at sea occurred.

Financial Review, 8 June 2013

THE LAST 100 DAYS

The remarkable recovery of the Gillard government's fortunes began in the last 100 days of office, in a political phenomenon that has since become known as the "Julia Curve". In recalling the most amazing turnaround in modern political history, it is difficult to remember just how dire things were for Australia's first female Prime Minister only three months out from the election that was to see her stunningly vindicated and returned triumphant to the Lodge in a landslide win on September 14, 2013.

Often compared to an Olympic marathon runner who saves all their energy for the last 100 metres, Julia Gillard's final dash to the finish line began in the most unpredictable fashion.

During a school visit in mid-June, a student threw a sandwich at the beleaguered Prime Minister. To the astonishment of all, she caught it with one hand. And much to everyone's delight, she ate it.

Later that day, a rogue pair of Telstra sub-contractors "digging a quickie" for the national broadband network in the asbestos-strewn streets of Penrith struck, much to their surprise, an unlikely substance. Gold. Within days, rich new seams of gold, platinum and diamonds were being dug up daily in Telstra pits the length and breadth of the country, sparking what has since been called the Second Great Australian Gold Rush. Almost overnight, public and private debt was eradicated, the national accounts flourished and the IMF declared Australia to be the wealthiest nation on earth, awarding the country an unprecedented AAAAA rating. To wide applause, a delighted Treasurer Wayne Swan announced "surpluses to infinity and beyond" and promised no Australian need ever pay tax again. Or ever work again.

Cheques for $9 million were swiftly sent to every citizen, with a multi-million dollar government advertising campaign explaining: "It's Yours. Because You're Worth It."

The Brisbane airport lounge where former prime minister Kevin Rudd and senator Stephen Conroy had planned the visionary NBN was declared a site of world heritage value at a ceremony in which Julia Gillard unveiled a gold statue of the two men huddled over the back of an envelope. By popular demand, the nation's flag was redesigned, replacing the union jack with a graphic representation of an envelope.

Hurriedly calling a doorstop interview, Kevin Rudd burst into tears and sobbed his heart out as he thanked Julia Gillard for not only the wisdom of recognising he was a dysfunctional psychopath, but also for her exemplary leadership.

In order to satisfy the sudden demand for people to drive buses, sweep streets, mow lawns and pick up kids from school while their parents galavanted around Las Vegas and Europe, Australians from all walks of life demanded that immigrants, refugees and asylum-seekers be given 457 visas as quickly as possible to fill the demand for menial jobs, by which they meant those involving any work.

A contrite Tony Abbott, sensing the sudden shift in the public's mood, belatedly introduced a new slogan for his flagging election campaign, BRING ON THE BOATS! Alas, it proved too little too late.

In late July, CSIRO scientists working on ways to safely dispose of asbestos made an accidental but startling discovery, when a chemical compound they were analysing mysteriously came into contact with a large double-soy skim latte. To their astonishment, the solution dissolved asbestos fibres into harmless water vapour.

Within days, the formula was being lauded as a miracle cure for not only mesothelioma, but all forms of aggressive cancer. Gillard and the CSIRO were promptly shortlisted for a Nobel Prize.

In early August, police investigating the detention of an Egyptian man living behind a swimming pool fence in the Adelaide hills were incredulous to discover a laptop containing the personal details of all al-Qaeda operatives throughout the world. Within a few weeks, the terrorist organisation was eradicated and Australia and her Prime Minister were formally thanked in a lavish ceremony at the Great Hall of the United Nations for their contribution to world peace.

In early September, whilst spring-cleaning his shed in the grounds of the Lodge, Mr. Tim Mathieson stumbled across a box of old unopened documents from the 1930's underneath a discarded pile of Kevin Rudd speeches. His curiosity piqued, the nation's "first bloke" quickly realised it was the set of plans for a revolutionary combustion engine that ran purely on air and water yet was capable of generating unlimited kilojoules of energy.

Dubbed the "Tim Engine", within weeks Ford had re-opened all its plants and the discovery was being lauded as a global solution to climate…

"Wake up, honey. You spilled your latte all over the pillow. Mr. McTernan's here with your daily briefing notes. I'll mop up."

Julia Gillard made a speech to a newly-formed 'Women for Gillard' group criticizing men in blue ties and claiming abortion was back on the political agenda.

A crude joke menu supposedly from a Liberal National Party fundraiser three months earlier appeared on twitter, making fun of various members of the cabinet, including a reference to Julia Gillard and a recipe for quail.

Rumours of an imminent return to Kevin Rudd reached fever pitch.

Financial Review, 15 June 2013

NOT ONE TO QUAIL, I'VE A MENU OF MY OWN …

As the Prime Minister of this country, I am often asked: "What is the best way to serve up quail?"

My response is always the same: There are many exciting and unusual ways to put quail on the menu, and they all make a great way of distracting your guests from talking about any awkward topics.

Below is a list of my favourites:

Afghan Quail: This is a highly-prized dish in many remote parts of the Middle East. Although it is very expensive – each dish can cost around $10,000 – I have made sure it is as hassle-free and easy to implement as possible. First, the quail must be imported into this country via aeroplane to Indonesia and then by boat to any of our northern shores.

Note: Dispose of any paper wrapped around the quail and it's important to put sugar on the table or some other suitable sweetener. (Avoid drowning the quail in salty brine as this can lead to unpleasant and impertinent questions from pesky reporters, which you must not answer under any circumstances).

Asbestos Quail: A national dish that deserves to be rolled out as slowly as possible to maximise the flavour. The best way to cook the quail is in a deep hole dug up in the pavement or the front yard. If you're planning an extra large banquet, dig lots of them. My friend Stephen always recommends lighting a bonfire in the hole using lots of hundred dollar bills and seasoning with dieldrin and asbestos powder (blue is best but white or brown will do). It's best to remove the asbestos entirely before you serve, which is a thoroughly unpleasant job, so first cover yourself completely by employing a dodgy subcontractor.

Pink Quail and Bats: When I was doing my apprenticeship as sous-chef to Mr. Rudd, this was one of his most spectacular failures. Although by no means his only one. To get the bats nice and pink they need to be hung first (any old roof space will do) and then exposed to a high flame as rapidly as possible. The beauty of this dish is that it requires no preparation whatsoever, indeed, the less the better. The results are devastating.

Quail a la Gonski: An exotic dish, so don't be surprised if it ends up costing way more than you anticipated. Originally dreamt up by (but since disowned by!) the eccentric and flamboyant Chef Gonski as a way to give everybody as much as they could ever want to eat – and even more besides!

In preparation, it's important to first cut and divide the public schools from the rest, then stuff the universities completely.

Roast the Catholic and independent schools, dispose of their charred remains. Although popular in parts of NSW, for most people the dish is impossible to swallow due to its lack of details.

Quail a la McTourniquet: Not to be confused with haggis, this stomach-churning dish is not for the faint-hearted. Indeed, you must be prepared to get down and dirty and kill the bird with your own bare hands, baste it thoroughly in misogyny, rip out its integrity, squeeze the life out of it and dismember it as thoroughly as you can.

Spin it in a spinner for as long as possible or until it no longer knows who it is or what it stands for. Often referred to as an 'abortion', this vomit-inducing dish is best served wrapped tightly in a blue tie.

Quail in Shorten-ing: A quick and easy dish to prepare, this is a great stand-by when all else fails. Quail in Shorten-ing is a very malleable dish, so it will become whatever recipe you say it is going to be even if it doesn't know what that recipe is. The Shorten-ing can be melted or softened into a suitable centre-left mixture. Since it is predominantly unionised fat, it usually produces the most tender and crumbly results in a Labor leader, but it does not have the unique flavour of Gillard, nor can it impart the flakiness that Rudd can give to, for instance, a doorstop interview. Make sure you place the Quail in Shorten-ing suitably close to the source of power.

Carbon-free Quail: The ideal way to cook this healthy dish is by wind-blown fan or simply by leaving it out in the sun. Even though the meat remains completely raw, the dish will give you a warm inner glow. Just don't look at the bill!

Beijing Quail: (or 'Mandarin goose' as it is sometimes known). The most dysfunctional dish that has ever been served in this great nation of ours. Entirely indigestible, it keeps coming back up every time you think you've finally got rid of it. Popular with psychopaths.

Quail stuffed with Swan: Swan is the perfect stuffing for virtually any dish. No matter how much of it you think you are eating, you're still starving at the end of the meal.

The stand-off between Kevin Rudd and Julia Gillard continued, with her refusing to resign and him refusing to challenge. Every day there was more speculation about who was in whose camp and who wasn't. ACTU boss Paul Howes came out in support of Gillard.

James Gandolfini, the actor who played Tony Soprano in the hit TV series The Sopranos, died unexpectedly in Italy.

Financial Review, 22 June 2013

THE RUDDRANOS

Tributes continued to pour in throughout Friday for the man described as "the greatest actor of his generation" after his unexpected demise at the tender age of 55.

Famous for his role as a powerful, conniving, ruthless Labor Party boss, the actor Kevin Ruddolfino struggled throughout his career to separate himself in the public's mind from his fictional counterpart; the dysfunctional earwax-munching psychopath he played for over a decade in Australia's longest running soap opera *The Ruddranos*.

Indeed, to many, the actor and the character were one and the same person.

With its distinctive theme music and opening credits – in which Kevin Ruddrano can be seen endlessly driving in circles, carefully navigating Canberra's famous roundabouts, churches, pizza bars and strip-clubs until he arrives at his destination, the Lodge – *the Ruddranos'* plot line and major dramatic themes captivated an entire generation of adoring political fans.

A staple of contemporary Australian popular culture, the series has been the subject of much critical analysis, controversy, and parody, and has spawned a video game ('Angry Kevs') a high-charting soundtrack album ('Unhinged Melody') and a large amount of assorted merchandise (including a cookbook of authentic Sicilian earwax recipes.)

Several members of the show's cast and crew, who were previously largely unknown to the public, have since seen their careers spectacularly fail.

"Everybody knew who he was. He couldn't even go for a walk to the local shopping mall in downtown Fairfield without being mobbed," said his fellow co-star Chris Bowensanti, who played the part of Ruddrano's doomed protégée "Christopher", who kept shooting himself in the foot during the notorious "people-smuggling" episode.

A key pivotal part of the series was the "night of the long knives," when Kevin Ruddrano was betrayed by the tough guys, including union mobsters Paulie and Joey.

"We buried him way back in 2010, and we're looking forward to burying him again next week," Paulie said on Friday night.

A common theme in the series was the relentless quest for power by Ruddrano – regardless of the cost to those who pledged their loyalty to him. A key part was the psychological relationship between the protagonist and his psychiatrist, played by the Australian public.

"There was this amazing underlying tension between what Kevin said he was going to do and what he actually did," said one die-hard fan. "In one incredible scene Kevin returned triumphantly to the Lodge, after murdering all his enemies in caucus and disemboweling them one-by-one with his bare hands. But, of course, it turned out to be just another figment of his imagination; a forlorn dream in the never-ending cycle of revenge."

"Basically, the plot never changed," said renowned TV critic Bazza "Sundance Kid" Cassidy. "In every episode I'd predict Kevin would make a dramatic comeback the next week, but of course he never did."

Central to the byzantine plottings, schemings, violence and torrid machinations of Canberra's longest-running soap opera was the tense stand-off between Kevin Ruddrano and his long-suffering, redhead wife Carmulia.

"At the beginning, they were quite close, but the hatred grew to the point where they couldn't even be in the same room together."

The series premiered on premium cable network HGO (Howard Government's Opposition) on 4 December 2006 and ended its original run on 23 June 2010. Since then, it has been on endless replay across most free-to-air networks.

"When Carmulia finally knifed Kevin in the back and took over running the 'waste management' firm, we had to transform her in the public's mind from this sweet, popular, docile redhead into a lying, manipulative, egotistical tyrant suffering from a severe case of tin-ear," said the program's executive producer, Jonny McTarantino.

"Many viewers struggled to understand her distinctive nasal twang, but, by introducing themes of sexism and class warfare, I managed to make her the single most divisive character on TV. Which, of course, allowed us to make Kevin Ruddrano look like the good guy again. That way the show could just go on and on – and we never had to resolve it."

Kevin Ruddolfino is rumoured to have suffered a fatal heart attack in what those close to him have denied was brought on by a massive loss of ticker. "Basically, he wasn't even sure he wanted to keep playing Kevin Ruddrano any more. The series is nearly at an end and the last thing he would have wanted was to spend the twilight of his career hanging around in discount stores and remainder bins."

On Wednesday 26 June, following rumours of a petition demanding a leadership spill, Julia Gillard called a ballot for 7 pm that evening. At 6.30, Bill Shorten announced he had switched his support to Kevin Rudd. Three years and three days after his own knifing, and vowing there would be 'no paybacks, no retribution', Kevin Rudd returned to the Labor leadership by a vote of 57 – 45.

He was sworn in the next day as Prime Minister. A third of the cabinet resigned and/or announced they were leaving politics altogether.

Financial Review, 29 June 2013.

THE RUDD RECONCILIATION

Kevin Rudd has offered a broad apology to all single, female, childless redheads and the Misogyny Generation for their "profound grief, suffering and loss" in a carefully worded statement that was greeted by a standing ovation of elated media commentators on Friday.

Thousands of unwed out-of-work atheists and Scottish spin doctors gathered in Canberra to watch the historic apology, which was televised around the nation and shown at special outdoor settings in remote Welsh villages, Rooty Hill focus groups and at shocked gatherings of union bagmen.

Prime Minister Rudd used the word "Abbott" 33 times in his 360-word statement. He said there came a time in history when people such as himself had to reconcile their unhappy circumstances with their unbelievably good poll ratings.

A clearly humbled Mr. Rudd, wearing a traditional blue tie and clutching the trashed and tattered remnants of a knitted kangaroo in his hands, fought to control his complete lack of emotions. "We come together today to deal with an ugly chapter in our nation's history. Australia has reached such a time and that is why the nation's press, particularly the ones I regularly leak party political information to, is today here assembled," he said. "To deal with this unfinished business of mine, whereby I was knifed in the back by some feminist union hack lawyer with a degree in corporate slush funds.

"To remove a blot lodged like a piece of wax in the nation's ear-hole and in the true spirit of revenge to open a new chapter in the history of this great career that I have got planned for myself.

"To the 45 Gillard voters, I say the following: As Prime Minister of Australia, I am back where I belong. And I offer you the chance to make this heartfelt apology to me without any sense of dire retribution whatsoever.

"Please repeat after me: 'We apologise unreservedly for the dreadful hurt, the pain and the grievous humiliation that the back-stabbing actions of successive governments run by Julia Gillard and Wayne Swan and ourselves – a bunch of vile, despicable, spineless creeps that obviously I have no desire whatsoever to wreak any kind of merciless revenge upon – for having inflicted such profound grief and suffering onto the entire electorate. We apologise especially for the removal of a popularly elected prime minister from the Lodge, from the gated community he belongs in and from his unlimited expense account and for the pain inflicted upon his family left stranded at the $5 million beach house on the Sunshine Coast.

"And for the indignity and degradation thus inflicted onto an otherwise psychopathic prime minister with a proud culture of chaos, dysfunction, tantrums and treachery, we are most profoundly sorry."

To illustrate his point, Mr. Rudd told the moving story of an unwed Welsh woman, part of the Knitting Generation, who he decided not to visit a few days ago in her office. Her minders tried to hide her from the "faceless men" by digging in and refusing to call a ballot. But luckily, at the last minute, she was betrayed by Little Billy Come-Shortly, who removed her from her office just before 8 o'clock that evening.

"There is something terribly primal about these first female prime ministers; the pain is searing, it screams from the pages, the hurt the humiliation, the degradation and the sheer brutality of the act of physically separating a prime minister from her caucus is a deep assault on our senses and on our most elemental humanity," Mr. Come-Shortly said, as he wept openly and uncontrollably on the shoulder of a clearly deeply aggrieved Penny 'I guess I got it' Wrong, herself struggling to fight back the tears by clinging on to a large, peeled onion.

Mr. Rudd said the pathetically low poll results and woeful judgment calls of Ms. Gillard "cry out" to be heard and "cry out" for an apology.

"Last week I sat down with Billy Come-Shortly for a cup of tea at his office here in Canberra. He told me he had five MP's in his back pocket. His mother-in-law was a governor-general who, in Billy's words, wanted him to have a 'decent job' post-September 14.

"When Billy was boss of the AWU, he remembers being taken to the steps of the local police station with his lawyers and told to wait until this woman with a nasal twang, who had promised to set up slush funds for all, came out.

"As Billy recalls, 'I never got my slush fund'. A fortnight later, he was offered pre-selection to a safe Labor seat, and later got into politics to help escape the psychological torture he suffered through years of so-called industrial disputes.

Said a tearful Mr. Rudd: "Billy has led a tough life. But Billy is a survivor.

"Just like me."

Having resumed the Prime Ministership, Kevin Rudd found himself having to finesse many of the positions he had previously held. Accusing Tony Abbott of causing a potential conflict with Indonesia over boat people, Rudd headed off to meet president Susilo Bambang Yudhoyono, challenged Tony Abbott to a debate on 'debt and the deficit', removed the word 'Gonski' from the political lexicon, and 'reformed' the NSW Labor party. All in his first week. Meanwhile, a Queensland coroner found that with the Pink Batts program the Rudd government had been partially to blame for the deaths of four young tradesmen by "putting economics ahead of lives." The mother of one of the men wished that Kevin Rudd "would just disappear."

Financial Review, 6 July 2013

TANTRIC POLITICS AND THE KEVIN SUTRA

Being a leader involves having to make love to the electorate as often as possible, but doing so puts you in extremely compromising positions. Ancient scripts written thousands of years ago by a group of reincarnated psychotic monks reveal the sacred positions of the Kevin Sutra.

The Position of the Polls: This is the position of admiration. Place a few polls under caucus to prop them up and prolong the electoral arousal. Force the man in speedos down on his knees by offering to debate him whenever you can, so you can control your own polling figures and set and maintain the tempo.

The Weeping Damsel: In this position, the woman lies on her back where the knives are to be placed and bends to the will of the caucus and, of course, her feet are in the air as she has been rolled by her own side. This is an amazing avenue for quick elevation to leadership, not to mention the view of the Lodge. The man should then drop to his knees in front of the electorate, begging forgiveness, and promising to change his ways.

The Germinated Seed: Keep planting the idea of your return to the Labor leadership month after month, year after year, until all those who would try to stop you are thoroughly spent.

The Lower Union: This position, which is also a deep penetration by extreme left-wingers, is optimal for the feel of tightening polls by getting on top of the unions and corrupt factional leaders. Place your feet on their chest and pretend to grind them down, then bend over backwards and do whatever they tell you to do.

Towing the Boat up the River, (also known as The Drowning Man): This is the most contorted position of the Kevin Sutra. First, say: "I shall tow back the boats." Then immediately change your position, dismantling all border protection to allow the floodgates to open. Then, when the woman arises, you must say there will be no lurching to the right. Then when you arise again, you must say there will be no lurching to the left. Keep rocking from side to side, remembering in the heat of the moment to declare war on Indonesia, and then beg them for help. But don't hold your breath.

The Turning Man: The positioning of your Gonski in this one is important because it opens the electorate to an array of exciting sensations. Spread yourself prone before the media so that your Gonski is no longer in view. Allow time beforehand to soothe the Catholics (also known as adopting the Missionary position) by promising them whatever they want. Remember, your Gonski is asymmetric and can be manipulated both independently and in public. Note: Ladies, get over the fact it was all your idea in the first place, the man loves to pretend it was his. Rest assured that the sudden voting urges it induces is extremely attractive.

The Suspended Congress: If you are frightened of exposing your inner weaknesses and appearing dysfunctional, this position allows you to achieve an election without getting any legislation up. Pin caucus against the wall, then climb on top of them. Try to sustain not calling an election for as long as you possibly can.

The Swing: After extended amounts of time performing physically rigorous alternating positions, this is good for revamping voter intimacy. The swinging voter in a mall stands before you. This position allows face-to face interaction and allows the TV cameras to see you promising the swinger everything they want.

The Perfumed Garden: Find two people of the same sex who want to get married and tell them you are opposed to it. Then sniff the breeze and hop into bed with them.

The Pink Bitts: This can be an extremely uncomfortable position to attempt on your own, so it is best if you have a partner with you, preferably a tall, bald man. Lock yourself in a tight embrace in a dark attic until you feel the flames of desire. Then escape as quickly as you can, leaving your scape-goat to take the heat. If you get caught, apologise profusely.

The Fiscal Embrace: This is how to stimulate your economy, and also makes room for good pork-barrelling. Start by saying you are a "fiscal conservative" and whispering "This reckless spending must stop" before splurging billions on the most reckless spending you can think of. Hours of fun, but your coffers may soon be depleted.

The Great Moral Challenge: The voter lies on its back with its knees up and feet flat on the bed after having opened their electricity bill. But soon they will feel a warm, gooey feeling all over. Ladies, don't forget the dirty coal talk, and tell Kevin how much you love everything he's doing. The same goes for Kevin; tell the voter why you love giving them your renewable energy and how good it feels to you both.

THE END

POSTSCRIPT

Your most Magnificence Monsignore Rudd,

I doff my cap to your glorious victory and the humiliation and torment of your foes; offering the most sincerest of flatteries for the brilliance of your political machinations.

As you know, my own humble talents in teaching such delicate arts of persuasion have found much to commend them. "If an injury has to be done to a man it should be so severe that his vengeance need not be feared," is, I believe, one of my sayings that is a favourite of yours, and I am told you proudly adhere to my most famous admonishment: "I am not interested in preserving the status quo, I want to overthrow it."

However, despite the keenness of my pupils, who number the scions of the Medici family of Florence, a smattering of Popes of Rome and my beloved Borgias of Valencia, none of those I have thus far tutored have displayed anything like your own exquisite cunning.

Perhaps now it is a case of the apprentice having more expertise than the master.

Imagine my delight upon learning of the success of your latest venture this past week. The precision with which you achieved your goals in such a short space of time leaves one breathless in admiration. When we first entered discourse as to the ways best suited for you to achieve your triumph over the woman of red hair, she of the shrill voice and tin ear; and in doing so overturning the established order of your pitiful party and gaining the purity and fulsomeness of the sweetest of revenges, I had imagined a campaign of many years, nay, a decade at the very least. Such an exquisite triumph you have so swiftly and expertly achieved; of which I am most envious. A double pleasure to so deceive your deceivers.

Allow me also to praise the brilliance of your cunning strategy of subterfuge. The ability to shape events through the circumspect whispering of secrets to chosen scribes and others of the chattering classes, the canny spreading of privileged information at the most opportune moment of the campaign, the consistent denials of personal ambition. These are all proper methods with which he who desires success must oft resort, as never was anything of substance achieved without danger or duplicity.

Of particular genius, may I hazard to suggest, was your heart-felt commitment that "under no circumstances would you return to the leadership of the party." For this clever and beguiling ruse, I tip my cap to you in sincerest admiration. Such a strategy of denial, I now appreciate, allows the deceiver to parade himself in broad daylight rather than scurrying furtively in the shadows like a filthy Venetian water rat. Even I, in my most inspired moments, have never devised of such a ploy. It is kind of you to credit me with the inspiration for the idea – you refer to my well-known observations that "a prince never lacks legitimate reasons to break his promise" and that "politics have no relation to morals" – but alas I fear my skills pale beside your own. With your permission I may suggest such tactics to my good friend Cesare, who will be mightily impressed by their audacity.

Equally noteworthy, if I may be allowed to opine, was the cunning scheme of not challenging the woman some three months ago when all expected you to challenge her, and tricking the old fool to step into the breech. Wrong-footing the enemy allows a key tactical advantage, and executed as efficiently as you did on that occasion is even deadlier than the vials of apothecaries so beloved of my eager student Lucrezia in bringing an unsuspecting opponent to their knees.

My highest praise, however, I must reserve for the exquisite deployment of your finest strategic weapon. I speak of course of that which you and I laughingly referred to as the "imaginary petition." How I look back fondly on the many hours we spent with a bottle of Tuscan red discussing and preparing such a scheme. As well we both recognised, the enemy had she so chosen needed simply to sit still and deny you your challenge, and in doing so she would surely have prevailed. That this famed petition – a weapon as devastating as any Da Vinci ever devised – only existed as a rumoured whisper, a figment of imagination let loose upon the breeze to torture the souls and minds of frightened, greedy politicians, will of course remain for all time our special secret.

I salute you, as ever, my dearest pupil,

Niccolo Machiavelli

P.S. I raise a glass to your next venture; the devious plan we dreamed up to wrong-foot the man you call Abbott. Remember; whosoever desires constant success must appear to change his conduct with the times.

ROWAN DEAN

Rowan Dean is the political satirist with the *Australian Financial Review* and co-editor of *The Spectator Australia*.

He is familiar to Australian audiences as a regular political commentator on ABC's *The Drum* and on Sky News with Peter Van Onselen's *Contrarians*, David Speers' *The Nation* and *Paul Murray Live*. He also has weekly spots with John Stanley and Paul Murray on radio 2UE and was a panelist on *The Gruen Transfer*.

He is also one of the most respected creatives in Australian advertising circles, having won Cannes Gold and Silver Lions, co-written one of the "world's greatest commercials", and been an award-winning film director, copywriter and Creative Director.

Rowan's advertising background includes creating the famous Paul Hogan Foster's lager ads for the UK, one of that country's most successful ever alcohol launches, and a three year stint as Chairman of AWARD, the Australasian Writer's and Art Director's Association.

His passions are politics, "proper" rock music and advertising. He is not a fan of the nanny state.

Rowan was born in Canberra, educated in France, Germany, Britain and Australia, and speaks French and German. He lives in Sydney, Australia.

Follow Rowan on twitter @rowandean